DATE DUE

Morality in America

RANDOM HOUSE · New York

MORALITY
in
AMERICA

J. Robert Moskin

To my father, who taught me to question

"Here is not merely a nation but a teeming nation of nations."

Walt Whitman, 1855

An Acknowledgment

Even though it will not interest most readers, I wish to acknowledge the help of many people in the creation of this book, especially those who talked with me about the perplexing moral problems dealt with here. In all cases, the individuals quoted are responsible only for what they themselves said, not for the conclusions I have drawn from their ideas.

I wish also to pay some small measure of my debt to those at Look who helped: the late Daniel D. Mich, for giving me the opportunity and encouragement to dig deeply; William B. Arthur and Robert Meskill, for their faith in this project; James Hansen with whom I made this and many other journeys for Look, and to Gardner Cowles, for publishing a magazine for which a writer is expected to report exactly what he finds. And, in addition, to Phyllis Jackson and Nan A. Talese for their continual help. Finally, my apologies to Mark, David and Nancy for the time this book has taken me away from them and my thanks to my wife, Doris, who has contributed her good sense and taste and an infinite amount of patience.

Contents

Introduction

You Are Not Alone

THIS book is a report based on interviews with more than a hundred thinkers and authorities, including many of the most probing minds of our age. They look boldly at our society, our values, our hypocrisies. They examine the baffling new moral problems that confront us. When they confirm our ideas and prejudices, they can be comforting; when they contradict what we have been taught to believe, they are disturbing, even shocking. They dare us to re-examine ourselves and our lives.

Each of us faces moral dilemmas. Our problems may be economic, social, scientific, political, but at their core they demand of us moral decisions—decisions of right and wrong. By reporting the insights of these thoughtful men and women, this book tries to pinpoint and clarify our dilemmas. If we understand our real problems, we can seek real answers.

The book began back in 1957 when I suggested to the

editors of *Look* magazine that we analyze the moral con-
fusions of the American people—of you and me—through
the perceptions of some of our leading thinkers. Over the
years I collected notes and finally began months of inter-
viewing—from Berkeley, California, to Berlin. The *Look*
article received more mail than any other published during
1963, except two pages of pictures of rare coins (money
still outdraws morality). The letters showed that many
Americans are deeply troubled by new moral questions to
which they can find no answers.

The brief magazine article could touch only a few of the
peaks. I dug further, talked with many more people and
spent months researching and writing this book. All the
quotations, except for the few clearly indicated, come directly from personal interviews.

The story told here is optimistic and challenging. These
men and women are saying that we have a unique opportunity today: the chance to discover moral answers for ourselves. We are blessed with the freedom to hold our beliefs
up to the light, debate them and even change them. We are
free, as perhaps human beings have never been before, to
arrive at moral decisions based not on taboos or cant or
dictation, but on the world as it is. We are free to bring together morality and reality.

None of us is alone in his search for answers. All of us
grope for the realities behind the puzzles we live with. The
same moral questions that trouble you in the lonely silence
of your mind also disturb many others. Only by meeting
these unsolved questions can we better understand our fears
and our hopes.

Morality in America

««« *1.*

The Moral Crisis

We Americans are members of a tremendously large, impersonal, money-motivated, sex-obsessed society. We are faced with moral decisions with which we can hardly grapple. We are in the midst of a moral crisis.

Conditions in our world are changing so swiftly that they have kicked out from under us our traditional props of ancient religious tenets and humanitarian principles. We are left to make urgent moral decisions virtually on our own. This is a burden many find too heavy.

Morality is the most intensely discussed subject in the United States. We argue about Elizabeth Taylor's love life, Billie Sol Estes' and Bobby Baker's deals, "Bull" Connor's brutalities, Adam Clayton Powell's junkets, Jimmy Hoffa's power. We debate drinking by youngsters in Darien, Connecticut; sterilization by doctors in Virginia; welfare restrictions by politicians in Newburgh, New York; the right to lie by officials in Washington; slant-well digging by Texans in Texas, and gouging by slumlords in Chicago.

Rarely will two Americans agree on who is immoral or what is the moral thing to do. We are adrift without answers to our moral problems. We want to know:

Am I immoral if I don't want a Negro living next door?

Am I immoral if I pad my income-tax deductions?

Am I immoral if I let my daughter go on an all-night beach party with her high school friends?

Am I immoral if I object to giving economic aid to a lot of primitive, probably lazy, countries?

Am I immoral if I let a friend "take care" of a speeding ticket for me?

Am I immoral if I believe that the poor ought to lift themselves out of the slums?

However you answer such questions, many Americans will disagree with you.

Each of us has moral decisions to make constantly. When we can see clearly what is right and wrong, these decisions are easy—even if we decide to act immorally: to cheat, to exploit, to hate. We know what we are doing; we can rationalize the act for the end. Moral decisions become tough when the distinction between right and wrong is blurred, when we can find valid arguments for several courses of action, when good and evil seem hopelessly tangled. Today these distinctions are more confusing than ever.

In other times and in other societies, the answers were clearer, the problems simpler, the ground rules sharper. But in our world of concentrated masses of people, jet-age travel, nuclear power and fragmented families, the established moral guidelines have been yanked from our hands. We are witnessing the death of the old morality.

The clergymen, educators, politicians, sociologists, scientists, and others with whom I have talked, speak in many voices and from many special fields of knowledge—from sex mores to business ethics. But a single idea runs like a steel thread through what they say: America is changing swiftly. We are losing our trusted anchors that have given us security. The sea is dark, as the Pope said, speaking of Columbus' first voyage, "where hitherto no one had sailed." And although our ship is luxurious and the food and fun plentiful (at least for those on most of the decks), we are heading into danger.

These eminent thinkers and leaders are not Doomsday prophets but people deeply worried by the way America is deserting its familiar moral shores and steering into unknown seas. They warn that we are in a moral crisis because the great majority of Americans, who want to try to live moral lives, must figure out for themselves how to apply the traditional moral truths to the problems of our times. Scientist J. Robert Oppenheimer expresses the dilemma of our nuclear power: " 'Thou shalt not kill'—but a general says we can kill 400 million human beings." Man has always killed; now he can exterminate himself.

We are not in this crisis because we are more immoral than people were in the past. Only a romantic would insist that in the good old days Americans were always good. We need only to look at our own history: the intolerance of many of our early colonists; the Americans who owned human slaves; the Andrew Jackson who slaughtered the Indians; the William Randolph Hearst who promoted a war to exploit the decay of the Spanish empire; the Harry Bennett who fought the unions with guns and clubs. We need only remember the concentration camps in which we imprisoned Japanese-Americans during World War II. We need only remember that four American presidents have been assassinated and that Franklin Roosevelt and Harry Truman almost were. And the racist pronouncements of Eugene "Bull" Connor reminded us again that Americans too can lack a moral conscience.

It is the essence of democracy that the people will work out their problems for themselves, but the American experiment with the freedom of the individual is under pressure. From without, it is challenged by authoritarian systems that say: "Give up your freedom, let the state decide and it will lead you away from the edge of privation." For masses around the world to whom hunger is a more immediate enemy than tyranny, this appeal can sound attractive. Many men are willing to sell their freedom if the price is right. The renowned Protestant theologian Paul Tillich, who died in October 1965, warned, "In periods of great upheavals people fly into authoritarian forms of life." Internally, the American experiment is challenged by the urbanization and industrialization of our society, by the impersonalization of our cities and our big organizations. Under these strains, our moral fabric stretches and sometimes rips.

Most Americans hate to believe we are actually in moral trouble. We habitually regard ourselves as "the good guys in the white hats," a modern "chosen people," superior in ability and morality. We talk disparagingly of the French, their sexual myth-image and their failure to pay taxes; of the Germans, who supported the Nazis with 11 million votes in 1932; of the British and the Profumo sex scandal that almost toppled their government. But what we are witnessing in America today suggests that we may not deserve a self-flattering image of ourselves. This is hard to admit. Most of us try to pretend that the moral crisis is an illusion, that it does not exist.

But it is real. We try to ignore it, keep it buried in our ghettos and our hearts. When we dare to look, it can be seen: in the parent who worries in the night for a child, the worker whose job is gone, the Negro whose hope is gone, the businessman who fears his heart is gone, the minister who preaches and is not heard. The minister's agony is perhaps the most tragic. His has been the greatest failure. He often feels himself a traitor to his faith, a slave to his congregation. He has failed to sell the life of good to those who seek only the good life.

The bitter fruits of our moral crisis are all around us: the beatnik, the racist, the wild kid, the price-rigging executive, the bribed athlete, the corrupt union leader, the uncared-for aged, the poor, the criminal. We shake our heads in horror when police dogs are used to control children, when a drunken driver kills and goes free, when young hoodlums destroy a school or a cemetery. We say these are not us. The good people of Dallas said President Kennedy could have been assassinated anywhere.

But television shows us that shoot-'em-up violence is the American way, the "hate groups" roar like vigilantes and the movies proclaim that stardom and success are warrants for four husbands and a lover.

Figures do not reveal the agony of the human heart but they can define the extent of the crisis. Here are a few surprising statistical examples of the scope of immorality in America today:

• Major crimes in the United States have increased five times faster than the population since 1950.

• Juvenile arrests have doubled since 1950.

• More than two million major crimes are committed each year: one for every 90 persons, one every 15 seconds.

They include 9,200 murders, 20,500 forcible rapes, 1.1 million burglaries.

• Divorces have averaged 380,000 annually since 1950, one for every four marriages performed each year.

• Automobile thefts surpass one thousand per day, an estimated 65 percent of them committed by teen-agers.

• Venereal disease cases (those reported) now number more than 400,000 a year.

• Vandals smashed 181,306 school windows in New York City in one year. A railroad, the New Haven, said that stonings of trains that same year required the replacement of 4,736 broken windows.

• Stolen property now is worth in excess of $600 million annually.

• Pilferage runs higher than $1 billion a year.

• Alcoholics now total five million, including 3 percent of the whole U.S. work force.

The gap between what we profess and what we do makes our immorality even more ugly. We claim to believe not only in the Ten Commandments and the teachings of Christ but also in the Preamble to the Declaration of Independence and the Constitution's first ten amendments.

Speaking of his country and ours, the Most Reverend Arthur Michael Ramsey, the Archbishop of Canterbury, says, "I think general lawlessness is greater—a breakdown of the sense of duty and of obligation and of truthfulness. I think two wars have contributed to it and the rapid change to a more industrialized society has uprooted people. People are living in a new world where they find it difficult to get their sense of duty."

The moral rules of an agricultural, parochial, small-town world have to be taken apart and reassembled in new ways if they are to be useful guides in our massive society—our U.S. population has doubled since 1912—in which size and speed dominate our lives.

The questions we must face are endless: What would you advise a college girl, pregnant by a boy she does not love but who wants to marry her? Would you testify against a close friend's son who caused an accident you had witnessed? What would you tell the local merchant who says he will have to go bankrupt if he tries to meet the lower prices of a new competitor? Would you mail in the fine for a parking ticket you received in a distant town? Would you sell your house if a Negro family was moving in nearby?

The moral questions no longer challenge only an elite. Willy Brandt, the mayor of West Berlin, says, "We have lived through greater changes during the last two decades than two hundred years before. It is taking place not only faster but for many more people—now that the masses are engaged in our civilization much more than in the past."

The moral confusion created by change worries Michigan's Governor George W. Romney. He says: "One reason America has excelled is because we have given a better expression to moral principles. It's slipping. Our greatest danger is the decline in religious conviction and moral character. This is more serious to our future than the external threats we face. Weakness within is always more serious. It's reached a level that should be a great concern."

The Reverend William Sloane Coffin, Jr., the chaplain of Yale University, sums up his view: "The trouble in America is we do love our neighbors as ourselves and that is why we are trying to do them in." He adds, "Martin Buber said there are people and things in this world, and people are to be loved and things to be used. But in American society I think we are using people and loving things more and more."

Each man is saying that our moral values are being seriously questioned, that we face a moral challenge unique in our history and that the real threat is within ourselves.

What makes this crisis exceptionally difficult is that we seem to have a "crisis morality." Too often we face up to a moral problem only when it reaches the point of crisis. It took Fidel Castro to make us think seriously about conditions in Latin America; it took the Negro's pressure to make us admit the moral core of his plight. Apparently, it requires a crisis to turn us from material goals to moral principles. As Professor Philip M. Hauser, chairman of the Department of Sociology at the University of Chicago, puts it, "The human animal resists thinking. You never think until you come to a crossroads."

The event which most startlingly awoke us was the assassination of President Kennedy. On November 22, 1963, each of us came face to face with the question of morality in America. We were forced to ask whether his death was the result of the moral attitudes we had permitted to flourish.

Was it significant that his assassination occurred in Dallas —a booming Southern metropolis, a city renowned for its big oil-depletion money, its right-wing fervor, its shining new bank buildings? Certainly the grotesque opinions of some of the men in the pointed boots and the string ties had inflamed hatred. They had spat upon Lyndon Johnson in 1960 and Adlai Stevenson was clobbered with placards only weeks before President Kennedy drove into Dallas.

In an important way, Dallas symbolizes the realization of the American dream of power and wealth. "Big D," ruled by a tight paternalistic business circle, is a city of bravado, pride and incredible fantasies of success. It is a financial center; money is its purpose for being. As a Dallas banker told me: "All we've got down here is money." If Dallas represents the dream of material success, then we must ask: Does the dream lead to this end? The question must be asked, not to slap a sentence of guilt on Dallas, but because the answer has meaning for every would-be Dallas.

The murder of the young, glamorous President shocked us into a fresh awareness of the hatred and violence that sit in many American hearts. A Dallas newspaper editor called the local hate-Kennedy attitude "a haunting presence—the ghost of our own bad conscience." Why are the haters so loud in America today? Because, it seems clear, we are not able to have our own way in a complex and frightening nuclear-armed world. We must live with tensions. And because we are struggling through an internal social revolution that began in the 1930's when we started using federal power and funds extensively for social purposes. Today this internal revolution is complicated by the bloody battle over human rights and the looming incomprehensibility of automation. This social revolution is broader than the fight over civil rights for the Negro. He is only at the tail end; the Negro is coming in last again.

Those who cannot find peaceful and rational adjustments to these social changes thrash out and destroy and kill. Those un-Americans called Kennedy a traitor ("Wanted for Treason") the day he was killed. They defaced shop windows with swastikas, demanded the impeachment of Chief Justice Earl Warren and smeared the memory of General George C. Marshall. They terrorized a Dallas minister for publicly complaining that some school children had cheered the news of the President's death.

In the months between Kennedy's murder and the 1964 election, there was widespread fear that we had given way to the wild-eyed. The radicals rose to a peak of pre-eminence when Senator Barry Goldwater accepted the nomination for the Presidency at the 1964 Republican National Convention in San Francisco and made his declaration: "I would remind you that extremism in the defense of liberty is no vice. And let me remind you also that moderation in the pursuit of justice is no virtue." Newsmen reported that this was the only passage underlined in the copies of his speech handed them by Goldwater workers. Immediately after the convention, Goldwater defined extremism by saying, "Extremism in politics is either fascism on one side or communism on the other." Following the logic of his definition, he was saying that fascism or communism in the defense of liberty is no vice.

Today we run the risk that one man—a General Jack D. Ripper or a Lee Harvey Oswald or a Jack Ruby—will decide that he alone sees the moral issue plainly and will act. The bombing of Sunday school children in Birmingham, the murder of Medgar Evers in Jackson, Mississippi, and the shooting of the President in Dallas were such ultimate acts.

A thoughtful academic leader said of the assassination: "This stark encounter with evil has shaken a disturbed people. I don't think we need lose faith in our culture because this has happened. It has shown us the price of freedom. The risk is one you have to take."

Out of today's moral agony and confusion must come either a society of license, godlessness and brutality, or (if we are wise and lucky) a new moral code based on the realities of our new world. Only by hammering out a new code can we give the enduring principles—the Ten Commandments, the Golden Rule, the teachings of Christ, the American Creed—relevance to the conditions of the world we live in. In our age this code will be radically different from anything the past has known and extremely difficult for many of today's older generation to swallow. But only by working out such a new morality can modern America hope to survive without exchanging its romantic ideal of the good guys in the white hats for the authority of a strong man on a white horse.

Our challenge is to discover how the ancient moral answers fit today's moral questions and to create a moral code within which we can live and rear our children. Such a code must deal with the new forms of the age-old problems of money, sex, prejudice and power. "The growing forces in this country are the forces of common human decency and not the forces of bigotry and fear and smears," President Lyndon B. Johnson said in accepting the Democratic nomination on August 27, 1964. "This nation, this generation, in this hour has man's first chance to build a great society, a place where the meaning of man's life matches the marvels of man's labor."

We have two hopes for the future: first, the fact that we Americans are becoming concerned about morality, and secondly, we are free to choose. Says Professor Hauser, "There was never a time in the history of man, when man was as free to exercise his own intelligence and make his own decisions."

According to Professor Lester A. Kirkendall of Oregon State University, "We are approaching a new moral code in which there is genuine honesty and concern for other people. Relationships have rules that govern them. Our problem is to discover what these rules are and how to put them into effect." Our search must seek new guidelines for everyone, from U. S. senators to theater owners, from cigarette manufacturers to high school students.

Labor leader Walter P. Reuther describes our opportunity: "This is the most dangerous but most exciting age in human history—the most exciting time to be alive. Now we have the tools for the first time to conquer poverty, ignorance and disease. We as a nation are too smug, we are too complacent, we are too apathetic. The crisis essentially is a moral crisis."

The potentialities are enormous. "It is not impossible that this could be a Golden Age," says J. Irwin Miller, past president of the National Council of the Churches of Christ. "We have solved our technological and economic problems. We only have moral problems left."

ᚎᚎᚎ 2.

Who Has Enough Courage?

For most human beings the determination of moral standards was always relatively simple. Someone told them what
to do, what was right or wrong; or someone stood up as a
model of moral excellence and inspired imitation. Often the
mores of the community, evolved over generations of trial
and error, have dictated moral behavior. At other times, an
overlord, usually armored with divine support, has imposed
standards. These standard setters have ranged from Popes
to Chinese warlords, and they have possessed the spiritual
authority or temporal strength to enforce their edicts.

But science has loosened many men's ties to their priests,
and industrialization has altered many men's relationship to
their secular superiors. We in America live in a society without a supreme moral authority to rule our conduct. No
church lays down the moral law for all; no tribal customs
and taboos define the limits of all our immoralities. We are
free to be prejudiced or promiscuous, to cheat or chisel.

Whether this is for good or bad, no man can punish all

of us if we disagree with his view of morality. The Catholic priest who tries to prevent steady dating in his parochial school may not win compliance from his students and he certainly does not control the conduct of youth of other faiths. The judge who decides that a novel is obscene may be overruled by his superiors. When one group is strong enough to impose its will on others by law—like Prohibition on the national level or the birth-control laws in Connecticut and Massachusetts—it is resented and circumvented.

The vacuum of authority reaches even further. The authority of the parent within the home is undercut by the increased economic freedom and the mobility of many young people.

We get little moral leadership from the churches. Says Dean Samuel H. Miller of Harvard University's Divinity School: "The church has become almost as monastic as the orders of the Middle Ages. There seems to be no connection between what happens in the church and what happens in society, except that people living in a desperate age use it to tranquilize their disturbing experiences—like some kind of lullaby."

And we have no elite setting a moral model. Says Dean Miller: "Morality depends on images of excellence. Every society tends to fall to lower levels unless these images are present. In the Middle Ages, this is what the saint was. We know what a rich man is, a scientist is, an astronaut—but we don't have an image of moral excellence. The fact that we don't have these images means we have lost the moral sense. To the degree that we have them, we are saved by them."

The late Dr. Leo Szilard, the atomic scientist whose contribution to our destinies has been so little recognized, was greatly concerned by the paucity of moral leadership. To amplify our discussion, he wrote me some months before his death: "The individuals who make up our society are rarely guided in their actions by moral considerations alone or by considerations of expediency alone. Mostly their actions are influenced by both considerations. Those individuals who give moral considerations a much greater weight than considerations of expediency represent a comparatively small minority, five percent of the people perhaps. But, in spite of their numerical inferiority, they play a major role in our society because theirs is the voice of the conscience of society."

Every mass society needs recognized heroes. But heroes are rare in our massive American culture. A John Glenn will flash across our sky. A John F. Kennedy will be idolized after his death, not so much as a moral model as for his courage, his vigor and his charismatic youthfulness. Vice-President Hubert H. Humphrey says, "This country needs heroes—moral heroes."

To fill the vacuum, we venerate actresses who have acquired a string of husbands, baseball players who brawl in night clubs, football players who are later suspended from play. To a surprising degree, we have replaced the hero by the celebrity. "They are waxworks carved by public relations men," says Dr. David R. Mace, executive director of the American Association of Marriage Counselors. "It is the people who can act, entertain, who become the rallying point of the people's need for heroes. They are essentially irresponsible people." He adds, "Our young people must be very hungry for heroes."

We cannot look to the creative artist for our images of excellence. Novelist Anton Myrer, who has given much thought to this problem, describes the change: "American fiction has had its heroes"—he cites Huck Finn, Ishmael, Silas Lapham and even Natty Bumppo and Jay Gatsby. "I call it the Private Morality of the American Hero: in a moment of crisis the protagonist resolves upon some eminently moral action—usually one in defiance of the prevailing political, social or economic codes. It is customarily a solitary decision, it is often made in the dead of night. It is reached after much anguish, in full view of the risks involved—and the hero usually suffers the consequences of that decision with calm resignation. He refuses to accede to rules he feels are incompatible with the moral dignity of the individual."

The revolt of these heroes, Myrer says, "is based on an arduous search for values and a troubled sense that these materialist, expedient values of ours are not all that they might be; and their consequent awareness that their action is in obedience to a truth more compelling—and quite possibly more valid—than the obligations of wealth or prestige or safety, helps sustain them in their ensuing ordeal. Nearly all of them survive, or at least achieve a modest triumph."

Then Myrer asks, "And what of those of us writing today, dogged by wars hot and cold, the dread of Armageddon and the slow extinguishing of individual idiosyncracy in megalopolis and manswarm? How are we faring? Well, you see bits of the thread here and there—but mostly you don't. . . .

"What one looks for, the soul greater than the rest of us, who succeeds where we have failed and who can touch all our losses with nobility. What is disheartening is that so many contemporary protagonists are so much less than most of us are, even in our bad moments."

Myrer explains why the American hero has been replaced in our time with something less: "How much of the country actually seeks something dangerous and exciting? Surfeited with wealth and leisure and material goods, we seem to long for some perilous, uncharted night-journey, a riotous descent into the sulphurous fires. Old Ahab would feel right at home in America . . ."

Harvard sociologist David Riesman believes that we end up getting our standards from the fanatics: "The fundamentalists whether in religion or politics are impressive because they are sure to people who are unsure."

Central to this problem is our affluence and the premium we place on security. Says Dr. Mace, "We can't offer people anything heroic. Life is so cushioned, so comfortable." He regards this absence of heroic challenge as "one of the major problems of the future of civilizations."

Our eagerness to replace the heroic with the glamorous may explain, for example, the attraction of the amorality of a James Bond, the fictional hero who combines the glamorous risks of sex and violence with heroic efforts for the common good. This almost suggests that we are beginning to admire social morality and personal immorality, or perhaps we merely enjoy the arm-chaired flight into fantasy. In either case, James Bond will hardly serve us as a model.

Without moral authority or moral model, the burden for setting moral standards now rests squarely on the individual. Several years ago I sat in a charming rectory in Paisley, Scotland, and over coffee and scones I talked with three pacifist Church of Scotland ministers about their deeply felt conviction that their country, Great Britain, should divest itself of nuclear weapons—should disarm unilaterally. They said they would rather be "Red than dead" because they devoutly believed that even if Britain were overrun by Soviet invaders, in time, good would ultimately triumph. When I asked them if they advocated unilateral disarmament for their country because it would still be under the protective umbrella of American nuclear power, they admitted they had not carried their thoughts that far. They caucused there before the roaring fire and agreed that if it were moral for Britain to disarm unilaterally, America must disarm too. Even these thoughtful ministers had no authority to turn to. They had to ask themselves the moral question and struggle to find their own answer.

"The greatest moral challenge is to think through what one really does believe and afterwards to begin to make judgments about what is right and wrong in that framework," says Professor Kirkendall. "This kind of a world we live in has multiplied the choices a person can make almost to the point of dizziness. Our supermarkets typify this. You are surrounded by choices. Many times we deny the individual any help in making a choice."

To John Cogley, editor of an extensive study of the American character, these myriad choices contain not only a burden but an opportunity: "The new morality makes it possible to make personal decisions without punishment. There are no more Scarlet A's. This may be a good thing. If they are not bound to the good traditions of the past, they may not be bound by the bad traditions of the past."

If the individual is left with this puzzling freedom to select his own moral standards from among dizzying choices, his problem is then to detect the moral act. Theologian Paul Tillich offered a definition that may help the individual choose what is truly moral: "For me a moral act is an act in which a person is constituted as a person. Not an act that is obedient to divine or human laws. Our moral act makes us a person. It has only one content, which is love."

This is a daring statement, because it preaches that it is not the act prescribed by divine law that is moral. In fact, it affirms that laws can be morally disobeyed. And it asserts that the test is not obedience: the test of the moral act is love. Jesus Christ was crucified for saying no more than this.

Left without minister or model, how can an individual act morally—with Tillich's "love"—in a crowded, competitive society like ours? How can the individual conscience make itself heard? "If it doesn't, God help us!" says the Most Reverend Paul J. Hallinan, Catholic archbishop of Atlanta. He is hopeful: "Any priest who hears confession week after week is exposed to the human soul and comes away from that experience with a high regard for human morality and human effort. The number of people who are trying. After all, that is the test."

Perhaps that is what we are searching for: the hero we must find within ourselves.

«« 3.

A Brand-New Age

C. P. Snow calls this "a major revolutionary age." Headlines blare at us about aggression and automation, discovery and delinquency, nuclear fall-out and narrowing freedoms. We worry about the loss of religious certainty, the revolt against discrimination and degradation, the blossoming of sexual license, the breakdown of controls and relationships within the family, the loss of personal concern in our cities. In this time of swift change, the forest of danger blinds us to the trees of hope.

Our country has changed spectacularly in twenty years. The 1940 census recorded 131 million Americans; the 1960 census listed 180 million. In 1940 the federal budget totaled $9.6 billion; in 1960 it reached $76.5 billion. In 1940 we spent $1 billion for defense; in 1960, well over $43 billion. In 1940 American business spent $2 billion on advertising; in 1960, almost $12 billion. In 1940 1.4 million students attended college; in 1960, more than 3 million. In 1940 our *per capita* income was $595; by 1960 it had zoomed to

$2,215. And these figures do not reveal the changes in attitudes, skills, science—or morality.

To grasp the nature and meaning of these changes, I talked with leading historians from Edinburgh, Scotland, to California. I returned with the awareness that virtually all these historians believe our days are marked by tumult and terror because we live on the brink of a brand-new age in history.

This is a time of transition, they told me: transitions in power, freedom, economics and morals. The British historian A. L. Rowse at Oxford University said, "The transformation of the modern world is so tremendous that the mere word 'revolution' does not describe it."

Arnold J. Toynbee, the historian of civilizations, believes this transformation confuses our ideas of morality. It reshapes the way we think about good and evil, about our role and our responsibilities. Toynbee says, "There are very few concrete rules of morality that are absolute. Someone said human beings always make the distinction between legal putting to death and murder, but they disagree about what is murder. They all agree there is right and wrong, but not what is right and wrong." This is our challenge—to determine how, in this new age, the moral verities apply to us and our lives.

The unleashing of atomic energy, for example, opens up the most fundamental moral questions about man's survival. In Toynbee's view: "The human race has not been in danger of extermination since man got the upper hand over lions and tigers. Mankind has had a period of thirty thousand years of security against destruction. Now, man is back in the state of his first million years. Since 1949, when Russia, too, got the bomb, it has become possible for the human race to destroy itself. If we are able to survive, we are going to live in danger from here on."

Walter Lippmann suggests that the politics of this atomic age add to our confusion: "The greatest change, in my opinion, is that for the first time we have a rival society to the Western world. Europe and America dominated the world until the Second World War. Even the two German wars were, in a sense, civil wars. This is the most recent thing in world history—the emergence of two world atomic powers."

Walter Prescott Webb, professor of history at the University of Texas, told me shortly before his death that he believed our time marks the end of "the great frontier" that lasted from 1500 to the 1930's. "This was," he said, "an interval of freedom—an interval that is over—the most abnormal age in history that I know."

To Webb, the end of the frontier was reached at the moment in 1953 when the first men reached the summit of Mount Everest. It was "the end of an epoch."

Historian Will Durant, who with his wife is writing *The Story of Civilization*, points to another historic change: "The changes of belief are to me more important than the changes in the balance of power. At the present time, there are millions of people in Western Europe and America who no longer believe in the old deity. Probably half the people in Russia no longer believe.

"What is going on is the formulation of a new moral code. The moral code we inherited was adjusted to agricultural life. The past twenty-five years have been an interregnum from an agricultural moral code to an urban moral code. This is an interval between two moral codes."

These changes affect all of us. Historian Samuel Eliot

Morison, in Boston, reminds us: "The most important thing that has happened in the last twenty-five years is the increased economic and social standing of the ordinary men and women, especially women."

When did we turn the corner? To most of the historians who, in Webb's term, look "down the long gun barrel of history," the period's first great political and moral crisis came when Adolf Hitler invaded the demilitarized Rhineland on March 7, 1936. Esmond Wright, professor of modern history at the University of Glasgow, explains: "In 1936, you get this passionate nationalist in Germany trying his first international experiment. And it comes off. It was the point of no return, the start of the problems we are living with." Wright says Hitler's troops had orders to turn back if France opposed them, but "France did not oppose." And Britain would not support her. Toynbee believes "it could have been done" if France and Britain had stood up to Hitler then. Such a dangerous response, he says, required American co-operation, but the United States had crawled back into isolationism. Americans played a crucial and unhappy part in the moral decisions at that turning point in history.

Harvard's Oscar Handlin looks back at what we were in 1936. Six or seven million Americans belonged to the Silver Shirts, the Ku Klux Klan and many other such organizations. As late as August 12, 1941, the U. S. House of Representatives extended the draft only by a vote of 203 to 202. Despite the efforts of Franklin Roosevelt to make us realize we could no longer live in isolation, we were not ripped out of our post-World War I cocoon until the Japanese made the fatal error of attacking Pearl Harbor. "They thought we were soft and they could get away with it," says historian Morison. They were wrong, and they shoved us, finally, into a new, irreversible era of national responsibility which led us to the wars in Korea and Vietnam.

Historian Herbert Agar also regards 1936 as "the high-water mark of American isolationism," and draws the contrast: "Look at us Americans today, our finger in every pie, realizing we cannot dissociate ourselves from the world's problems. This is a very great revolution."

Three overriding political developments have changed our moral attitudes toward the rest of the world, the historians assert: the spread of communism resulting from the Russian revolution, the rise of the United States as a world power and the radical changes in nationalism. Many Americans fear the consequences of these developments and resist accepting the reality of these historical events. But sitting before the open fire in his Texas ranch house, the late J. Frank Dobie, historian of the American West, said to me: "There's nothing remote any more. I don't regret provincialism passing."

Lippmann says the rise of communism is not comparable to the usual struggles between nations. It has a moral content: "I think the challenge and threat of communism are more like the rise of Islam, when it was a very militant, fighting religion that advanced to Tours and the gates of Vienna. That's more than the communists have done yet. If this comparison is correct, there will never be an end to it. The war between Christianity and Islam has quieted down but never ended."

Says theologian and political philosopher Reinhold Niebuhr, "Communism is a virulent form of the messianic dream."

The historians believe that the ascension of the United

States has shifted power from Western Europe across the Atlantic. Toynbee compares America's rise to a "son growing up and taking over the family business." A. L. Rowse says, "The great cycle of English history that began with the Elizabethan Age has reached its terminus. Now Europe is rather secondary to America. America is, after all, the greatest achievement of the English people."

Some of the historians emphasize the effect of the totalitarianism toward which nationalism has frequently swung in our day. Agar cites Hitler's "totalitarian solution of the Jewish problem" as a symptom of "the final disease of nationalism." He adds, "I sincerely believe this is the beginning of the end of nineteenth-century nationalism, which ended up in two world wars. I think it is over and done with, and the world is working toward some diminution of sovereignty." Will Durant says, "Nationalism in America now is very strong, but it will have to decline."

The emergence of the new nations since the end of World War II is recognized by the historians as another overwhelming political change of our time. Rowse points out, "The whole shape of things of the century to come will be determined by the problems of these new nations in Africa." And Willy Brandt, despite his years in the breach of the East-West struggle, believes that eventually the basic confrontation in the world must take place between the developed North and the underdeveloped South.

Toynbee, Wright and Agar see the nationalism of the new countries of the southern hemisphere as a passing phase. Toynbee says, "No local state is going to be effectively independent. Even the United States and Russia need allies." Eventually, he predicts, nations will become "municipalities of the world," without the right to make war and organized in confederations like the United Nations, the Organization of American States and the British Commonwealth. Associations such as these Lippmann calls "the great replacements of empire."

With political changes as basic as these, with events as momentous as these, with possibilities as radical as these, it is little wonder that we find ourselves face to face with baffling moral dilemmas.

"In the last twenty-five years," says Durant, "the world has advanced in science, knowledge and industry, but retrogressed in morals, art and manners." Morison also believes "man has progressed, as far as comforts are concerned, but his moral nature has disintegrated." J. Frank Dobie bluntly condemned "the decay of righteous indignation. People are lying more. We are more pretenders than we were."

We are ambivalent about lying. British Secretary of State for War John Profumo stirred up reactions less because of his sexual behavior than because he lied to the British Establishment about it. We get upset over lying about television quizzes and cheating on physicians' examinations. On the other hand, we condoned the Eisenhower Administration's lie about the U-2 plane and the Kennedy Administration's lies during the Cuban missile crisis. We seem to be saying that lies are okay when they help us.

The historians blame our moral laxity on the weakening of family ties, the increase of industrialization and the decline of the influence of our religious institutions. Harvard historian Crane Brinton calls this as dissolute an age as any in American history. "There has always been some sexual promiscuity," he says. "I know several periods that have been more promiscuous—but not in the United States." Mrs. Ariel Durant says of today's young people, "You would not have this epidemic delinquency if they had any kind of belief at home and in the churches. You can see the reaction to being denuded of religion."

The decline of religion is a scar on our age, according to most of these historians. "We have a great deal of religiosity that does not have any sense of majesty, mystery or contrition in it," says Reinhold Niebuhr. "If there is moral loyalty to religious institutions, that is because of fears and a need of a sense of community." Frank Dobie said wryly, "Thomas Jefferson couldn't be elected justice of the peace today if people knew how he felt about religion."

This lessening of religious influence has at times left a vacuum into which evil has seeped. Arthur M. Schlesinger, Jr., historian of the ages of Andrew Jackson and Franklin Roosevelt, says, "The rise of terror in this period has shown how ineffective religion has been." And Toynbee observes, "In all Western history, there has been nothing so wicked as what the Nazis did. Extreme cruelty and extreme humaneness are particular to this age."

No one can believe the moral character of our times was purified by the defeat of Hitler and the end of World War II, any more than one can believe that the myth of white superiority in our South died with the defeat of the Confederate Army. I have touched the barbed wire that cuts South Korea from North Korea, visited the bridge at Lo Wu where Communist China meets the free world, explored the wall that divides Berlin and walked the armed line that splits the ancient city of Jerusalem. I have seen the pitiful hunger of the refugees from the war between France and Algeria, and the hatred and distrust in the eyes of colored Americans in Harlem and Memphis.

At the Berlin Wall, late in 1962, an incident occurred

that brought home to me the brutality of modern scientific, civilized man—an incident that haunts me even now. *Look* photographer James Hansen and I had spent days photographing and talking with people along The Wall, and one bright, cold Monday morning, at the northern end of the city, in the French sector, we saw a pleasant-looking woman come out of a nearby shop, dragging a tall ladder. She put it up next to a lamppost, climbed the ladder and hooked her arm around the post to steady herself. Then she took out a pair of binoculars and peered over The Wall. She watched for a long time, and when she came down, we asked her what she had been doing.

She told us her story: The Wall began to go up on August 13, 1961, a Saturday night. She and her husband worked and kept a tiny apartment in West Berlin. Her parents lived in the Russian sector of the city, and that Saturday she had taken her little daughter to spend the night with the child's grandparents there in East Berlin. The child was trapped on the other side of The Wall.

The woman lived in hope that her child could be brought over into West Berlin. Every morning at 11 o'clock, through all those months, she had come to this spot and climbed the ladder and looked over The Wall. And each morning at that hour the grandparents walked with the little girl, who was now five years old, on the street on the other side. Because she and her grandparents would have been arrested, the child was not even allowed to wave to her mother. Here was a simple example of modern man's inhumanity.

The spread of freedom is another momentous change. In fact, Oscar Handlin, director of Harvard University's Center for the Study of the History of Liberty in America, believes that the improved position of minorities is "the big change in our lives." He says, "Terms of justification and resistance are different from what they were in 1935. Now it is a matter of expediency and how fast the change comes, rather than a belief in racial difference and inequality." As Crane Brinton puts it: "In our time, it has become clear that white men are not better than black men."

Western ideals of freedom have spread in our day into the underdeveloped, colonial parts of the world. Civil War historian Bruce Catton says, "People who have always had someone's foot on their neck want to get it off. They don't know where they are going or what they want, but they don't want people sitting on them any longer."

When the historians talk of the changes in our times that have come from man's achievements, they speak primarily of science: the splitting of the atom, the new understanding of the human mind and the virus and the exploration of space. Will Durant, who has bestowed names on the ages of history, predicts ours will go down as The Age of Science.

Walter Lippmann says, "The art of invention has become a deliberate and organized thing in our times. We cannot predict its outcome because we cannot predict what will be invented. All we know is that the changes will be great and swift."

To Toynbee, the great event of our era—second only to the development of atomic energy—is the discovery of the unconscious. He calls Freud and Jung "the Christopher Columbuses of the lower depths of the human psyche. They opened it all up." Of this new ability to manipulate men's minds, he warns, "It is a terrible threat to democracy; democracy believes that everyone is a rational human being. Even if it is used to condition people for good, conditioned human beings are like dogs. I am very conscious of Madison Avenue's and Hitler's devilish use of it."

Bruce Catton also fears this historical development. He

says, "We've gotten crusted over with something in the past twenty or thirty years. To pick an easy target, it is Madison Avenue, the cult of the big shot, the cult of the guy who always makes it. We judge ourselves and everyone else on the press clipping—the invented record."

Schlesinger takes a different view: "Certainly, some alarming techniques have been evolved, but so far they have only been used to sell soap—not in areas where people care very much, where their emotions are involved. This is a development for the fourth quarter of the century."

Thomas S. Kuhn, now professor of the history of science at Princeton University, sees the past quarter century as a period of scientific consolidation and exploitation, following the advances in our knowledge of the nature of matter and its relation to energy. ("This is what it took to make The Bomb.") Our use of science, Kuhn feels, is the critical development in the past twenty-five years. "Science had been a wonderful, useless thing, like art. It is only since the last war that it has become obvious to heads of state that science is a great social force to be treasured—or damned."

Science has also affected our moral ideas by advances in public health and the resulting population problem. Niebuhr says, "Modern medicine is making the population explosion inevitable. In many countries, the population explosion prevents them from getting ahead of the game." Walt Whitman Rostow, economic historian at the Massachusetts Institute of Technology and State Department policy planner, regards the growth in family size in the United States as "the most unpredicted fact about us." Of the explosion abroad he says, "We have the techniques in hand to feed these people until progress itself brings the birth rate down."

Thus, our Age of Science creates special problems. Lewis

Mumford puts the central point vividly, "The problem of our time is the control of quantity—of births, energy, knowledge. We cannot assimilate, much less organize, it in some meaningful pattern. We are victims of the accumulative process. We are even surrendering thought to the machine. We ask ourselves only questions the machine can answer."

Niebuhr looks candidly at the problems created by the machine: "The greatest moral problem that we face is that the employer is interested in automation and the worker is inclined to oppose it, out of fear of losing his job. Next to the nuclear dilemma, this is the great dilemma."

Science has wrought a revolution in war-making. Morison says, "The gun is almost obsolete and the bomber is almost as dead as a dodo." Dobie said, "The weapons have gone full circle. The primitive boomerang used to come back to you, and so does the atomic bomb with its fall-out. You get homicide and suicide at the same time."

Our era has also forced momentous changes in economics. Schlesinger and Durant both emphasize the evolution of a "mixed economy" in America. "This was an American invention," says Schlesinger. Durant says, "Although we are moving toward socialism, we are engaged in a merger of capitalism and socialism. I anticipate in Russia a growth of freedom and a diminution of regulation, and in America I anticipate a growth of regulation and diminution of freedom. This may make for more discipline in the family; parents will bring up their children, rather than vice versa."

Lippmann says, "It is just impossible to live in great cities and not be regulated." And Durant explains, "The ability and inventiveness of the few enabled the many to produce faster than the wage-price cycle permits them to consume.

We've been driven to take measures to alleviate the cycle. That is the main reason for the welfare state."

Rostow and Lippmann also point out that agriculture is posing an economic challenge to the new nations and making difficult problems for the major powers. Rostow says, "Because communism cannot deal with agriculture efficiently and because 85 percent of life in underdeveloped areas is agricultural, agriculture is going to be the problem for communism." Lippmann says, "The success of American agriculture is much more spectacular than the success of American industry. The one place where we are indisputably ahead of Russia and China is in agriculture. Our success is so enormous that we don't know what the hell to do with the results."

In art also, this is a time of change and perhaps the beginning of a new age. Art historian and critic John Canaday says, "Contemporary art is either the greatest revolution in art since the Middle Ages or the most bizarre blind alley. It is a very confused time. An absolute premium has been set on experiment *per se*. It is a period of search.

"The artist starts today with the assumption that he is working for himself and if people are interested in him they'll buy his work. The public must make all the concessions. The idea that the artist is a special person to be pampered and sought out, in a way, is a very vicious, dangerous thing.

"The art studio used to be a workshop where the artist supplied his services. Now the studio is sometimes an experimental laboratory for an aesthetician or a public confessional.

"Art has almost become a form of autopsychiatry," Canaday says. "Art is not needed as an integral part of life today, because contemporary living is crass. We haven't got religion any more. The cathedral spoke to everyone, but TV is a shoddy cathedral. The only faith we have left is in money. Art and money don't make a very good emulsion."

Peering "down the long gun barrel of history," these historians see this as a time of change and confusion in which mankind faces the possibilities of annihilation, years of tension or even a surprising new age—if men can learn to live together. What hope is there for us?

Some of the historians seek hope in the unexpected. Niebuhr says, "I don't think nuclear catastrophe or war is inevitable. History is so full of surprises." David B. Horn, professor of modern history at Edinburgh University, believes the possibility of disarmament is "remote," but he says, "If you change the conditions, something that has gone wrong ninety-nine times may go right the hundredth time. There are great men, and they change things. Efforts to get disarmament may be the most important of our time."

Schlesinger believes we are now "moving toward a pluralistic world—a much more stable world—a world in which peoples can have a sense of national independence, especially in a framework like the United Nations to set the groundwork." Crane Brinton agrees: "If we keep on at this rate, it is just possible that the Russians will mellow a bit, and it is possible that the United Nations can get strong enough to maintain order." Says Rostow, "What historians will write about is how Russia and the United States coped in the last forty years of the twentieth century with the diffusion of power from Washingon and Moscow."

Toynbee sees hope for us in another development. "In the past," he says, "we have failed to make changes without violence and bloodshed. Now Gandhi has shown us how. In the atomic age we will have to pursue our ideologies without using military power. That is perhaps the new thing."

Rostow banks on men's desire for freedom: "Democracy is a system that does not say, 'Papa knows best.'" He feels that the communist world is showing us that, in the long run, "human freedom is the natural direction of human aspirations. It depends, of course, on the vitality of the free world. Every failure in the free world shatters the people of Eastern Europe; every success gives them a little light at the end of the tunnel."

Niebuhr sees hope in the younger generation, saying, "This young generation is very impressive. They have no illusions. They have the maturity to ask if we have the maturity not to crack up."

Perhaps, in the end, all the historians would agree with Esmond Wright when he says, "Today, you don't solve problems. A historian knows that people and nations live with dilemmas all their lives." And the historians would agree with Morison: "We have got to get used to living without solutions. We have to get used to living in crisis after crisis, hoping for the best, but expecting the worst."

The enormous, unprecedented range and speed of change in our times has exposed, to each of us who will dare to look, the impotence and irrelevance of many of our moral attitudes and assumptions and has compelled us to seek new answers to our new dilemmas in this brand-new age.

"History will say," predicts Toynbee, "they created the atomic age, but continued to live as if they were still in the pre-atomic age—and in doing so endangered the whole human race. People will not understand how we could live in the old, violent, obstreperous sort of way."

≪≪ *4.*

Conformity and
the Individual Conscience

"It is getting more difficult in our highly organized society for the individual conscience to break through," says Arnold Toynbee. "Think of the number of religions that came out of the farmers of Vermont. But it would be harder to get prophets out of the offices of General Motors. It's very hard to have an individual morality. It is a question of individual conscience for me. If you do it just because the group demands it, I don't call it morality."

David Riesman, author of the seminal study *The Lonely Crowd*, asserts, "The leviathan of the population makes the individual seem very small. By turning subjects into citizens at the rate we've done, we have increased the scale of human enterprise very much and reduced the importance of individuals."

Mass alone makes an enormous difference. To make clear the effect of a mass society, Professor Philip Hauser conceives of a circle with a ten-mile radius: "In aboriginal America," he writes in an unpublished paper, "a person moving within the ten-mile circle could potentially make only 313 different contacts with other human beings. In contrast, the density of the United States as a whole today would make possible 15,699 contacts in the same land area. The density of the average central city in the United States would permit over 2.5 million contacts, the density of Chicago over 5.3 million contacts, the density of New York City over 7.8 million contacts, and the density of Manhattan over 23.5 million contacts in the same land area." This concept provides, he concludes, "in a simplistic way to be sure, a basis for understanding the difference that city living makes." He believes the impact of this difference on us is as important as a genetic mutation.

The urban mass, for example, offers one explanation of the case in New York City where on March 13, 1964, thirty-eight persons heard or saw a young woman being murdered in the street and did nothing to help her—did not even call the police. When we are exposed to so many people, it is impossible for many of us to be directly concerned about any anonymous one of them. Overwhelming numbers of people can, at times, extinguish our ability to be concerned about each other.

One demonstration of this dehumanization of the individual is the present push to tag people with numbers. An American today is virtually tattooed with numbers: social security number, all-number dialing for his telephone, postal Zip code for his home address, account numbers stamped on his bank checks, and, for millions, a military service serial number. A recent cartoon showed a tombstone that identified the deceased solely with a series of numbers. Some people, worried about the confusing multiplicity of numbers, propose that each of us be given one number at birth to serve all these functions. Then we won't even need names.

Professor Hauser explains, "We have come from a folk society to a mass society. In a mass society the individual is a very small fish in a big pond. Bureaucracy is a function of the mass society. It is unnecessary in a rural society and indispensable in an urban society. In a mass society the authority behind the moral code disintegrates."

The bureaucracies of big business and big government can squash the individual's sense of moral responsibility. Today government often makes moral decisions. It was the government from which the Negro leaders demanded a moral stand against discrimination and segregation. The judicial arm of the government, the Supreme Court, determined in 1954 that public schools should not be segregated. The government decided it was proper for the Project Mercury astronauts to make money out of the space program. Says Dean Samuel Miller, "The center of conscience seems to have been transferred to government." And Barry Goldwater asserts, "Government itself to me is the enemy—by virtue of its power."

Vice-President Humphrey, who was interviewed when he was a senator, believes America depends on both private and governmental efforts: "When you see the amount of charity work being done, you can't say everything is ugly in America. Voluntaryism is the key to our democratic way of life. It is citizen participation in many parts of life. I wouldn't want to be in a society that merely taxed people for a public welfare program. Hitler had one of the best public welfare programs. Our voluntaryism keeps our welfare system honest."

But the problems of the mass society have changed private charity too. The charitable organizations have been forced,

in great measure, to replace free-will giving with highly organized arm-twisting fund drives. They justify this distortion by saying that high-pressure tactics get results. Maybe
so, but no one can pretend his motivation for giving is to
help his fellow man when actually the driving force is em-
barrassment, shame, or a response to business or social
pressures.

Senator Abraham A. Ribicoff of Connecticut explains:
"There has always been a streak of humanitarianism and
brotherhood running through the fabric of this country. If
a farmer's barn burned down, his neighbors might call him
shiftless or lazy but they would help him rebuild the barn."
Then the Great Depression made problems too vast for
private charity to handle alone; the federal government
stepped in. "The federal government did it because they
weren't going to allow there to be mass starvation," Ribicoff
says. "It would be preferable if the federal government did
not have to step into all these fields. The federal government should only come in as a last resort." But, as a result,
he adds, "We have a different kind of society."

Despite all the difficulties involved in high taxation, social
welfare programs and even collective bargaining, we have
evolved an economic system that produces more wealth—
more widely distributed—than any system yet discovered.
But its complex problems are hard to solve; for example, the
arms race affects unemployment, which in turn affects attitudes toward civil rights for minority groups. These problems interlock and none can be solved in isolation.

It seems certain that the government will play an ever
larger role as our moral arbiter. The population explosion,
if it continues, will create more congestion, air and water
pollution and water shortages, and will add more people to

the labor force than we can put to work. "Dealing with the problem raises a moral dilemma," says Philip Hauser. "It becomes necessary to match death control with birth control. Should a person be forced to limit his family? In our society we want people to learn enough to make decisions compatible with themselves and the social order." Will the government eventually have to make a moral decision to depopulate, as it has sought to desegregate?

Irwin Miller, both a businessman and a church leader, is concerned about this problem of bigness: "One of the dangers of bigness is the smothering of the individual. This is not avoiding bigness. Few could have an automobile if we didn't have General Motors. We must find how an individual finds increased personal freedom and increased opportunity for achievement in a big society. This is one of the big debates going on in our society now. I am an optimist on these problems. I could be too optimistic; it is possible that we could crash."

But soar or crash, we cannot expect bigness to disappear. Niebuhr calls it "the new feudalism in economic life." It was no historical accident that the social welfare ideas of the New Deal came along after the frontier was closed to people who needed an escape from failure and from the inability of the established economy to use them. Those who yearn for the earlier eras when American society was divided into more manageable units are wishing for something that is gone forever—and has been disappearing ever since the Civil War galvanized our power and industrialized our society. Those who condemn all bigness—private or public—and who refuse to face up to the realities of bigness fail to make any constructive contribution to our problems.

Inside the big organizations, moral decisions can be compromised and individual responsibility crushed. Committee morality emerges, and the committee member learns to survive by becoming a "team player." He learns to avoid individual responsibility when a moral question arises; he learns to go along with the rituals and taboos of the industrialized society. He can rarely rule; why should he risk?

We call the result "conformity." The conforming "organization man" may be creating a new kind of tribal "moral" code—one in which the individual is swallowed up by the organization and loses any conscience independent of the machine-age tribe.

This is a frightening prospect. A morality of conformity must be dehumanizing, slavish, irresponsible, fearful and undemocratic. Eichman demonstrated this. Chris Argyris, Yale University professor of industrial administration, worries about the problem: "Morality is going down and will slide further unless we change the basic guts of the organizational world we have created. We are spinning our wheels with bigger and bigger organizations, not realizing that this kind of organized life we are creating is deteriorating our freedom."

Dean Samuel Miller reminds us, "The Nazis and Fascists tried to impose social order on the individual. They contained both a termite colony and the overexaggeration of the individual as the Führer."

And George Romney says: "The Nazi Party and Fascists did things as a group they would be aghast to do as individuals. We have [such] groups in the United States—this applies to business, unions, education, race relations—you pick the field.

"I think people are less and less able to distinguish between individual responsibility and group activities, whether the activity is public or private. Membership in a group doesn't excuse the individual from his responsibility. There is a growing tendency to overlook this."

Individual moral courage does not totally disappear in a mass society, but it does become rarer. Commented Paul Tillich, "The critical gadfly is caught and put into a beautiful prison, but he is not permitted to criticize the whole structure of society." We accept the critic of our society, but we do not allow him to go, suggested Tillich, to the very roots of our problems. Too often an intellectual who questions deeply the premises most of us accept is smeared with labels designed to throw him outside the pale of debate.

Those with the courage to set their own moral standards belong, in Tillich's phrase, to a "personal elite." He said, "They have the courage to say 'No!' and this is a very great courage in certain societies.

"The individual has in himself, essentially, the responsibility to form his convictions and act accordingly. If conflict with society cannot be avoided, he has the responsibility to sacrifice himself. This is my liberal Protestant principle. All totalitarian systems deny it, even the Catholic Church, the oldest authoritarian system."

Here Tillich went to the heart of our dilemma. We do not live in an authoritarian system—not even the Catholics among us. The American system permits the individual to do battle with society, if he has the courage. But the price of courage, Tillich noted, can be self-sacrifice. The rebel in a big organization, the parent who repudiates the neighborhood norms, the businessman who opposes the unethical practice of his competitors or associates—all risk self-sacrifice. But to Tillich we have the responsibility to form and act on our convictions.

There is another root question here that must be faced. If, in our society, each man should "form his convictions and act accordingly," are we justifying the man who decides that morality requires him to break a law he finds unjust or to take justice into his own hands? Because we justify the farmers of Lexington, Massachusetts, do we justify too the farmers of Oxford, Mississippi? If it is right for the individual to oppose the law or the rule of an organization of which he is a part, if the individual's moral conviction supersedes society's laws, are we not approving the assassin and the disobedient?

Certainly the Negro's direct-action protest against his condition in America violates local laws. Surely the radical who resorts to violence believes his convictions are superior to the law of the majority. But the distinction between these two social protests is clear. The Negro demonstrators do not resist paying society's penalty; they are supposed to sacrifice themselves. And this applies as well to the white college students who have gone South to teach and register Negroes to vote. This resistance is passive and nonviolent. Our society can accept this kind of rebellion in which decisions ultimately have to be reached peaceably.

Erwin N. Griswold, dean of the Law School of Harvard University, makes this point: "Thoreau acted illegally only by refusing to pay his taxes. He didn't burn down people's houses and insult people." In Dean Griswold's view, three fourths of the civil rights demonstrators have merely expressed their rights. "The Court," he says, "has made it perfectly plain that all these local ordinances have been invalid, and it is a sham for local officials to be relying on them." And he adds, "There is nothing in the Civil Rights Bill that hasn't been part of the Wisconsin and Ohio law for years." Griswold asserts that because local segregation ordinances are unconstitutional, the state officer acts illegally, not the individual disobeying the local law.

The enormous material success of our industrial society has brewed this conflict between the organization and the individual conscience. It has given some men the means and courage to fight for their rights as it has drained others of their sense of individuality and their courage. It also presents us with another serious moral problem: How can all Americans share our affluence?

To build a successful industrial society, we have frequently acted immorally. Perhaps this has been the unavoidable price of the material success we treasure. And to make an amoral judgment: We have gotten results. Today we have the capability to feed, house, clothe and care for every American at a level of human decency.

But despite our success, we still have with us a good share of "one third of a nation ill-housed, ill-clad, ill-nourished," as President Roosevelt put it a quarter of a century ago. Today 38 million Americans have family incomes under $4,000 a year. One fifth of all U.S. families have an average income of about $1,500 a year. Ten million people over sixty-four years of age receive $1,000 or less a year. It is estimated that 14 million American families live in bad housing, in urban or rural slums. Seven million Americans depend on public assistance for at least part of their living. One economist figures 40 million U.S. citizens live below the poverty line. In our society the majority enjoys a surfeit of material goods, and a large minority, whites as well as non-whites, suffers poverty and deprivation.

To the political liberal, the moral problem is how to get the prosperous to spend more to help the silent poor; to the conservative it is how to get the poor to help themselves. However this problem is to be tackled, the disturbing fact is that privation, hunger, unnecessary disease, despair do exist in the richest nation on earth. People are locked in ghetto slums, both urban and rural, from which few escape. They hardly ever vote. Their children attend inferior, overcrowded schools—insuring the inability of the next generation to share our work and our affluence. They lose all motivation to make an effort—all hope to climb out—because for them opportunity in America has disappeared. And some of us, the affluent, release our vague feelings of guilt with the puritanical idea that the poor and the unemployed have only themselves to blame.

Walter Reuther says caustically: "We are so far advanced that we know enough to go hungry when there is too much to eat. You have to be smart to do that."

Sociologist Philip Hauser points to a specific example: "Take the slumlord. The city lowers his assessment on the building he has milked. Then he can sell it at a profit without matching the [building] code. Society has decided to get rid of slums. We have slums because there are profits in slums."

Says the Reverend Coffin of Yale: "In a competitive society, there have to be losers. We haven't faced up to what we're going to do about these things. There are endless pockets of need—millions of urban poor, rural poor, people in mental hospitals, people in jail. It's immoral not to do something to help these people."

To most of us who share America's affluence, America's poor are quite invisible. Is it good enough just to keep them out of sight?

««∙5∙

The Day Work Disappears—
Man vs. Machine

We have only begun to face the moral implications of
automation. It already is changing our society and threatening the economic disruption of all nations, whether industrialized or still underdeveloped.

Ironically, the accelerated replacement of men by machines has become a threat at this particular moment in
history when the vast underdeveloped areas of the world
are beginning their first industrial revolution. The newly
emerging nations are desperately trying to convert from
exploited, raw-material-exporting colonial economies to
more self-sustaining, industrialized economies that can provide work for their people and compete for a share of world
markets. While these nations experience the painful-enough
pressures of the industrial revolution, directly ahead of
them looms the automation revolution.

No sooner will these new nations begin to take pride
in their industrial progress, than automation will cut down

their need for manpower. Instead of trying to convince their people that progress depends on work, the leaders of these nations will have to whirl around and deny the Western idea that work is good. But these new nations will have one advantage over us: Their people who are sent back to sit under a coconut tree will still be able to remember when work was not the only path to heaven.

Arnold Toynbee told me of meeting an old Bavarian-born farmer in Kentucky who had worked hard all his life and now, looking back on his years of toil, felt both satisfaction and independence. Toynbee said, "That's what America meant to him. He had his chance." But now automation will force many Americans to abandon their deep-set conviction that work is essential for a moral life. Our Protestant ethic of work goes back to the beginning of the American story. This ethic, which helped make our nation great, came out of an economy of scarcity, in which every man's hand was needed. Today automation promises to destroy this need.

Our industrial revolution exploded a hundred years ago, during and after the Civil War. But we will not benefit from the time gap between our industrial and automation revolutions; this breathing spell makes the psychological about-face even more difficult. We now have to uproot our belief that work is moral. Paradoxically, says Irwin Miller, "It's what man has aimed at all his life—getting out of work."

The problem is already upon us. We can make more and more goods with less and less work. Only a fraction of our labor force is needed to produce the goods we consume. And this is true in agriculture as well as industry. We have, economists tell us, at least four million workers who must be classified as permanently unemployed; some are second-generation jobless. We have created a workless class. There are simply no jobs for them.

Automation now eliminates from the working labor force as many as 40,000 men a week, either laid off or retired and not replaced. Our steel industry in March, 1963, turned out a million more tons of steel than in the previous March with 25,000 fewer workers. In 1957 the iron and steel industry employed 719,900 workers; by 1962 this was down to 591,900. In 1963 the automobile industry produced 1.8 million more cars and trucks—all more complex than the earlier ones—with 162,700 fewer workers than it needed a decade before. The bituminous coal industry employed 425,000 in 1947; because of extensive automation, as well as competition from other fuels, this was down to 139,800 by 1962. In 1946 coal production was figured at six tons per man per day; in 1964 it was up to sixteen tons per man. Similarly, employment in the lumber and wood-products industry dropped from 845,000 in 1947 to 588,700 in 1962. The railroads employed 1,352,000 in 1947 and 700,200 in 1962 because of technological change and losses in business. And beyond all these examples, an enormous number of companies reportedly have stopped adding workers.

If you look deeper, the picture is even more shocking. Only 25 million workers, one third of our employed labor force, are actually in productive work. Of the rest, 12 million workers live off the defense effort, without which, of course, our economic growth would be even slower than it has been. One study says that one in every eight workers is employed in government work.

Another report charges that in the last decade private enterprise in the U.S. has not, on balance, added one new manufacturing job to the economy and transportation has not added a single net new job for 35 years. Economists figure that between 1950 and 1960, seven of every eight new jobs in this country were created not by the free-enterprise, profit-motivated economy but by government expenditures for defense and space.

According to U. S. Department of Labor calculations, of the 4.3 million non-farm new jobs created between 1957 and 1963, private, profit-motivated business provided only 900,000—one fifth of the total. Those elements in our economy which free-enterprise proponents condemn have taken up the slack. Of the remaining 3.4 million new jobs created, state and local government added 1.8 million, the federal government 200,000, federal purchases from private industry 300,000, state purchases from private industry 500,000 and private non-profit institutions 700,000.

There are many reasons for this snail-paced growth of our traditional private economic institutions—taxation, which reduces free-choice spending; the failure of industry to dream up new products, and, above all, the increased rate of per-man productivity resulting from our advancing technology. How fast automation will continue to wipe out jobs depends on scientific progress and on such economic influences as the volume of investment and marketing prospects. But the trend is clear. An ice-cream manufacturer today uses electronic data-processing to compute his daily requirements and control the valves which govern the flow of ingredients from bulk storage to his blending tanks. The U. S. Post Office is preparing to use optical scanners that will sort mail automatically by reading the five-digit Zip codes. The Veterans Administration already uses a data-transmission system that transcribes insurance-premium information onto magnetic tape in St. Paul, Minnesota, and transmits it to Philadelphia over special wires.

At the same time that technology is cutting the number of production jobs, our labor supply is rapidly growing. Four million babies are now born in this country each year, and scientists predict that in the 1970's we will have five to six million births a year. The task of creating enough jobs for this next generation is awesome; some authorities fear that private industry is not ready to meet this challenge.

The problem will not wait a generation. Economists say that from now until 1970 we must employ 1.3 million new workers a year—almost double the annual increase of the past five years. Very shortly four million youths will become eighteen years old every year. The market for their labor, especially those who are inadequately educated and trained, is shrinking. We are beginning to wake up to the problem of the unschooled and the unskilled. But as the market for unskilled labor diminishes, 35 percent of high school sophomores in our five largest cities still become drop-outs and kill their chance for skilled jobs.

President Kennedy warned that we must find 22 million new jobs in the next decade. The Labor Department says that to keep unemployment at 4 percent will require 3.75 million new jobs by the end of 1970. Walter Reuther figures we must create 80,000 new jobs a week: "Every five weeks for the next decade we have to create a new General Motors Corporation. Four hundred thousand jobs every five weeks just to stand still."

The figures vary but the experts agree the problem is enormous. "This may be the most serious challenge our economy has faced in peacetime," says Philip Hauser, "and may result in a great extent of government interventionism." They don't agree on solutions. Some believe that if we put everyone to work, wages will increase consumer demand, which will in turn consume the products of automation. Others argue, however, that full employment will only drive up wages and reinforce business' desire to accelerate automation.

Of course, we have unmet needs—teaching; slum clearance; the building of low-rent housing, adequate hospitals and enough schools; the construction of modern transportation systems and roads. They apparently can only be tackled by increased government effort, and we have demonstrated our reluctance to turn more of our economy over to government supervision, unless we are pressured by military dangers or the fancied specters of Sputniks. We seem, on the record, to insist that the government mobilize its pump-priming "public works" activity in the areas of defense and space, where the only private competition is over public contracts, and where we can rally Congressional appropriations by blowing the bugle of patriotism.

Perhaps the domestic programs of the Johnson Administration, implementing the ideas of the Kennedy era, are the first break in this pattern. On top of the Peace Corps and the Hill-Burton hospital construction program, we are now getting federal aid to education, federally directed health insurance for the aged and anti-poverty expenditures. They begin to add up to one kind of answer to the problem.

What are the moral challenges that automation holds for us?

First, of course, automation threatens a man's job—makes him insecure and stimulates him, through his union perhaps, to demand job security even when it conflicts with economic efficiency. Says the Reverend Coffin, "What is immoral about Americans—and for that matter always about all people—is the way we are constantly trying to secure ourselves against insecurity. Right now this is particularly true, I think, of America, which is faced with a lot of new forms of insecurity." And Walter Reuther asks: "We know how to make the tools of abundance but not how to manage abundance so we can share it. What good is productive power if people don't have the money to buy the things we know how to make?"

We don't have the answers yet. The urgency of the need to find them is suggested by the prediction of some economists that in ten years we will produce all life's necessities without a single man on the production line. The speed of change is almost supersonic. Philip Hauser says, "If our society were completely frozen, moral issues would be solved in time. But society keeps changing." We need answers now.

Automation threatens the livelihood and morale not only of the sweating worker in a steel mill. The industrial revolution put the workingman on the production line and took away much of his pride in a product he himself had made. Similarly, this new automation revolution will upset the role and the morality of the managerial class. Yale's Professor Arygris reports that the machine is beginning to create apathy (and featherbedding) among industrial managers from whom it strips the responsibility for decisions. He says marketing vice-presidents of some large corporations now have computers to program their sales campaigns. As a result, he reports, "Managers are knowingly distorting data that goes into computers because they fear losing their jobs or some power they had. This is understandable, but not good." He foresees the eventual emergence of unions among middle management, and he warns, "We will need an army of psychiatrists to take care of these people."

"Our subjection" to machines, says the Archbishop of Canterbury, "has a dehumanizing effect."

Dean Samuel Miller of the Harvard Divinity School says, "If we have a God, it's the machine. The machine saves us labor. The machine gives us status. The machine determines how fast we go, and carries us. The machine gives us the means to manipulate—to force the world to do what we want it to. This even gets down to birth control."

The second moral question posed by automation is: How can a society like ours, which does not have jobs for all those who are willing and able to work, continue to regard work as an essential part of moral living?

To enable men for whom there is no work to earn their living, some claim, we must develop new kinds of work, if only because work is moral and necessary for a satisfying life and because idleness is immoral. Reuther believes the solution cannot ultimately come from cutting the work week or having workers share the profits of automation with their employers. For him, the only long-range solution is to create enough jobs for full employment. He asserts that if we were willing to attack our unmet needs, we could achieve this: "The solution has got to be the fact that when you replace a man with a tool, it gives you the opportunity to use him somewhere else to meet the unmet needs of our society." Reuther adds, "Providing a socially meaningful and useful job provides income to sustain a worker and his family, and the worker, in the process of working, has a sense of belonging, participation, dignity and worth. He can't get this unless he works. Man is more than economic. He is social, spiritual."

Others leapfrog the debate over wages and hours and say we must separate entirely the idea of work from the idea of income, so the nonworkers can still be consumers. We begin to hear responsible thinkers speak of "the right to consume" in a society that does not have jobs enough for all. If a man is born into a society that has no need for his work and cannot provide him a chance to earn his way, should he be left starving and in rags? To anyone who believes work is moral and the growth of government is evil, this is a fearsome question.

Automation raises still another moral question: In a society that may eventually have a twenty-hour work week or income without work at all, what will people do with their new leisure? Automation will create a leisured class from the least-skilled, lowest-paid, least-educated part of our society. This will be a strange aristocracy. Warns scientist J. Robert Oppenheimer, "I don't think we are making the proper preparation for the use of the time technology releases."

To some, leisure will become a burden, as work has been toil. Suggests Professor Kirkendall, "Las Vegas may be a preview of what we are coming to. It's a community in which everyone works very hard to have fun. They are almost grim about it. We make more and more out of having fun."

To others, who see automation stirring new activity in the arts, teaching and such, the future promises an exciting creative opportunity—if only it will be grasped. The French political scientist Raymond Aron says, "Our industrial society is the first that has a chance to integrate into society all of the people. The present revolution of expectations is made possible by modern technology and [gives us] the possibility of integrating a large part of society. There is a vague consciousness that a new form of human organization is necessary."

Says Luis Muñoz Marin, the longtime governor of Puerto Rico, "This is the ideal civilization of the future. You free men from just earning their living and you liberate them to justify their lives to themselves."

«« 6.

The Scientist as God and Devil

Our society stands on the scientific notion that man, independently and individually, can approach some approximation of the truth. This concept cuts the ground out from under those who claim authoritarian possession of The Truth. When men believe they possess ultimate truth, they cannot adapt to change. In a world changing as rapidly and drastically as ours, change itself throws into doubt even those who are convinced they hold the final answers. The lesson of our scientific age is that we have not found truth but we are searching for it.

In great measure, the scientists have created our moral crisis as well as our material comforts. They have changed our world. Automation is only one gift which upsets our moral traditions. Medical scientists have made the population explosion possible by slowing down the death rate. Science's discoveries—the computer, the Bomb, the oral contraceptive, the subconscious—have damaged men's sense of individual responsibility.

These achievements pose moral questions. As the Reverend Coffin puts it: "The computer says, 'Here are all the facts. Now what are you going to do about it?' " Scientists, like gods, have given us the potential for heaven and hell, and then, too often, have solemnly turned their backs.

Science has, to a momentous degree, diminished the individual. It has shown man that he lives on an insignificant planet in the suburbs of a not-too-prominent solar system— one of countless galaxies, many of which may contain life more intelligent than ours. It has shown man that his subconscious and the laws of probability control much of his activity and success. It has shown man that he can never again hope to master all knowledge. And, by destroying the comforting myth of racial superiority, it has demonstrated to the white man that he belongs to a minority that hardly affords him a basis for arrogance.

Science has damaged our beliefs in a personal God and a life beyond life and cut us off from some of the hopes and superstitions that have succored us. The laws of probability cannot replace this loss nor fill the void nor reduce the finality of death. In sum, science has threatened our feeling of individual moral responsibility. Some scientists claim that science itself is neutral, but, as Philip Hauser says, "The knowledge we have undermines social mores."

Dr. Glenn T. Seaborg, chairman of the Atomic Energy Commission, a Nobel Prize laureate and former chancellor of the University of California at Berkeley, says we have gone through three revolutions: the first, democratic; the second, industrial, and the third, scientific. "The third revolution," he says, "creates a much greater movement toward complexity."

One example of the difficult moral problems with which scientists have bombarded us is the glamorous space race,

A surprising number of scientific leaders charge that the crash program to put men into space and onto the moon detracts from national security and diverts us from the fight against such evils as cancer and mental illness. They point out that we need 125,000 more teachers and a million hospital beds. Should we race the Russians to the moon or spend the same talent and money fighting disease, ignorance and poverty? The $20-billion space race, engaging 250,000 scientists and engineers, compares less to Columbus' voyage of discovery than to the building of the Pyramids as symbols of the magnificence of kings.

The late Dr. Leo Szilard, who played a major part in helping Albert Einstein convince President Roosevelt in 1939 to build the atomic bomb, and who later opposed its use against unwarned Japanese cities, put our choice about space bluntly to me: "This is a moral issue and we are making the wrong choice. To race the Russians to the moon and let our old people live on almost nothing is immoral. Putting men on the moon has nothing to do with science— it is a circus. Our astronauts play the role of the gladiators of ancient Rome. I think we should not race. What are we trying to prove? It's lunacy, I say."

Dr. Oppenheimer, on whom the Atomic Energy Commission in 1963 bestowed the Enrico Fermi Award, says of his friends who work in this field, "The more competent they are, the more troubled they are." In London, British scientist and author Sir Charles Snow regards the space race as "misguided—really rather a pity." He describes the choice: "The solar system is desperately dull. We could make South America a decent part of the world with the same effort." Arnold Toynbee adds, "We'd better clear up the world before we go into space."

Possibly, suggests Dean Samuel Miller, "the big boys will

bump each other, and a little nation not interested in the space race at all will create a sane society and inherit the earth." The hope of our scientific age, in truth, could depend on the meek.

"I broke with the ideas of progress and the perfectability of man early," says Reinhold Niebuhr. "There is progress in education and mastery of nature, but the nuclear age has completely refuted the hopes that this was for the good of man."

Says Professor Leroy G. Augenstein, chairman of the Department of Biophysics at Michigan State University, "Science is now presenting vast new potentialities. Society must make the decision of how you use these things. Society is going to miss the boat unless they grapple with this question: Why is man here? In the past, this question was a luxury. Now with the population explosion, this question is no longer a luxury but is being forced on society. It will be answered by default, as it is now, or by active discussion." He adds, "Our society is no longer chained to exerting 85 to 90 percent of its efforts to producing survival goods and is now free to devote more than one half of its productivity to services which we normally associate with the good life. If we only build color TV sets and make sexier movies and electric can-openers, and we don't do something about the question of why is man here, we are being amoral as all get out."

Men like Augenstein worry that such moral decisions will be left to the scientists. He wants society to decide when population growth should level off and how this is to be done. He warns, "It is a terribly important thing that we scientists not be put in the position of being dictators."

Snow, however, believes that scientists must ready themselves to participate in these decisions. He says, "Scientists have to deliberately train themselves for the world responsibility they are bound to have thrust on them. Some scientists must take the risks and horrors of politics. I'd like to see some scientists as senators of the United States—not one but several, and preferably of different opinions. Otherwise, the real decisions are going to be made in back rooms and translated by politicians acting as press-relations officers. If we are going to make democracy work, we have to have these arguments, but in public, so people can know what is being decided about their fate."

The most dangerous problem that science has lobbed up to us is whether we shall use nuclear weapons. The scientific world has been torn apart over the responsibility for making fateful decisions in nuclear science. Oppenheimer says, "I'm a purist. The scientist's job is to find the truth and to tell it." He believes the scientist must help people understand, but, he adds, "There would not be a 'bomb' in the world if it were for the scientists. That's government!"

Snow suggests, "A scientist has to be neutral in his search for the truth, but he cannot be neutral as to the use of that truth when found. If you know more than other people, you have more responsiblity, rather than less."

Americans live with a special moral problem as the only people who have used the atomic bomb to kill. Oppenheimer, who had a part in that decision, explains, "We had already done Tokyo [with fire bombs]. We were already debauched. The notion that we could have a great war and not use the stuff is even more dangerous. Virtuous nations are not virtuous when at war, although this is still a view held by some—despite Hiroshima."

Snow feels differently: "I still think it was done without

any real sense of that present or this future. It obviously meant that the whole East thinks we are entirely heedless of life." And he regards the second bomb dropped on Nagasaki as "utterly needless."

His wife, Lady Snow, the novelist Pamela Hansford Johnson, comments, "I felt the night the bomb dropped we had put ourselves outside the moral pale."

As Pope Paul VI told the United Nations, "Today as never before, in our era so marked by human progress, there is need for an appeal to the moral conscience of man. For the danger comes, not from progress, nor from science— indeed, if properly utilized, these could rather resolve many of the grave problems that assail mankind. No, real danger comes from man himself, wielding ever more powerful arms, which can be employed equally well for destruction or for the loftiest conquests."

While the moral problems of nuclear power attract our attention and stir our fears, we have hardly become aware of the equally shattering problems that are now being posed by discoveries in the biological sciences. A concrete example: the need to decide who will live and who will die in the distribution of transplanted organs and the use of such instruments as artificial kidney machines.

Scientific progress is forcing new moral judgments on those men of science who are in closest contact with the public: the doctors. We no longer regard medical care as a luxury. As never before, medicine has the power to cure the ill and prolong life, and, as a result, medical care is in great and growing demand. This demand has created immediate problems of quantity. We don't have enough doctors, nurses, laboratories or hospital beds. We don't have enough of the tools of medicine that can save lives. In good part, we have these shortages because we are not yet prepared to pay enough to buy the facilities and train and hold the skilled personnel.

Modern medicine has grown so fantastically expensive that now, between the people able to pay for care in major illness and those who must resort to charity, we have a new class of the "medically indigent." These are people with incomes large enough to meet normal expenses but inadequate to pay big medical bills. The present struggle in the medical world is over how these people can receive and pay for high-quality medical care.

It is estimated that if everyone bought as much medical care as families with incomes of at least $10,000 a year, Americans would spend 30 percent more for medical care.

It was a slow and frustrating battle simply to permit people to contribute a fraction of their earnings to a federal government system that would help insure medical care for the aged. The American Medical Association, seeing the bogeyman of so-called "socialized medicine" under the bed, spent millions of dollars trying to prevent the creation of such a medical payment system for the aged. The AMA succeeded in delaying the plan for years, during which people suffered and died; but it finally lost the battle.

The AMA, in fact, presents a case study of an organization so frightened by change that it refuses to face reality or its own moral responsibility. The AMA's record of blind opposition to change is virtually unbroken. Its leadership of doctor-politicians has, over the past thirty years and more, fought every organizational and economic change in medical practice in the United States. The careers of many doctors have been damaged because they opposed the AMA's negativism. Almost every time, the AMA has fought a retreating battle and ultimately lost, because it offered no constructive solutions to real problems. The total effect, of which many doctors are only now becoming aware, has been to increase rather than reduce the very danger the AMA fears—government-controlled medical care and medical practice.

The list of AMA negativism is shocking. It opposed Blue Cross and other voluntary health insurance ideas until the threat of compulsory governmental health insurance became visible. It opposed, initially and often for long periods, Blue Shield, group practice, closed-panel practice and various private health insurance plans. It opposed financial aid to medical students and federal loans to medical students. It opposed the Public Health Service report on smoking until June 1964, meanwhile accepting a ten-million-dollar grant from the tobacco industry to conduct further studies. It opposed letting doctors work on salary in hospitals and corporations. It has long sought to limit medical care for veterans and even to curtail the facilities available for service-connected disabilities. And the AMA has wielded considerable power to influence the size of medical-school enrollment and control the supply of doctors at a time when conservative experts say we need 50 percent more first-year places in medical schools.

The AMA is a trade association and, like so many similar organizations in other industries, has sought to maintain an obsolete status quo. It has failed sadly to lead the way to sound and desirable solutions for the problems surrounding health care in a mass society. Too many doctors have abdicated their moral responsibility and left the field to the professional doctor-politicians who would like to see the world stand still.

Because some powerful medical leaders battle against changes in the availability of good medical care, many

Americans receive inferior care. One study found that 90 percent of the appendixes removed by some doctors prove to be healthy. In one New York hospital in 1962 only 16 percent of the surgery was performed by qualified surgeons. Our failure to reduce the national infant death-rate has dropped us to eleventh among nations. In our urban slums, infant mortality is as much as three times greater than among babies born to patients who can afford private prenatal medical attention. In our slums, too few doctors care for the poor; in some 3,000 small towns in the United States, there are no doctors at all. Despite all our scientific advances, 74 million Americans are afflicted with chronic diseases. We have some of the best medical care in the world, but we also have some of the most inexcusable.

The medical scientist faces his own moral dilemmas. The growth and complexity of scientific knowledge has forced doctors to specialize. A single doctor can no longer know enough to treat every ailment. This "knowledge explosion" is leading to the disappearance of the traditional family doctor and is making medical care in America increasingly impersonal. Most medical students today become specialists and tend to think more in terms of disease problems and less in terms of human patients. "At a time when amorality is rising," says one thoughtful doctor, "we have to work harder to make sure the doctor is protected against his culture, by strengthening his obligation to people who entrust him with questions of life and death."

Now that medicine is able to keep the dying alive longer, a doctor must also decide whether to end a patient's apparently hopeless pain or to continue the artificial processes which stretch out his life in a terminal coma. A California doctor, telling of keeping alive a patient in the last stages of cancer, asks: At what point shall I remove the life-sustaining tube and end the patient's life? Says one respected health insurance expert, "Too many people are kept alive when their situation becomes terminal. They become vegetables after their usefulness and enjoyment of life ceases."

This new power leads to still another dilemma. Should medical researchers experiment on human patients? If not, how will doctors learn which treatment works and which does not? Where shall the medical scientist draw the line between the number of deaths a new drug may cause and the number of lives it may save? Since almost all drugs are toxic and can cause death, is it moral to risk a few deaths to save many lives?

The booming growth in the world's population, which science made possible, has intensified the religious debate over birth control. The Roman Catholic Church accepts the need to limit population growth and the desirability of achieving family planning, but the Catholic Church has firmly opposed birth control by mechanical means. Church leaders have opposed the use of welfare funds to give birth-control information and devices to the poor. In 1960 the bishops of crowded Puerto Rico declared it a sin to vote for Governor Luis Muñoz Marin because his government had permitted the dissemination of birth-control information. Archbishop James P. Davis, then archbishop of the island, said to me, "The side effect of this approach to it on the human being who has little enough self-respect and dignity is that his self-respect will be less. And out-and-out contraception lends itself to a question: Is a favored class afraid they will have to share with a less favored class? Is this part of the fear? If so, it should be taken out and examined."

Governor Muñoz told me, "There is no law against birth-control information. Doctors in public health centers can give information to married women who request it for reasons of health. That depends on the doctor's convictions. He may believe poverty is bad for health."

The development of effective birth-control pills has now changed the terms of the controversy and required the Church to re-examine its interpretation of the morality of contraception. The pills made the Church's position against "mechanical means" suddenly less clear.

The revolution in the biological sciences has even deeper ramifications. Scientists are beginning to explore the possibilities of "genetic surgery," by which they may eliminate diabetes or give a patient a new heart—or shape mankind to some master's model. Several scientists have already achieved human fertilization in a test tube, a form of experimentation that has been condemned by Catholic authorities. And the subject of artificial insemination has moved on from the medical to a legal frontier. Other biological scientists are exploring the mechanism of the human mind and devising new methods of persuasion. Says one, "The Chinese did brainwashing all wrong [in Korea]. There are methods available now where you can erase the old and put in the new."

Most dramatic and potentially far-reaching of all these biological investigations is the effort to crack the "code of life" and discover precisely how human characteristics are handed down from one generation to the next. With such knowledge, human characteristics could be manipulated; it is predicted that in less than a generation the scientist will be able to create life itself. He will transform dead chemicals in a test tube into living material that can grow and reproduce itself. He will perform an act of God.

Because this biochemical frontier is so little understood and because it contains such enormous moral meaning for mankind, this research deserves attention in any consideration of the moral problems on our horizon. Science is making life less a mystery and more a problem in chemistry and physics. The achievement of creating living matter promises to overshadow even the most optimistic benefits of the better-publicized race into space. If scientists succeed in unlocking the secret of life—and they have already made startling progress—their efforts will affect everyone on earth. They will gain the power to control cancerous growth, to battle virus and mental disease and to manipulate the development of living things, including man himself.

Scientists are proving that all living things are created from inanimate matter. They have put together nonliving chemicals to form complicated units just like those units which comprise living things. When the biochemists completely master the techniques of making the complex building blocks of life, and when they then fit together the blocks themselves, they will have created living matter.

To do this, the biochemists are trying to understand what goes on inside the cell. A single cell is as complex as a city, contains at least 10 billion atoms and uses energy to perform thousands of chemical jobs inside itself. In the healthy cell these activities are organized and regulated.

The most crucial materials inside the nucleus of the cell are molecules called nucleic acids. And the most important of these nucleic acids, scientists believe, is a huge molecule called DNA (deoxyribonucleic acid). Without DNA, no cell can grow or reproduce itself; with it, the processes of life are set in motion. Some scientists think the first living thing on earth was a blob of DNA. In all the world, it is said, only DNA has the power to make exact copies of itself.

DNA serves as a blueprint. A cell follows this blueprint to make protein—the chief material of living cells—out of some twenty chemicals called amino acids. Since the human body is said to contain 100,000 different proteins, the DNA blueprint determines precisely which kind of protein will be made, and thus the nature of each cell and its descendants. DNA is called "the master molecule of life." To create life artificially, scientists must construct DNA from dead chemicals and enable it to manufacture amino acids into proteins.

The scientists have been battering at the fortress of the cell. Some have carefully mixed a soup of chemicals, exposed it to electrical energy and dramatically made some simple amino acids, the raw material of proteins. Other biochemists have been building artificial proteins.

But making DNA—the master molecule—has been more difficult. To build DNA that carries useful blueprint instructions, scientists must understand the arrangement of its parts which carry the inherited message. Many scientists are working at the heart of this problem—breaking the code of DNA. When they can achieve this, the secret of life will be secret no longer. Says Linus Pauling, two-time Nobel Prize winner at the California Institute of Technology, "There is no reason why nucleic acid, proteins, genes should not be synthesized—why genes should not be introduced into living things." But, he adds, "the chemistry of nucleic acid is in a primitive stage."

Some believe the control of cancer lies down this same road. It has already been shown that some cancers in animals are started by viruses (containing DNA). Outlaw

DNA may turn out to be the cause of many cancers. If scientists learn how to alter the DNA, perhaps they can stop cancer. They may discover anti-cancer chemicals, perhaps man-made forms of DNA.

Others dream of the day when, by manipulating and making DNA, man can control his inheritance and change human characteristics. This dream raises controversial moral questions: Should society someday use these biological discoveries to improve the breed of mankind by purposefully changing genes? And if so, who is to decide what are improvements? These questions trouble scientists. Most insist that they are not questions for science but for public policy.

Some scientists also worry whether, by creating man-made life, they will unleash an uncontrollable monster. One Nobel Prize winner warns, "Synthetic life may be exceedingly virulent and strong and may destroy all other life on earth."

Another fundamentally moral question is: What will this new scientific knowledge mean to man's view of himself, his responsibilities, his universe and his God? One scientist says that perhaps someday man will learn "the molecular structure of God." He means that science may wipe out belief in a supernatural origin of life by finding chemical answers to all the mysteries of life.

Reinhold Niebuhr believes that life is ultimately not explainable: "You always have this mystery in the creative process—that a previous cause is never an adequate explanation of a subsequent event. This is the mystery of creation." He does not believe that science "can go the whole way."

Linus Pauling says, "There is no area of the world that should not be investigated by scientists. There will always remain some questions that have not yet been answered.

In general, these are questions that have not yet been posed."

The scientists' attack on "the code of life" illustrates the enormous impact scientific advances are having on our thinking about ourselves and our relations to our fellow men. Science has given us unprecedented choices. And if scientists have already raised baffling moral questions and shaken some of our old beliefs and certainties, there is more to come—much more.

Pope John XXIII wrote in his encyclical, *Pacem in Terris:* "The progress of learning and the inventions of technology clearly show that, both in living things and in the forces of nature, an astonishing order reigns, and they also bear witness to the greatness of man, who can understand that order and create suitable instruments to harness those forces of nature and use them to his benefit."

The Reverend Martin Luther King, Jr., president of the Southern Christian Leadership Conference and recipient of the Nobel Peace Prize of 1964, points to the work unfinished: "We have made of the world a neighborhood through our scientific genius, and now through our moral commitment we must make of it a brotherhood. We've got to learn to live together as brothers or we'll perish together as fools."

⫷ 7.

America's New Imperial Morality

As never before in our history, we are involved now in the fate and future of the world. "The extraordinary fact," says Raymond Aron, speaking of Americans, "is you have got extreme power without wanting it. You discovered your own security at the same time as you came to the first rank. When you are powerful, you cannot stay outside."

How morally are we using our vast new power in the world?

This question must be answered in two ways: first, specifically in relation to our power to make nuclear war; and second, more generally, in relation to our wealth, our resources—and our ability to wage any kind of war.

Perhaps all international power is rooted in the ability to make war, but that seems a narrow definition. (Where are the Pope's battalions?) Our power to strengthen the periphery nations against communist expansion—the power of our ideals and our dreams of government and man—must not be depreciated just because of the nuclear sword hanging over us.

Whatever the morality of those acts at Hiroshima and

Nagasaki—and people are still dying from them—nuclear power has changed the nature of war, and the morality of war, for all time. I have stood in the port city of Hiroshima at 8:15 on an ordinary gray morning. I watched the men bicycling to work through the park that now covers Ground Zero and heard the children's tinkling laughter as they walked toward school. Hiroshima must have been much like that at 8:15 on the cataclysmic morning when the *Enola Gray* let go her bomb and fused the city into a mass of rubble and left behind the dead, the scorched and the insidiously crippled.

Before Hiroshima, war had become less and less catastrophic economically. A defeat in modern pre-nuclear war need not eradicate a nation's economic base. To see this we have only to look at the swift revival (with our help) of West Germany, Italy, Japan, the Soviet Union and Great Britain since World War II. It is not surprising that weapons have been suggested that will destroy populations without harming property. For some, this makes the big war once again conceivable.

Lewis Mumford says our crucial moral decision in World War II was not Hiroshima at all but "the decision in 1942 to take over the Fascist policy of extermination bombing. Fire bombing roasted alive thousands in Tokyo in one night. It was more terrible than what we did at Hiroshima. The atomic bomb only gave us the means to do this, once the taboo is gone." And Bruce Catton points out that we Americans have practiced total war ever since Sherman marched through Georgia.

A cynic might claim that if God is all-knowing and just, war may be a Malthusian way to increase the death rate (of young potent males—no homosexuals allowed) to counteract a rising birth rate. World War II proved that gun-

powder could no longer do the job. "You could argue that
World War II resulted in the greatest increase of population
the world has ever seen," points out demographer Philip
Hauser. Birth rates went up; wartime medical advances cut
death rates; nations even evolved furloughing policies to
keep up their birth rates. So, in His wisdom, perhaps God
gave us new power and will lead us to use it if ever the death
rate must be raised drastically.

Nuclear weapons have now made human annihilation possible and a planned major war insane. The concept of
"overkill" may be efficient but hardly moral. Says John
Cogley, "One man made the decision to plunge man into
original sin, and now we are where one man may again make
the decision." The man whose finger is on "the button"
holds vast power. Aron points out, "Your deterrent is con-
vincing other persons that you are willing to perform an
irresponsible act." Today we fear most the irresponsible act,
whether it be performed in Moscow, Peiping or Dallas.

Said Dr. Leo Szilard, "How many governments are sane?
Professional politicians are more afraid that they may lose
an election than that the country may lose a war."

"Do you think anyone at the Pentagon knows what a
nuclear war is?" asks Walter Lippmann. "Poor things, they
can't know. What we do know is we cannot have a direct
military conflict. We can have indirect conflict as we have
in Southeast Asia.

"Atomic weapons have changed the nature of war. Now
there are two powers that have the absolute power to destroy the other. Fifty million Americans killed would be the
end of the American Republic, and 50 to 100 million Russians killed would be an end of Russian society. War cannot
now be used as a means of policy. The two great powers

cannot go to war. It would be the mutual destruction of each other." And President Kennedy described the 1963 nuclear-test-ban treaty with the Soviet Union as "a shaft of light cut into the darkness."

How close we came to nuclear war during the Cuban missile crisis has been reported by Roger Hilsman, then State Department intelligence chief. The most fantastic incident occurred when one American plane, through a navigational error, approached Soviet air space during the height of the crisis and was turned back only at the last moment. Echoes of *Dr. Strangelove*.

Oscar Handlin says, "It is inevitable that we will live for a long time with this threat. Even if we had a communist regime in the United States, we would still have missile bases in Kansas."

"We go to endless pains to keep alive almost dead bodies in hospitals," says Mumford, "and at the same time we are preparing to wipe out sixty million lives. This is insanity."

Secretary of State Dean Rusk, judging nuclear weapons' effect on international relations, sees hopeful signs: "The nuclear situation has tended to make voices a little less strident. It's had a sobering effect on national ambitions and appetites. It reminds people there are problems that make pigmies of us all."

Perhaps the danger of annihilation would not seem so terrifying to many Americans if they had not lost the promise of heaven.

But, Rusk adds of The Bomb, "It has not affected our ideals of freedom or our working in our national interest. It has changed the style, the tone, in the direction of caution, because it is a dangerous situation."

From a historian's perspective, Arnold Toynbee says,

"If the British and American anthems were written now, they would have fewer images about war. There is a great change going on about war all over the world. It is regarded as an evil rather than glorious.

"Making war was not regarded as a crime or wrong, but now it means the destruction of the human race. Unless we could develop a loyalty to the human race as a whole, we shan't survive. We must not regard anybody as a foreigner, a 'nigger,' or outside the pale. We must all be part of the human family. If it hasn't changed our ideas about right and wrong in international situations, we shall not survive."

It has been said that no nation can any longer defend its people; it can only revenge them.

Luis Muñoz Marin believes that one hundred years from now the Cuban missile crisis will be seen as a turning point in the history of the world. He notes that "the world was deeply changed by the Cuban crisis of 1962, profoundly changed for the better, because of the firm, steadfast way Kennedy handled it—not only firm but wise. He left Khrushchev a way out, which Khrushchev took. . . . The mass of the people now have a consciousness of what they are living with. The Cuban crisis changed the world."

I have spent weeks with the crews who man the Polaris submarines at their advance base in Scotland's Holy Loch. I found them men of courage and balance, who saw war not as glorious but as final. These men lock themselves up, for a month at a time, inside a submarine armed with 16 nuclear-warheaded missiles, each one 25 times more powerful than the bomb that devastated Hiroshima, each one able to destroy a city. These men did not swagger. They dreaded the day when the coded signal to fire might come to them, submerged somewhere deep in the sea. They would perform this act with the knowledge that before their weapons were launched, everyone they loved, everything they dreamed of returning to, would be gone—wiped from the earth.

Reinhold Niebuhr calls this "a period of tragic maturity. We have always had our way when we were weak; now we are very, very strong and cannot have our way." The rise of the extreme right in this country is one result of the frustration caused by our inability to dominate the world and bend other nations to our will. In his speech in the Senate on March 25, 1964, Senator J. William Fulbright, chairman of the Foreign Relations Committee, made this point. He said, "We are confronted with a complex and fluid world situation and we are not adapting ourselves to it. We are clinging to old myths in the face of new realities . . . the United States is not omnipotent and cannot be."

Certainly nuclear weapons have increased man's moral concern and frustration. "You cannot wage foreign policy without threatening to wage this immoral atom war," asserts Professor Aron. "Politics is more immoral than ever. Many people are crushed under the burden of this contradiction. In this horrible game, the big player must be respected by his opposite number. If Kennedy had accepted the missile bases in Cuba, he would not have been respected.

"The common denominator is that politics is a dirty business, and we cannot be sure that illegal action is not sometimes useful and lying is sometimes necessary. . . . Your President was quite ready to use force against a small country with good conscience and with the approval of most of the people."

Although disarmament and a nuclear-test ban are among the few issues in international affairs on which many Americans have expressed moral indignation, unofficial movements to achieve them have had little effect on the arms race. It is controlled by more pragmatic considerations. David Riesman warns, "We have to step up the pace of moral development if we are not going to put an end to the moral experiment." He reports that 20 percent of the seniors in a middle-class New England high school recently voted for preventive war. They had, Riesman says, "no sense of moral catastrophe."

The threat of nuclear disaster affects people in many different ways, and those who are concerned with such frightening matters offer us some idea of the range of reactions:

Oppenheimer says, "If you prepare to suffer—or prepare to inflict—such monstrous and irreparable damage, it's hard to take small considerations seriously. We do, but it produces a sense of unreality."

Walter Reuther warns, "If you can't preserve the peace, everything else is academic. What good are higher wages if someone pushes the button?"

One American minister notes, "It's putting the man in the street into a foxhole religion: 'God, save me and I will believe.' "

AEC Chairman Seaborg says, "It has presented us with life-and-death problems. It has presented us with problems we have never faced before. It might be that it demands a higher moral standard if we are going to survive."

But Willy Brandt expresses hope: "This problem of living with uncertainty includes the danger, for some people, that [it] may lead to the dissolution of traditional things, but if looked at in the right way [living with uncertainty] may lead to better things."

Says the Archbishop of Canterbury, "A lot of people are

so oppressed by the possible destruction of the world, they ask why should they worry. But Christians know we are always under divine judgment, and that braces us to the service of our fellows."

One escape from the nuclear danger is the use of non-violence as a technique for achieving change. So far, non-violence has been tried only for civil change: by Mahatma Gandhi, Martin Luther King, Jr., the Buddhists of South Vietnam. But some believe that it has future relevance for international relations as well, in a world in which we cannot afford a war that may go nuclear. If this be so, here may be one moral gain out of the immorality of The Bomb.

We have not reached such a morality yet. U Thant, Secretary-General of the United Nations, speaks for the necessity of force in the world as it is: "When you appoint a policeman in Manhattan to maintain peace, his function is to maintain peace. If a woman is mugged, he cannot stand by without using force. When there is a disturbance of the peace, this is the function of the policeman—to use force." Similarly, "When the Security Council decides to send a UN force to the Congo, if breaches of the peace occur, the function of the police force is to preserve law and order."

Nuclear power is not our only moral challenge in world affairs. Perhaps even more tangible is the leadership that has been thrust upon us. Hubert Humphrey voices optimism: "The best thing that happened in the United States is we have had to take up the burden of leadership after World War II. A struggle is now going on in America whether we're going to have leadership of the warrior or of the philosopher and teacher. After the war we had to give leadership, and isn't it funny that the more we've given, the more we've had? We have helped ourselves at home and we have done more abroad. Some say we should quit this; it isn't appreciated. It's difficult to be a rich man in the city of the poor."

Toynbee believes we have established a new standard of "imperial morality" which is not exploitive. His term offers us a new vision of the rich and strong nations acting morally toward those who have less and are weaker. Some time before his death Adlai Stevenson spoke to me of this, from his experience as United States ambassador to the United Nations: "We are in the twilight of imperialism, and the death of every imperialism has been followed by a new one. Our imperialism is dying, and the Russian is rising. It is, in effect, a form of Roman imperialism—a universality of authority. It has the force of military power and the great force of an ideal especially attractive to the underdeveloped countries. The conflict is: Is the Soviet Union going to prevail—as the new imperialisms always have? What we are experimenting with now is whether we can make a transition from the old imperialism to a new era without imperialism. This is really what the United Nations means. Can it enable us to pass from this imperialism to a new order without a new imperialism and new violence?"

Secretary Rusk agrees in essence: "We don't have a special morality we are trying to impose on other people. We are part of a mainstream." Rusk says our actions and attitudes today are based on the fundamental American political idea that governments should derive their power from the consent of the governed: "This is deeply rooted in a moral concept, and at the same time it is the most explosive idea in the world today. This is why we don't like what is going on in Eastern Europe, why we get along better with democracies than dictatorships. Since World War II, United

States power has been put behind the concept that men don't like to be pushed around."

Rusk asserts the realism of moral power: "On the level of political action, moral ideas are of the greatest importance. These moral ideas are themselves an elementary ingredient of power. Any analysis of power must make room for a large component of what people want in the moral field—what's worth dying for."

Arnold Toynbee looks back to the Nazi era and confirms this thought: "Certainly the Germans' defeats have been moral defeats. They defied the world's conscience."

Walter Reuther believes it is essential to our own survival that we understand and live by our moral values. He says, "If the contest with the Soviet Union is to be waged solely on the economic level, the Soviets are going to win. Their sets of values are geared to that end. We provide an opportunity for achieving a sense of worth and purpose." And he adds, "The crisis in this country is a crisis in our values. We profess to believe in a system of values different from the Russians'. Our free society will only survive if we live by our true values."

No one would argue that we always use our great power to express our true values. Many times our acts fail to include Rusk's moral component. We have been criticized severely on moral grounds for our support of dictators, for our participation in the arms race and for such specific actions as the Cuban Bay of Pigs invasion. Many have voiced desperate doubts about the morality of our military intervention in Vietnam and in the Dominican Republic. And we have been blamed for failing to act—during the Hungarian revolt and during the construction of the Berlin Wall, for two examples.

Our failures have not only been at the leadership level. Our actions as indvidual private citizens can also affect deeply how the world sees us and our power.

Several years ago I went down to the tiny colony of British Guiana on the northeast coast of South America, to research an article on Cheddi Jagan, who had been elected the colony's premier by a free vote of the people.

Cheddi Jagan is a charming, handsome man. He grew up in British Guiana on a sugar plantation where his father, whose forebears came from India, worked. Jagan got a break and went to college at Howard University in Washington, D.C. One day he and a classmate—a Negro—rode into Virginia and were ordered to the back of the bus.

Jagan spent his summers working. He sold patent medicine in Harlem one summer—peddling stuff that cost a dime to the poor for a dollar. Scholarships enabled him to go to dental school in Chicago; there he worked nights as an elevator operator in an apartment building where, he remembers, some rich businessmen kept their mistresses.

Cheddi Jagan became a communist, and in his home late one night he told me at length and with great fervor how his experiences in the United States had convinced him that our system could not help his country—it was exploitive. Jagan came up with the wrong answers, but what he saw of our society, what he saw of how we acted toward each other, made a Marxist of him. What we do morally as individuals can have repercussions around the world.

During the war in Algeria, I visited the refugee camps for Algerians who had fled across the border into Tunisia. At the Tunisian border province of Le Kef, Governor Bechir Bellagha arranged a dinner, a formal midday affair in exotic surroundings with strange foods and cordial conversation. At one point, the young governor, regarded as one of the most able leaders in Tunisia, blamed the French-Algerian war on the United States. He charged that without American military supplies the French would have to stop the fighting. He regarded the United States as aiding the enemy of his brothers across the nearby border.

I tried to explain my country's dilemma. France was an ally, I said, an important member of NATO and partner in the effort to prevent Soviet expansion. I explained our fundamental belief in the self-determination of people, and spoke of our own revolution for self-government, Woodrow Wilson's ideals and Franklin Roosevelt and his Good Neighbor attitude toward South America. But the governor waved me off. He said, "That's all a long time ago. That's ancient history." He was convinced that we do not practice what we preach.

Secretary Rusk realizes such contradictory problems exist, but he says, "There is a decency about the long-range policies of the United States that is recognized around the world. We see this in moments of crisis."

Senator J. William Fulbright told the Senate in a speech on September 15, 1965: "We are not, as we like to claim in Fourth of July speeches, the most truly revolutionary nation on earth; we are, on the contrary, much closer to being the most unrevolutionary nation on earth. We are sober and satisfied and comfortable and rich. . . . We must try to understand social revolution and the injustices that give it rise because they are heart and core of the experience of the great majority of people now living in the world." And criticizing U.S. intervention in the Dominican Republic, he added, "The movement of the future in Latin America is social revolution. The question is whether it is to be communist or democratic revolution and the choice which the Latin Americans make will depend in part on how the United States uses its great influence."

Goldwater goes further and defends the Bay of Pigs invasion: "When we are seeking freedom for other people, I don't think there is any immorality in getting the job done. It would become immoral if we invaded a country or caused a revolution for some trade benefit. I wonder sometimes if a nation can afford to live by this rule in this world. I think it is an immoral world. Communism is immoral."

One of the chinks in our armor of moral leadership is our Texas-like tendency to proclaim our own perfection and superiority. This is not a new American characteristic; Alexis de Tocqueville commented on it in 1831. But today, given our power and our wealth, these pronouncements sound like arrogance, and, at times, undermine acceptance of our decency. Paul Tillich made this point when he said of our power in the world: "I think we use it responsibly with one exception: to forget the ambiguity of our perfection as a nation." He says we cannot morally regard ourselves as perfect in a world where one of every three persons lives under communism. "We must understand why communism came and what it means to many millions of people. The purely propaganda attitude toward the communist world is ultimately evil because it makes us good and them bad."

Soviet expert and former ambassador George F. Kennan says it is an American error to "cultivate an image of your adversary as something inhuman. You assume he was born with horns and cloven feet. Some of these people on the other side are terribly dangerous people—especially the Chinese Communists and some Russians. But we should never forget they are people."

Of this desire to regard ourselves as perfect, U Thant says Americans "will always first say whether it is a gain for the democratic world. The Russians the same— whether it is a gain for them. This is expected in this struggle. . . . If you are to be strictly objective, you have to admit it's not strictly moral."

Thant makes his position clear: "The cold war is on, of course. Americans believe their way of life is far superior. I believe in parliamentary democracy, the dignity of man, the basic freedoms. I am not neutral. I'm always for democracy. I am against dictatorship."

In Paris, Raymond Aron carries Thant's thought a step farther: "There are immense differences between the way you act and the way the Russians act. You do not impose your own system on other people in the same way Russia imposed their system on Eastern Europe. You seem willing to accept a socialist regime in the Western Hemisphere on the condition it does not become a Russian military base— a combination of morality and necessity. I think it a very good compromise."

In all this vying among nations, what is the moral role of the United Nations? Says Secretary-General Thant, "There are some nations that believe the UN should only be a moral force. Another extreme position is that the UN should be a big power. It is somewhere in between. It is not now an effective instrument. It's at a crossroads. We can safely say, although there are no statistics, most public opinion wants the UN to succeed as a force for peace. . . . For most governments elected under democratic processes, the views of the government toward the United Nations can be construed as the attitude of the majority of people. In some states, in communist countries, it is difficult to make this assumption." Thant, who has visited many of the communist countries, says, "I came back believing the people in the streets want the UN to be stronger."

Is there a conflict between the interests of the United States and those of the UN? This question is frequently raised in terms of the system of voting in the UN General Assembly by which each nation, no matter how small or how large, has one vote. The vote of the U.S. weighs no more than that of little Dahomey. A State Department study of this question came to the conclusion that the system does not, in fact, detract from the national interest of the U.S. As Rusk explains, "This is because on the important issues the small, weak nations find themselves voting with us because they join us in their ideals."

Thant believes he detects a new moral attitude emerging in international affairs. He is convinced a synthesis of human endeavor is coming, despite the creation of many tiny new nations and such symbols of divisiveness as the Berlin Wall and the barbed wire that splits Korea. Thant, who is a Burmese, sees man becoming less provincial: "The parochial concept of 'our town,' 'our country' is disappearing. It should be the endeavor of the UN to aspire to do away with the parochial concept of society. This is another stage of human development." He urges, "We should aspire to this very much. I've been trained to be as objective as possible. If a Burmese boxer, maybe a middleweight, fights a U.S. boxer, I will not feel any emotion. I've reached this stage. It has taken much training and meditation. This should be our aspiration. I feel very strongly about it. If we can think of one human species, it is the only wisdom and vision."

Israel's former Prime Minister David Ben-Gurion told me, "I see a day when Russia and America will live together. I'm

sure they will. Then we will live together with the Arabs.
When Russia doesn't send arms to the Arabs, they will
know Israel is here to stay and they cannot destroy it. Then
there will be peace, and there *will* be peace. Everything is
a matter of man's will. Oh, not on the sun, but here among
people. This is my lesson from our history here. It depends
on the strength of the will."

Dean Rusk also believes there are forces in the world
working for synthesis. He sees nations passing through a
progression: from colonial period to independence and then
to co-operation among nations. But he warns that this is a
slow-moving historical process and says, "Immediate dangerous problems are not going to be solved by these trends."

One of the most moral acts in our nation's history has been
the giving of postwar aid to other nations—from the Marshall Plan to the Peace Corps—without imposing our political views. We gave $40 billion of aid to Western Europe.
(We still hoard a billion bushels of surplus wheat.) "The
American public view is one that approaches idealism or
morality," says Hubert Humphrey. "My people out home
don't understand why there should be hunger when there is
a nation with a surplus—want in the midst of plenty." He
thinks this anomaly is our greatest moral challenge: "It is
the paradox of a few people in this world having much and
the overwhelming numbers living on the brink of starvation. The fact that there are so many with so little poses
terrific political problems. When people saw the Sears and
Roebuck catalogue, it opened their eyes. People now know
they are not necessarily doomed to poverty and disease.
Now there is no escape for us. It challenges some of the old
moral concepts we have. The American people are a gen-
erous people, with all that's wrong with us. You can't just

go to Sunday school and church and ignore human want. When people hear there are people in want, they have to do something."

Rusk adds, "We have not only a responsibility but a very serious national interest about doing something about it." He observes that almost every developing country—"whether ally of ours or nonaligned nation"—is increasing both its productivity and social justice and becoming the kind of country we want in the world.

The United Nations' Food and Agricultural Organization has found that 10 to 15 percent of the world's people are undernourished and up to half suffer from hunger and malnutrition. Dr. B. R. Sen, director-general of the FAO, told the World Population Conference in August 1965: "Where there is maladjustment between [production and population growth], famine, pestilence, wars have in the past intervened to restore the balance. . . . The outlook is alarming. In some of the most heavily populated areas the outbreak of serious famines within the next five to ten years cannot be excluded. And if food output everywhere just kept pace with population growth at the present level of consumption, by the end of this century the number of people who would be subject to hunger and malnutrition would be double what it is today." He warned that the current balance between population and food supplies is "precarious."

Governor Romney thinks we have not gone far enough: "The most needed commodity on earth is food. We have surpluses that embarrass us, unused land, unused capacity, and we haven't thought through ways we can use this for the good of others and ourselves. In recent decades we have developed the greatest capacity for the production of food the world has ever seen and yet we're still following policies which prevent us from filling the need of hungry and starving people."

Of the poor in the world, Walter Reuther says, "We must show them they can get the wrinkles out of their empty bellies without putting their souls in chains."

As President Johnson put it in a speech, "For the wall between rich and poor is a wall of glass through which all can see."

Toynbee poses our moral choice: "Should people have unreal wants when other people are starving? One can see why it happened. But is it good? An Indian peasant doesn't need Madison Avenue to tell him what his wants are; his stomach does.

"My argument requires a revolution in the economy. In each of the wars, we have revolutionized our economies. We can do it if we choose, if we prefer to satisfy real needs. Those who are relatively rich could feel more satisfied if their surplus money was going to meet the wants of people who have less, rather than for a tenth pair of shoes."

In the meanwhile, we pay the calorie-counting penance of an affluent society.

In international affairs, our dilemma lies between gaining and giving, between economic interest and moral responsibility. In London, Sir Charles Snow sees the American problem not as selfishness at all, but as idealism: "You are not a materialist people. You are prepared to put up with a great deal of discomfort for a dream you have never fulfilled—a dream of happiness beyond human capacity to achieve. You have no sense of limits."

And in Washington, Humphrey adds, "Much of the success of American foreign aid is due to the Judaic-Christian background of our people—a blend of compassion and charity. But implementation of the program is too often the other way. Too many people trying to sell foreign aid as economics and national interest. Our people need to believe it's the honest, moral thing. There are too many clever people. You have to have politics of the heart in this country. If you don't, you don't get very far."

««8.

Is Dirty the Word for Politics?

In our country four institutions have the prime power—and the prime responsibility—to influence our morality: government, business and the labor unions, the press, and the churches. Each one has failed to provide moral leadership and has helped to precipitate our moral crisis.

Because we are a nation based on democratic principles and forms, our morality is, to a large extent, expressed in political terms and through political acts. These roots stretch back to the Mayflower Compact, in which, on November 11, 1620, at Cape Cod, the Pilgrims agreed to "covenant and combine ourselves together for the civil Body Politick" to create laws "for the general Good."

To be an American, one must uphold our covenant, the Constitution—not the Bible. In some societies, allegiance to official religious views is a prerequisite of membership. In America, it is legal to recite the Pledge of Allegiance in the public schools, but the government is prohibited from designating prayers for schoolchildren.

We believe that, despite repeated distortions of the people's will by their representatives and bureaucrats, our government exists of, by, and for the people. After the assassination of President Kennedy, the American people mourned the death not of some imposed leader but a man who represented them, who was part of them. Our politicians carry a special burden. They may be neither more honest nor more farsighted than politicians in other lands, but they must answer directly to the people. They may forget that they are public servants and swell up with a sense of power and the arrogance that power fosters. They may pull the wool over the people's eyes. But only if the people let them.

The fact that more than one in every three Americans of voting age failed to vote in the 1964 Presidential election and one in two did not vote in the 1962 Congressional election suggests that we are not living up to even our most basic political responsibility.

In a nation as vast and mighty as ours, the moral decisions of individuals with power can move mountains. "Politics is the method by which a political society like this carries out its intentions, whether they are moral or immoral," says Professor Robert G. McCloskey of Harvard. And as a result of his study of the American character, John Cogley makes the point that today there is "not much difference in the quality of moral decisions made, but they can have much more effect than in the past. A decision by the President or the Soviet Premier can destroy the world. A decision by a banker can throw many more people out of work. A decision by a member of Congress may mean people in India aren't going to eat."

Because government converts conscience into action, the

courts often serve as our moral arbiters. Increasingly in recent years the U. S. Supreme Court has moved to protect the rights of individuals, racial and religious minorities and urban majorities. Professor McCloskey, an expert on Constitutional law, says, "There is more tendency to mingle law and morality in this country than anywhere else." As a result, our moral ideas are translated into legal forms. He adds, "The law itself is an expression of moral intent."

Judges have moved into the vacuum of moral authority, but judges are not always the best moral arbiters. In 1963 New York state's highest court ruled Henry Miller's novel *Tropic of Cancer* obscene in a 4 to 3 decision. The book was also declared obscene in Connecticut and Pennsylvania, but state courts in Massachusetts, Wisconsin, Illinois and California came to the opposite judgment. Finally, in June, 1964, the U. S. Supreme Court ruled that the book could not be constitutionally banned—by a 5 to 4 decision. Obviously, the line between literature and obscenity varies for judges. Often a judge's personal idea of morality becomes law.

After the Supreme Court decision, Francis Cardinal Spellman issued a statement saying in part: "I would ask you to join with me in a plea to those judges who have weakened America's efforts to protect its youth to reconsider their responsibilities to Almighty God and to our country."

Of judges and morality, Professor McCloskey says, "In some ways they are ill-fitted for their job. Judges are always lawyers and the law is not the most broadening profession." He adds, "Lots of judges just don't read books. They are just amazed when they pick up D. H. Lawrence. They haven't read anything since Tom Swift. Judges may not be the best arbiters of morality, but they are better than none at all."

Judges are prey to personal prejudices and even conflicts of interest, particularly when they serve as part-time dispensers of justice and part-time lawyers in private practice. Some cynic once said that a judge is a lawyer who has known a governor. But judges at their best, as exemplified by the majority of the justices of the U. S. Supreme Court in recent years, have been the bulwark of our liberties and our democratic ideals. Despite the apathy and even hostility in the other branches of government, the justices have advanced our understanding of morality. Perhaps history will say that the recent Court has been our greatest because of its concern for the individual in our mass society. The Court said all children have the right to go to public schools without segregation as to race. It said no child shall be forced to recite a government-prescribed prayer. It said that no man's vote shall count for more than any other's, and that improper actions of public officials can be reported and criticized without fear of gagging libel suits. It upheld in the states the Fifth Amendment's guarantee against self-incrimination. It strengthened Constitutional rights in areas of state jurisdiction. In a time of cold-war fears and momentous change, the Court has strengthened the moral heart of our democracy.

And it has achieved these things in the face of vigorous opposition. The Congress has tried to overrule the Court's decisions on school prayers and political reapportionment. The attack on the apportionment decisions was a blatant attempt by elected representatives to preserve an obsolete status quo and careers and power for themselves and their fellow politicians.

In the light of conflicts between the Supreme Court's decisions and local laws, we debate whether there is a moral right to disobey a law. The point can be briefly made: The proper way to oppose a disliked law is to have it repealed through the people's legislative power. However, if those who object to a law are either disenfranchised or malapportioned so that they have no effective voice or if they are too weak a minority to limit a legislative majority, then they must seek redress through the courts. The test of a law in the courts usually requires a violation of it. Therefore, it seems logical that people have a right to disobey the law when their conscience is violated or rights destroyed—as long as they do not invoke violence and are willing to pay the penalty if they are proven wrong. In the end, the Supreme Court will be our conscience.

This touches the central moral question in American politics: Do the politicians carry out the moral intention of the people; how much is this intention distorted and perverted?

A political leader can reflect the moral purposes of the citizens he represents. He may also reflect their greed, avarice, selfishness and fears. (He may, for one example, represent, above all, their interest in oil-depletion allowances.) But if we are to believe that our political system works, we should expect him to articulate the people's moral desires.

At times, a political leader will actually lead—he will see the moral implications of a problem before they are sighted by the people he represents. The late Senator Estes Kefauver's investigation of the drug industry is a good example. Then, if the politician has enough courage (perhaps if he has a law practice or business he can return to if he is politically disowned), he may show his constituents the way.

What are the realities in American political life that distort the people's moral intentions? If we put aside for the moment the immorality of some individual politicians, there are three major conditions that tend to distort the people's will:

The first is size. Liberals and conservatives alike complain about this problem. Says Hubert Humphrey: "The government is a big impersonal mass. You have to find some way to personalize it. If the federal government gets too impersonal, it becomes not a citizen's friend but his enemy." Humphrey says that as a senator he spent an enormous share of his time simply serving as a bridge between government in Washington and people back home.

Barry Goldwater feels as strongly: "Government has done almost irreparable damage. Why do people downgrade patriotism? Why are people suspicious of anyone who works for government? The whole darn country is spread thin by immorality spawned by the federal government."

Humphrey recognizes the problem that the massiveness of our nation imposes on our representatives: "We don't have Plato's Republic. You are not drawing people from a governing class. A wheat farmer doesn't want to give up his farm and come here [to Washington]; he doesn't know how long he'll be in Congress. He'd vote for his price support of wheat. In a sense, there may be a conflict of interest, but he may also be wise. People aren't mean. It's difficult for a congressman to understand the North Dakota farmer or for the farmer to understand the Puerto Ricans' problems in New York."

Massive impersonality breeds moral dilemmas not only for the elected politician but also for the government bureaucrat. Two and a half million people work for the federal government alone—plus 3.7 million under the Department of Defense. When one joins this vast bureaucracy, he commits himself to a world with its own problems of security, ambition, gain. And the largest of these is security.

The infinite number of anonymous Washington bureaucrats whose first intent is to hang on to their jobs, to avoid sticking out their necks, and who consequently duck decisions and pass the buck, lies like a dead hand on government efforts to serve the people.

I have found too often that when I complain to the New York Public Service Commission, I receive a reply from the railroad it is supposed to oversee. When I ask a question of the federal Food and Drug Administration, I receive a call immediately from the Pharmaceutical Manufacturers Association it is supposed to police. And on at least several state commissions, I have found ardent partisans of the giant telephone utility they are supposed to regulate. These experiences confirm the often-stated thesis that regulatory bodies tend in time to protect the special interests they were created to control.

A study made at the request of the Bureau of the Budget showed that the Federal Communications Commission "has not been entirely successful in providing reasonable protection of the public interest, convenience and need. This is particularly true of the attempt to regulate the telephone industry." And in 1964, when Representative Walter E. Rogers, Democrat of Texas, introduced a bill prohibiting the FCC from adopting a rule to regulate the amount of time a radio station could devote to commercials, Jack Gould wrote in *The New York Times:* "So long as the commissioners nibble on the periphery of broadcasting problems, theirs is the illusion of autonomy. But when the tough bread and butter issues seem threatened, the FCC discovers it is fundamentally without meaningful authority. . . . Novices in broadcasting may fight the FCC at a Washington hearing; sophisticates neutralize it on Capitol Hill."

Bureaucracy extends into our enlarged military complex

as well. The length of the red tape between the lower members of the military hierarchy and the policy-making echelons is now enormous. This again is the result of size, and it disturbs some of our most thoughtful military professionals. Air Force Colonel Robert N. Ginsburgh wrote in the January 1964 *Foreign Affairs:* "Taking full advantage of modern communications and computer techniques, the decision-making authority has become more centralized. As a result, the military professional faces many more roadblocks—more people who can say no and fewer who can say yes." This very centralization was accelerated by Secretary of Defense Robert S. McNamara's effort to create some cohesiveness within the military bureaucracy that civilian leadership has found so difficult to control.

"The trouble is that almost all the government is run by bureaucrats," say Senator Ribicoff. "What worries me is not its deliberate misuse, but I am apprehensive about a great bureaucracy doing anything. I think a bureaucracy is to be feared. It gets stultified. It gets inefficient. It lacks imagination."

The second present-day condition that has distorted the moral intentions of the American people is malapportionment, by which a rural citizen counts for more in the Congress and in the state legislatures than an urban or suburban voter. We began as a rural nation and when our cities grew, rural politicians clung to power long after their power no longer matched the political facts of life. They twisted the American political system so that the vote of a man in a rural farmhouse could be worth ten times as much as the vote of a man in a big-city apartment or a suburban home.

Virtually all attempts to unhorse the rural politicians failed until 1962 when the U. S. Supreme Court, in a landmark decision, *Baker v. Carr*, decided that the federal courts could intervene if urban voters were denied equal representation within a state. That opened the dam, and a flood of supporting decisions followed. Although rural partisans shouted that such intervention by the federal judiciary would swing all power to the urban population, *Baker v. Carr* promised the coming of age of the legislative process in twentieth-century America.

At the time of the *Baker v. Carr* decision, the idea that in America everyone had an equal vote was a fake. One third (or less) of the people could elect a majority of the state senate in 27 states, a majority of the lower house in 18 states and a majority of both state houses in 13. District lines had not been redrawn for 25 or more years in 27 states. The 383 residents of Union, Connecticut, sent as many representatives to the state legislature as did the 161,000 residents of Hartford. In California, the state senate could be controlled by 10.7 percent of the population. In Florida, 12 percent could elect a majority in each house.

On the northern peninsula of Michigan, the late Congressman John B. Bennett then had 177,000 constituents, the fewest of any man in the Congress, while Congressman John Lesinski of Detroit and Dearborn in the same state had the nation's third most populous district and represented 803,-000 people. These two men cast votes of equal strength in the Congress.

In February 1964, in a Georgia case, *Westberry v. Sanders*, the U. S. Supreme Court ruled that the Constitution requires Congressional districts to be, "as nearly as practical," equal in population. This decision promised to revolutionize the U. S. House of Representatives. In its 6 to 3 decision, the majority of the Court stated: "Other rights, even the most basic, are illusory if the right to vote is undermined. . . . While it may not be possible to draw Congressional districts with mathematical precision, that is no excuse for ignoring our Constitution's plain objective of making equal representation for equal numbers of people the fundamental goal for the House of Representatives. That is the high standard of justice and common sense which the founders set for us."

Four months later, the Supreme Court ruled in *Reynolds v. Sims* that both houses of a state legislature must be apportioned according to population. It declared unconstitutional situations such as that in New York state where one man in the lower house in Albany represented 314,000 people and another 15,000.

Where the rural minority dominates even one legislative house, it can block urban housing projects, urban transportation improvements, state aid for urban schools. Sometimes a conservative minority in the cities, wishing to avoid higher taxes to solve urban problems, will ally itself with the rural legislators to keep the state malapportioned. (I am told that for every dollar the New York legislature spends on an upstate school child, it spends only 63 cents on a child in New York City's schools.) As a result, state governments have been less and less responsive to the growing needs of urban people, who then, ironically, turn to the federal government for help. This makes Big Government in Washington bigger.

Malapportionment enables legislatures to distort the moral intentions of the majority of the American people by enabling one minority—the rural minority—to hold onto entrenched power in the state capitals and the U. S. House of Representatives. Today an American can no longer be legally disenfranchised for reasons of race, creed or sex; but until the Supreme Court began to act in 1962, his vote could still be diluted for reasons of geography. Malapportionment, to a significant extent, helped disenfranchise not only the Southern Negro, who often has been kept away from the polls by the ruling rural politicians, but also the great urban masses, whose votes are discounted and cheapened.

How corruptive malapportionment can be was clearly seen in the desperate efforts of U. S. congressmen and senators to preserve the power of the rural minority by blocking the Supreme Court's decisions with a Constitutional amendment.

The third condition that distorts the political expression of the people's will is the seniority system in Congress and the state legislatures. Through this system, control of the vital committees is often held in the fists of veteran, aged politicians from one-party-dominated states, usually in the South, and one-party counties, usually rural. The seniority system gives undue power to the aged and the reactionary. As a result, the intentions of the majority of people are frequently suppressed in favor of the interests of those few represented by men whose right to power is based primarily on political longevity.

Observers like George Kennan and Walter Lippmann have warned that the executive can be paralyzed by the legislative power of a few determined old men. Lippmann, in his writings, has proposed that the houses of Congress pass a rule that any measure sent up by the President and certified as important must be put to a vote. He blames the seniority system and the misuse of the committee system for creating the need for such a rule.

Another special force working to distort the moral intent of the majority of Americans is in those ardent and vocal groups we now call extremist. In our society the heretic is not religious but political, and as Raymond Aron says, "Since 1945 there has been a popular explosion against heretics." He, like others, sees the brief rise of Senator Joseph McCarthy as a "violent reaction against heretics in society—communists who deny the content of the American creed from God to the American Constitution." And he adds, "Now there is sort of a vague revival of this indignation in the right-wing organizations like the John Birch Society. But you [Americans] have received 'a shot' from McCarthy and will not fall into the illness a second time."

Aron points out, "We [Frenchmen] are used to being divided on the fundamentals. But every American has a different background. In order to be an American, you have to have American ideas. How else can you be an American? We Frenchmen don't have to have the same ideas about the organization of society." Because of this, some of our more recent immigrants and their offspring go to extremes to prove their Americanism.

Many observers are deeply concerned about the damage done by McCarthyism and the present right-wing movement. Said Paul Tillich, "I'm worried about the effects on people. In California I was told ministers had to leave their pulpits when they disagreed with these societies." In the arts, film maker John Huston notes, "The most shameful thing in my time was the McCarthy incident. I hope it's over with and the last convulsive signs of the struggle are evidenced by such absurdities as the John Birch Society. I'll be a long time getting over the sense of common guilt when we look back on the innocent sufferers—people only guilty of having an opinion. The American people invariably come around, but sometimes it takes a hell of a long time."

Of McCarthy, historian Oscar Handlin says, "I knew as soon as somebody blew on him, he'd fall down. The distressing thing was that nobody was willing to blow."

There were few in John Huston's Hollywood willing to blow McCarthy down. The moral failure of the movie industry was recorded in a poignant obituary distributed by the Associated Press on August 23, 1964. It was the story of a man named Louis Pollock, who became a motion-picture writer in 1945, wrote the scripts of a number of films, including *The Jackie Robinson Story*, and died of a heart attack at the age of sixty. Here is his story as told by the AP:

> During his first nine years as a screenwriter he was said never to have regretted his decision to gamble on his writing ability. His name was becoming known within the industry, and his price was creeping upward steadily.
>
> Disaster struck him from an unknown source in 1954, just as he was beginning to believe that he had arrived as a top-flight film writer. His output remained as high as ever but everything Mr. Pollock wrote was either dropped or returned with no explanations.
>
> His savings dwindled and disappeared. For a time, he supported his family by mortgaging his house, but eventually he had to sell it. He lost all professional contacts and Hollywood made it clear to him that he was finished.
>
> For five years, Mr. Pollock lived in a state of confusion without an inkling of what had happened. Then, near the end of 1959, he met an old friend from the entertainment world who asked why he was no longer turning out scripts.
>
> Later that afternoon, the friend telephoned to inform Mr. Pollock that his name appeared on a widely feared Hollywood blacklist.
>
> Further investigation revealed that on April 21, 1954, a

man named Louis Pollock, a California clothier, refused to reply to questions before the House Un-American Activities Committee.

Belatedly, he sought and was granted a letter of full clearance from the House committee in December, 1959.

When he received the letter from Washington that was supposed to erase his five years of unemployment and anguish, Mr. Pollock folded it carefully and shook his head as he put it down.

"Now I feel numb," he said at the time. "But I can't help feeling that in those five long years, nobody ever asked me once: 'Are you this man? Could you be this man?' Nobody ever asked me."

Despite the clearance, Mr. Pollock found Hollywood doors still closed to him, and during recent years he turned to writing television scripts under an assumed name—the only way, he said, that he could sell his work. . . ."

George Kennan sums up the danger of McCarthyism: "People are terribly sensitive to the charge that they are not sufficiently anti-communist. The Right Wing has had an influence—it silences its opponents and makes everyone desirous of not being criticized from this quarter. A great part of the country stands silent on this."

And commenting on the exaggerated fear of an internal communist danger, Kennan adds, "This reminds me of the sort of thing that was being said in Germany in 1932 and '33. This is a totalitarian device. I've seen too much of this sort of thing. When anyone creates a myth to cast suspicion on thousands of people, I'm on the alert."

United States Attorney General Nicholas deB. Katzenbach also does not want the threat of internal communist subversion overplayed. "There is no danger the United States is going to be overthrown by the Communist Party. But they can make trouble and disruption," he says. "We've kept high officials of the Communist Party so tied up in litigation for fifteen years that this has had a salutary effect on what they're able to do." And he adds, "All our big spy cases have involved professionals—often with diplomatic immunity—and Americans who have no ideological orientation but are short of cash."

And, finally, the morality of American politics is affected by the morality of the individual politician and public employee. It has been fairly said that in a democracy the people get politically pretty much what they deserve. If they care enough to insist on moral standards, they have the power to do so. But they care enough only sporadically.

Corruption starts at the local level and is accepted there. The corruption in our cities includes pay-offs for liquor licenses and taxicab permits, bribes to health inspectors and building inspectors. Numbers rackets are widely protected. Police get paid off for everything from ignoring illegal parking to controlling strikes. The police are the most vulnerable to temptation. As one New York City official said, "The problem is not police brutality but police venality."

"Some of our local police methods and organizations are very horse and buggy," says Attorney General Katzenbach. He wants police officials to become more professional. "One of the problems of fighting organized crime is you always get the police chief or lieutenants involved. In some cities you can give a bit of confidential information to the police and get it back in twenty-four hours [through underworld tipsters]." He wants police chiefs and heads of detective departments to be freely hired from one city to another, like school superintendents, so that they will value a reputation for integrity. He adds, "If you think the mayor, police chief, cop on the beat is on the take, you don't have much respect."

Corruption goes right to the top. High city officials rake

in not only cash for their "little tin box" but shares of stock from companies to which they grant profitable franchises. And to attract conventions, for example, city fathers cannot clamp down too tightly on liquor or prostitution.

The attitude that serving the public means special privileges was exemplified by the proposal in 1964 in New York state that federal and state legislators be given special blue-and-gold automobile license plates—to inflate their egos and, presumably, to make them easily identifiable to all police.

The dubious use of public power on the local and state level is shockingly widespread. Here are just a handful of examples from a single period of a few months: In New York a state court judge was sentenced to a year in prison after pleading guilty to charges that he had conspired to bribe State Liquor Authority officials. The New York senate's majority leader admitted that his wife had received 3,000 shares of stock in a New York City finance company a year after he had voted for a bill allowing small loan companies to raise interest charges; the legislator denied any cause-and-effect relationship. New York City's Bronx boss, Charles A. Buckley, then a congressman, was accused of padding the federal payroll; *The New York Times* editorialized: "these revelations of payroll padding are scandalous." Massachusetts has won a national reputation for political corruption that ranges from paying inflated prices for land for federally aided highways to bribery and larceny. A special grand jury there indicted 26 men, including prominent state officials, after investigating crime and corruption in government. In Boston several city councilmen were accused of violating the state conflict-of-interest law when they accepted campaign contributions in return for a promise to vote for an urban renewal plan. In Illinois one veteran observer estitmated that one third of the members of the state's lower house accept pay-offs. Oklahoma's highest court was rocked by the conviction of a retired justice for income-tax evasion. In Arizona a $100,000 slander suit against a former water company owner who had accused officials of seeking a bribe was settled for $1 when the defendent admitted that he had slandered them.

This list could be extended, but it does not mean that all politicians are "on-the-take." Many—hopefully, most—are honest men and women. But in our legislatures, the battle between morality and power is not always won by the forces of morality. As President Kennedy told the Congress: "Public officials are not a group apart. They inevitably reflect the moral tone of the society in which they live."

Money is the root of much political evil. The headlines are peppered with charges of favoritism in stockpiling contracts, defense contracts, and the placing and sustaining of military bases, federal hospitals and space program centers. The motivation of some congressmen who fought vigorously against a bill requiring merchants and loan agencies to provide customers with detailed facts on finance charges is suspect. The reason given—that it would place a burden on businessmen—seems spurious.

Efforts to get United States senators to reveal their financial holdings have been repeatedly blocked—by United States senators. Although the proposed rule was so mild that it did not cover financial holdings of a lawmaker's wife, in July, 1964, the U. S. Senate voted down, by 59 to 27, a plan for senators and leading Senate officers to file copies of their income tax returns. And the Senate scrapped by a 62 to 25 vote a plan requiring senators to disclose their outside earnings.

Professor Gray Thoron, former dean of the Cornell University Law School and a member of the Citizens Committee that recommended revisions in the code of ethics for the New York state legislature, says of his earlier experience with practical politics in Texas, "Texas politics is a liberal education. I've seen a lot of political infighting. There was a total lack of morality on the part of people who were otherwise perfectly good citizens." He tells of one able candidate for a Texas judgeship whose friends, it was widely believed at the time, "found" a couple of thousand votes for him and he was thus elected.

Politicians are most reluctant to impose codes of ethics on themselves. The code that the New York legislature passed in March 1964, after rejecting the Citizens Committee's more realistic recommendation, did not even try to close the barn door. This is only surprising in the light of the realism of one state legislator's comment: "Did you ever see a bill that a bunch of lawyers couldn't figure out how to get around one way or another?"

The drive for political success matches the American regard for material achievement. The Kennedy Administration was often accused of putting political victory above all other considerations. Governor Romney, an experienced businessman now in politics, observes, "I find a good deal of thinking that the political end justifies the means. I believe it would be accurate to say the predominant political attitude has become that of winning, regardless of what it takes to win—that victory is the primary consideration. I think this is wrong. I think there are many things more important than winning an election." And he adds, "The spirit of victory regardless of means is more prevalent in politics than it is in business. I think the low regard the general public has of politics and politicians is an indication they [the politicians] haven't conducted politics in a manner to demand higher respect."

The politician's dilemma was dramatized after the nomination of Barry Goldwater as the Republican candidate for the Presidency, when many "liberal" Republicans who disagreed with him had to weigh their principles against a belief in party unity or their own political futures. As James Reston wrote in *The New York Times*, they had to face "the moral ambiguity of Goldwater's racial and foreign policies."

Their dilemma was demonstrated when, in an NBC television interview, Dean Burch, the newly appointed national chairman of the Republican Party, said, "The Republican position on the Ku Klux Klan and any organization is that so long as this organization is not attempting to overthrow the government of the United States by violence, such as the Communist Party, that we're in the business of getting votes. We're not in the business of turning away votes, and this to me is much as a tempest in a teapot."

When one New York City Republican congressman repudiated Presidential nominee Goldwater, the Republican chairman in his area cried, "We gave him his career and this is how he pays us back."

It is generally agreed that politicians today are less free-wheeling than in the past, when the big interests (steel, railroads, etc.) owned their puppet senators and the big-city bosses ruled their domains with all the immoral callousness of divine-right kings.

Professor Thoron suggests a reason why politics may be more ethical today: "I think it's the wide increase in education plus the work of newspapers and magazines. As poor as college education is in some ways—with its athletics and fraternities—it is raising standards." And he adds, "You can't steal votes or operate the smoke-filled room under the glare of TV and newspaper publicity today."

Raymond Aron agrees: "If you look at American politics in the nineteenth century, you had many big bosses who were worse than today. I'm rather inclined to think American politics is slightly better than it was." Hubert Humphrey credits this change to the weakening of the hold of the political parties on their candidates, particularly with the decline of political patronage—the pay-off.

But we still have congressmen who are indicted for taking bribes and who tour the world at the taxpayers' expense, and city politicians and "county courthouse gangs" who manipulate the law. As Professor Thoron puts it, "If Senator X makes an inquiry of the Immigration Service, the Immigration Service jumps. Administrators are susceptible."

Goldwater takes a less critical view and says, "I haven't found any dishonest people in Congress. The closest you can come is people like [Adam Clayton] Powell who is in this for his own good." John Cogley suggests that the press covers up much immorality. He notes, "We never hear of sexual aberration or alcoholism among congressmen."

But the buying of legislative influence goes on. Professor Thoron points out that someone seeking to influence the fate of a bill need not buy legislators *en masse*. "It only takes buying a few people to get legislation through. If you get certain votes, it goes through. A chairman of a powerful committee can give the green or red light to legislation coming through his committee. He has the power."

Sometimes, Thoron points out from his own experience, the techniques used can be "awfully crude." He says, "In

Texas, it's widely believed that when a young legislator wins a primary, he is called by certain railroads and trucking lines and put on retainer to handle personal injury suits. This is called conditioning the legislator."

Conflict-of-interest problems gain public attention when Cabinet officers must sell stock holdings, but congressmen are not required to do so. New Hampshire's Republican Senator Norris Cotton had a minority interest in a Bernard Goldfine-controlled mill, and Cotton's law firm, from which he was then still drawing a salary, represented several Goldfine enterprises. And Goldfine had other good friends he cultivated on Capitol Hill and in the White House. A Secretary of the Air Force in the Eisenhower Administration was dropped for using Air Force stationery to solicit business for an engineering firm in which he still had an interest. Kennedy's Secretary of the Navy Fred Korth had a surprisingly parallel experience when he tried to help a bank back home in Texas. The *Times'* James Reston wrote: "Korth wasn't crooked; he was morally insensitive and stupid, but the President [Kennedy] insists Korth wasn't fired, which raises the question: Why not?"

On the other hand, the late Senator Robert S. Kerr of Oklahoma, for example, was well known for proposing gas and oil legislation while holding great gas and oil interests himself. And two New York state legislators who sponsored a middle-income housing law were revealed by the *New York Herald Tribune* to have connections with companies that earned hundreds of thousands of dollars in legal and architectural fees from builders utilizing the law.

In a page-one story on August 5, 1963, the *Herald Tribune* reported that the then New York State Senate Majority Leader Walter J. Mahoney was chairman of the board of the City Title Insurance Co., which "writes insurance and receives premiums on millions of dollars worth of mortgages purchased by the giant, multibillion-dollar state and city employee pension funds . . . and the company walks off with the lion's share of title premiums on state-aided Mitchell-Lama housing projects." The connection violated no law or any formal code of ethics.

It is illegal to offer a legislator a bribe but it is perfectly within the law to give him legal or insurance business. Congressmen and senators commonly receive $1,000 or more for making a speech. Political contributions come in various ways from everyone from businessmen to union leaders and gangsters. (One congressman is known for saying, "Just leave it on the mantel.") And it is normally not the politician who demands the pay-off; the influence buyer is eager to dump out the dollars. Maybe he wants an open-door policy when he comes calling, maybe he wants some self-benefiting legislation passed, maybe he wants an ambassadorship. All three are for sale in our America.

The most notorious recent case of immorality in the capital centered on energetic Robert G. Baker, secretary of the Democratic majority in the Senate, who, under fire for wheeling and dealing, resigned on October 7, 1963. A lot of political smoke rose out of the reluctant and incomplete investigation of Baker and his senatorial friends by the Senate's own Rules Committee; some fire could be seen and a stench could be smelled.

Baker was charged with having made $2 million as a result of his connections. No one doubted he was a powerful young man whose word carried weight with many senators, including Lyndon B. Johnson, then majority leader, and oil-tycoon Kerr. But the Senate committee walked a tightrope and steered clear of involving any members of the Senate in its inquiry. Since "Bobby" Baker's only leverage for building a fortune on his $19,600 salary was his influence with powerful men in Washington and his control of hundreds of thousands of dollars of campaign funds (in cash), the committee's avoidance of dragging any senators into the investigation necessarily undermined public confidence in the moral integrity of that legislative body.

It proved too much to ask the exalted U. S. Senate to police itself. The press kept Baker on the griddle, with help from Republican senators, some of whom hoped to make partisan hay. Baker's own business dealings did get public attention; they included borrowing large sums from James Hoffa's Teamsters Union; borrowing more from Senator Kerr's bank in Oklahoma City; sharing in land speculation with Senator George Smathers of Florida; investing $28,700 in a Milwaukee insurance company and seeing his money zoom to a value of around $400,000; and owning a piece of a vending-machine company that turned up with contracts in major aerospace companies doing business with the federal government.

The biggest headlines of all were made by a Washington insurance man who said that Baker had enabled him to place $200,000 worth of life insurance on Lyndon Johnson (after his heart attack had reduced his attractiveness as an insurance risk). The insurance man testified that Baker was actually his business partner and had brought him many prominent customers and that he had repeatedly paid Baker for services rendered. Baker claimed the payments were only loans. This lesser enterprise of the enterprising Mr. Baker made headlines because by then Johnson was in the White House, and the insurance man was saying that he had been urged to buy advertising time on a TV station owned by the Johnson family and to send Johnson a stereo phonograph worth more than $500. The President's spokesmen, trying to make the best of the situation, explained that Johnson had thought the phonograph was a present from his friend Baker, not a kickback from the insurance man.

The important thing about the Baker case was that a shrewd young man could make a fortune while working in the United States Congress and that the Senate could pretend to investigate itself and end up shamefaced and nervous with unsightly jam on its face. The Senate Rules Committee found Baker guilty of "gross improprieties" but proposed no punishment. A Republican minority report called the nine-month inquiry a "cover-up." The Senate's attempt to reform itself was a sham.

Veteran Washington correspondent Richard Wilson, writing in the Cowles newspapers on May 27, 1964, said, "The pattern set in these cases is shocking. The lesson taught to federal officials is that if they see mismanagement, wrongdoing or bad judgment they would be wise to keep their mouths shut if they wish to maintain or improve their job status. . . . Some kind of a new morality seems to have gotten lodged in official Washington. It is the morality of blind loyalty to superior authority and complete obeisance to the word from on high. It is the morality of cover-up in the Billie Sol Estes case and whitewash in the Bobby Baker case. . . ."

Although the American public apparently enjoyed the Bobby Baker show, few were indignant. The majority had long been conditioned to the premise that politicians will feather their own nests and that there are more spoils in politics than just careers of public service. Those had seen the late Senator John W. Bricker's law firm represent several large railroads while he was chairman of the Commerce Committee back in 1954. In 1961 Senator Smathers' law firm represented Pan American Airways while the senator was opposing a European airline's application for landing rights in Los Angeles. Such apparent conflicts have long been tolerated.

The Baker exposure did turn up one relatively small fish: Representative John W. Byrnes, Republican of Wisconsin, who in 1960 had pushed the Treasury Department into reversing an unfavorable tax ruling on the Mortgage Guarantee Insurance Company of Milwaukee and who had been allowed to buy $2,300 worth of stock in the company before it was available to the public. By the time Byrnes, ranking minority member of the House Ways and Means Committee, disclosed his gain, his stock was worth more than ten times what he had paid for it. This was the same insurance company in which Baker had invested and made a paper killing. (Byrnes said he did not know Baker.) It was reported that Baker had bought his stock in the company a month before Byrnes introduced legislation that persuaded the Internal Revenue Service to change its unfavorable ruling.

It was repeatedly pointed out that activities like Byrnes' broke no law and violated no ethical code. While it was said that Byrnes was doing what was expected of him by aiding a Wisconsin company (although it was not even in his constituency), *The New York Times*' Arthur Krock said Byrnes had "a privileged, sure-thing, money-making opportunity." The whole mess raised some nasty moral questions that few legislators were eager to seek answers to.

Another example of this kind of moral question was

brought to general attention when *The New York Times,* reporting on the nomination of Representative William E. Miller of upstate New York as the 1964 Republican candidate for the Vice-Presidency, said with delicacy: "After his election to the House of Representatives in 1950, Mr. Miller maintained the traditional alliance between Niagara County Republicans and the private power interests so important at Niagara Falls." And the following day the *Times* added: "House colleagues associate Mr. Miller most readily with militant advocacy of the causes of his constituents. The private power industry once politically influential in Niagara Falls and the phonograph coin-machines now manufactured near-by are examples."

One of the politician's most difficult moral dilemmas is to draw a line between legitimate campaign contributions and influence-seeking gifts. Every local mayor is exposed to the temptation of making decisions for which a businessman or contractor will gladly remunerate him. A senator may need a million dollars to get re-elected. Almost every congressman is obligated to big contributors, many of whom expect something in return.

Comments Professor Thoron: "It's perfectly obvious people don't give large campaign contributions to legislators who are going to vote against their interest. This was the way the railroads bought senators." He draws a line between moral and immoral political contributions at the point where "the degree of support you give is such that he [the candidate] is no longer a free agent. As soon as a lawyer has a client representing more than 25 or 30 percent of his practice, he is no longer a free agent." Corruption, he warns, does not always take the form of cash. It may fulfill the ambition of a legislator's wife to enter a certain country club or include a legislator or his family in a profitable business deal. "You don't cut a legislator in for five percent of a good deal without expecting a *quid pro quo.*"

Thoron suggests, "I would like to see elected public officials—state and national—voluntarily or absolutely forego representing clients before governmental agencies and be prohibited from representing clients with claims against their government. Not because there is necessarily any dishonesty or undue influence, but because the public and disappointed litigants suspect dishonesty and undue influence."

The Special Committee on Ethics, of which Thoron was one of three members, reported to the New York legislature in March, 1964. It recommended that members of the legislature and legislative employees be prohibited from practicing or appearing before most state agencies or the Court of Claims for compensation. It recommended that they be prohibited from soliciting or accepting gifts of substantial value, including loans, travel, entertainment and hospitality, under circumstances involving possible influence. It urged disclosure of financial interest in regulated activities.

Even this proposed code would not eliminate the problem entirely. It left loopholes by exempting from its restrictions on practicing and gifts a legislator's employer, clients, business associates or family. Nevertheless, the state legislature rejected the committee's proposals, and an ineffectual, watered-down version was substituted and passed into law. Robert Moses, New York's active public builder, piously told the committee: "Mental honesty is what is needed, not a rigid moralistic code advocated by do-gooders or by politicians . . ."

With parallel disdain of the public's interest, the U. S. Senate in 1964 overwhelmingly rejected the bills which would have forced its members to disclose their business and financial affairs.

Political ethics are almost impossible to control completely. Special-interest clients will retain a legislator's law partner for fees as high as $100,000. The legislation that interests them may have nothing at all to do with what the retainer is paid for. "That's the sophisticated way of doing things," Professor Thoron explains. "That's the problem. It's very hard to police."

Laws have failed to solve even the relatively simple problem of campaign contributions in this age of high-cost elections. An organization is allowed to spend only $3 million in a Presidential campaign, but Barry Goldwater says, "It's a laugh. I know about what the Republicans spent [in 1960]. It's in excess of the law—not legally but in spirit. It's immoral."

In a mass society like ours, we turn more and more to political means to wipe out injustices and to make moral reforms. The pressures on the men responsible for such judgments are varied and enormous. The special interests to whom they are obligated for their political lives sometimes threaten to smother their sense of responsibility to the moral intent of the people. This is recognized by politicians of every political stamp. Goldwater says, "If you realize that every government back to Babylon has fallen because of a decrease of morality, then you can understand the conservative's concern for the situation in America today." And Hubert Humphrey says, "It's important for congressmen to understand that all is not well in America. We have so many welfare programs—like opiates, to dull the pain. As long as these are all there, you can go to church on Sunday and say these people are being taken care of."

Professor Thoron concludes: "The practical politicians have not yet learned the impact of moral force and the public feeling of outrage."

And there is a clear warning from Arnold Toynbee: "We can't take democracy for granted. It isn't automatically the destiny of the Western World. We have to keep struggling for it all the time."

‹‹‹*9.*

Can We Mix Morals and Profits?

If any institution is central to our culture, it is business; if any single morality dominates us, it is the business ethic. Business is the next institution of power responsible for moral decisions in the American society.

Business often fails to provide moral leadership because profits and morality frequently clash. Since our economic organizations have no single standard—except that imposed by ever growing regulation by government—business ethics in America are varied, fluid and, at the same time, open to change and reform.

Barry Goldwater blames business immorality directly on government and sets the date of The Fall at 1913, when the creation of the graduated income tax made it possible for social purposes to be an objective of taxation. He says, "Government is the biggest enemy of moral values. Why did we see things we saw in General Electric and other companies—price-fixing? What does high taxation do? The little businessman starts to connive, cutting corners in order to get along. Moral values decline as government grows. We have a powerful government that bears on the daily lives of every American. This shouldn't be."

Most observers disagree. They believe government regulation "humanizes" free-enterprise capitalism and controls its business barons, railroad kings, oil tycoons and Wall Street manipulators. They feel that, to a significant degree, American business has become more ethical in our time under the pressure of government regulation. David Riesman has described what we now have as "the tamed managerial capitalism of today." As a result, American businessmen tend to be more concerned over moral questions—if not always for moral reasons. Few companies are more sensitive to their public image and government reactions than the American Telephone and Telegraph Company, the biggest of them all.

This is not to say that business has swept out its stable— far from it. The businessman is beleaguered with moral problems, when he faces up to them. One set of moral problems has been caused by the replacement of the individual magnate who could make decisions boldly and whose self-interest coincided completely with his business' welfare. Today's corporate manager might, for example, benefit more from manipulating an expense account than from increasing the company's dividends. He has little incentive to take risks. Says one successful businessman candidly, "The hardest thing to do today is to sell top management on a new idea."

This division between a company's interest and its managers' gain may explain, at least in part, the rash of complaints about industry's poor-quality performance in some of our defense and space programs. In the fall of 1963 the National Aeronautics and Space Administration charged that 50 percent of the spare parts delivered to Project Mercury were defective. Escape-tower wiring for John Glenn's flight had badly soldered connections; storage batteries for Walter Schirra's capsule were faulty; Gordon Cooper's back-up capsule had more than 500 mistakes attributable to poor workmanship and quality control. Vice Admiral Hyman G. Rickover, father of the atomic submarine program, has also complained of parts made of wrong materials, improper welds and mislabeled parts. He charged that some atomic subs were delayed because of bad workmanship and he blamed this on industrial managers "more interested in getting new contracts than in seeing to it that the things they have already contracted for are done well."

One corporate executive explains the economics of the gap between what is good for the manager and what is good for the company. He points out that stock options are often created to give the manager a stake in his company's success. If the stock's value rises, the manager will benefit personally. But, according to this executive, stock options are really inadequate. In his own case, he says, he has an option on 100,000 shares of his company's stock, an extraordinarily large option. If he works hard and makes the company grow, the value of its stock may rise $10 a share, and he can make a one-million-dollar profit on his option. But then he must pay a capital gains tax, reducing his profit to $750,000. If he invests this at five percent, he will receive a pre-tax income of $37,500 and will be able to keep about half of that after taxes. But he does not want to "play" for stakes of only $18,750 a year.

It might cost a company's stockholders $20,000 to provide a car and chauffeur so their president can ride to work in style. If the president decides this is immoral, he would have to earn at least $50,000 more to be able to afford his own car and driver.

A classic case of conflict of interest occurred at the Chrysler Corporation in 1960 when its president was fired for allegedly profiting from companies that supplied Chrysler with parts. The president, who later promised to repay Chrysler $450,000, claimed he was being made a scapegoat and the victim of a management conspiracy.

The managers operate almost universally without effective supervision from their stockholder-owners (an AT&T stockholders' meeting is a boring farce usually held in a barnlike armory in the bowels of the Bronx). They often hide behind a protective screen of public relations advisers who give their bosses' power the recognition it must have to be viable, divert public resentment from the managers and whitewash or hush up immoral incidents and policies. In his report on the first fifty years of the Graduate School of Journalism of Columbia University, Dean Edward W. Barrett, himself a former public relations man, wrote, "Rare is the corporation president, cabinet officer, or university president who does not have at his elbow a specialist in public communications." Machiavelli might be called the patron saint of press agents; and if Adam Smith could call England a nation of shopkeepers, we are, perhaps, a nation of salesmen.

Every businessman whose job it is to help his company make a profit faces moral choices. He must decide questions of employment, wages, contracts, production quality, prices, competition, taxes. He is pressured by government and labor unions and by a growing awareness that the public's opinion of his company affects profits. A simple example was the moral dilemma which the TV executive faced when 26 Southern stations dropped his network show because a Negro actress was seen on the screen arguing with white players. Would he compromise his principles to keep his show on the air? Textbook publishers meet the same problem when they publish integrated editions of school books for sale in the North and segregated editions for sale in the South.

More complex was the problem of the tobacco industry in reacting to the finding that excessive cigarette smoking causes cancer and heart disease. In 1963 Americans spent $7 billion to smoke 523 billion cigarettes and the industry provided a living for millions of workers and farmers. The industry tried to meet the medical charge by barring advertising from school and college media and by not aiming its ads at persons under twenty-one. It adopted a code that said in part: "Cigarette advertising shall not represent that cigarette smoking is essential to social prominence, distinction, success, or sexual attraction." But some companies continued to display good-looking girls in ads and one radio jingle proclaimed: "Lucky Strike separates the men from the boys—but not from the girls." The tobacco industry fought the Federal Trade Commission plan to require every package to carry a warning that cigarette smoking is dangerous to health. Senator Maurine B. Neuberger of Oregon, in a booklet, denounced the industry as "callous and myopic." In fiscal 1964-65 Americans smoked 533 billion cigarettes.

Another industry faced with conflicts between public health and profits is the drug industry. In 1963 the FTC accused six large drug companies of conspiring to fix prices on a widely used antibiotic. In his dramatic book *The Real Voice*, Richard Harris tells the story of the Kefauver hearings on the drug industry. He cites one drug that cost 1.5 cents a tablet, was sold to the druggist for 18 cents and to the patient for 30 cents. In another instance, an American firm bought a drug in bulk from a French firm and sold 11.7 cents' worth for $8.40—a markup of 7,079 percent, just for putting the drug into tablet form and bottling and selling it. No research was involved. One expert testifying before the committee pointed out that the development of the Salk polio vaccine was paid for by public donations, but five large drug companies made profits from $53 million in sales of the vaccine. Even the American Medical Association opposed Kefauver's drug-control bill, which was finally passed unanimously by the Congress in 1962—only after the thalidomide disaster had resulted in 7,000 deformed babies in Europe. Under the laws in effect at that time, thalidomide could have been sold in the United States. This tragedy made it possible to overcome the vigorous and effective drug-industry lobby that until then had virtually killed the new bill. But some experts doubt that the new law made any real change in the marketing practices of the drug industry.

One industry that feels enormous pressure to act immorally in its relations with government officials is the building industry. It must deal with zoning, building codes, inspection and many other regulations. A greedy politician spurned can be fatal to a builder. One building-industry executive describes how this problem is handled. Leaders in the industry never bribe officials themselves. But of handouts to small-fry inspectors, he says, "It is so much a way of life we don't even think of it any more." He explains that builders control the more important politicians through "bagmen." There are, he adds, two kinds of bagmen: the "class bagman," who is a highly reputable member of the community, and the "no-class bagman." Class bagmen receive large fees from a builder, and although they may never bribe an official directly, they and their employees spend a great deal of time and effort setting up fund-raising dinners and doing other costly favors for politicians. A "no-class bagman" actually takes money from the builder and hands it over to politicians and bureaucrats. He may not have "class" but he can be very effective.

This entire relationship with officialdom is rarely left to chance. The home building industry spends great sums each year on lobbying and entertaining congressmen and senators in Washington. It must be said, in fairness, that the builders are no worse in this respect than many others, from aircraft manufacturers to doctors.

Businessmen usually encounter the moral question of their relationship with government employees on the local level. One major retailer speaks proudly of how he paid off the policemen in a big-city precinct to hold his striking employees under control. He says he finally protested when policemen from other precincts, hearing of the windfall, came around in droves to collect their share. The sergeant in his precinct coolly told the businessman how to handle the situation: simply ask to see each grafting cop's identification card, which bears his precinct number.

Another recent example was what *The New York Times* called the "ugly mess of corruption" in the New York State Liquor Authority. The *Times* said that a man in the liquor business had to know the right people and pay a stiff price to lawyers, politicians and people connected with the authority itself. The small businessman who refuses to go along with this kind of corruption is rarely heard from. One restaurant owner on Long Island paid "under the table" to obtain a liquor license to serve drinks with meals. When he sought to upgrade his license to permit serving of drinks at the bar, he met demands for even bigger bribes. He balked; sold the business and got out.

The age-old problems of the small businessman are intensified and magnified by the vast anonymity of the big city. If you own a shop, should you pay off the fire, building and health inspectors, the union delegate and the police who come around with their hands out? Should you buy space in a publication that demands an ad before it will give you favorable publicity? Should you accept a kickback from a supplier competing for your business? Whenever you answer yes, you may be acting immorally. But whenever you say no, you can hurt your business.

These are just a few examples of the businessman's continuing struggle to reconcile morality and profits. The businessman who feels the strongest sense of responsibility to the public and to his employees is precisely the one who suffers the most when he wrestles with his moral dilemmas.

Many businessmen have become concerned about moral questions, but we still have with us the "operators" who seize companies through proxy fights, milk corporations and bilk customers, manipulate markets and conspire to control and rig prices, connive for excessives profits, and bribe politicians and public commissioners entrusted with guarding the public welfare. To these men, the Golden Rule is nonsense and the business world a jungle. "Everyone sells influence and you have to pick the right one," explains an important executive. "I worry more about getting the right person than about what happens afterward."

The dramatic chiselers who capture the headlines and end up in court are the scapegoats who carry our sins out into the desert and reassure the rest of us that, by comparison, we are moral people. The big-time operators make other businessmen seem respectable, not because the majority has not sinned but because its sins are smaller.

The ethical problems of American business today can be subtle and insidious. Speaking to an audience of law students, Mortimer M. Caplin, until recently the director of the Internal Revenue Service, said, "The law may permit your client to take a full giant-step toward the goal of realizing the highest possible profits, but is it wise for him to go all the way—taking into account the interest of his fellow entrepreneurs, his employees, his customers, his competitors, the community in which he lives, and perhaps even his nation? That the proposed action is 'legal' does not necessarily also mean that it is 'right.' " And Caplin admonished the future lawyers: "Never forget that, in a democracy, it is we, the citizens of this country, who determine the type of society in which we live, as well as its ethical standards and moral tone."

Raymond Aron identifies a crucial point when he says, "The paradox of a free economy of the American type is that people should want to make money, and at the same time the system can work only when you teach people to respect legality. This paradox is fundamental in American society. There has always been in America an underworld of illegality"—making money on the edge of legality.

Business also invites moral problems when it raises capital from the public. Seventeen million people now own shares in United States corporations. As recently as July 18, 1963, *The New York Times* found cause to assert editorially: "It is evident that the rules governing the financial community are inadequate to cope with the present mass market. The need to protect the public demands elimination of every last vestige of the days when Wall Street was a closed shop of professional investors and speculators. . . . The financial community cannot maintain privileges without responsibility." The newspaper charged that none of the financial institutions or exchanges "has fully acknowledged its responsibilities." In the spring of 1964, the New York Stock Exchange found it necessary to set up a $25-million customer-protection fund.

Edwin D. Etherington, who in 1962 became president of the American Stock Exchange to reform it, describes the dilemma facing a company that sells stock to the public: Is management obligated to get the highest price possible for its stock? If the public is eager enough to pay more than the stock is worth (sometimes because of high-pressure publicity), should the company hold the price down? Etherington, who dreads government control, believes that the only solution to this quandary is "full disclosure" of the facts and the "economic education" of the buying public. In view of the difficulty of educating people to stop killing themselves with automobiles and cigarettes, it promises to be difficult to educate them not to play the sucker for a quick buck. "Nobody likes to scare the public by hanging out dirty linen," says Etherington, "but in the long run, we'll keep the public if we are moral."

Moral problems are also caused by our ability to produce more than we can consume. This leads to making products that must be replaced after a limited life—built-in obsolescence—and to magnifying the role of advertising in our society. We cannot afford to let consumption slow down. Business urgently seeks more customers for more goods, and as a result, Madison Avenue has replaced Wall Street as the whipping boy of the reformers.

Competition is the key to our free-enterprise system, but

competition aims to eradicate the weaker competitor. The larger, more efficient company wipes out the smaller, the less efficient. The drive in big business is toward monopoly.

As far back as the Sherman Anti-Trust Act of 1890 and the Federal Trade Commission Act and the Clayton Anti-Trust Act of 1914, the thrust of government regulation of business has been to keep the big fish from gobbling up the small. As some see the problem, government must save our free-enterprise system by keeping competition alive. This was why a few senators tried to prevent AT&T from grabbing too much control of the Communications Satellite Corporation, why anti-trust suits have harried the steel industry, why bank mergers are often prohibited. Business does not generally object to government subsidies of airlines, shipping, farming, the electronics industry or the oil industry, but it battles government regulation of competition. One government regulator cites the example of the bicycle industry, which asked government protection from the importation of English bikes. When this was refused, the leaders of the American bicycle industry changed their style of management, imported foreign parts, made English-type bikes and are, he says, doing better than ever. Some observers believe that today international competition must provide the spur to drive American competition forward.

Anti-trust laws give the federal government weapons to police the economy: to keep it free from monopoly, to prevent price-fixing and bid-rigging and to control business mergers that would concentrate economic power in too few hands. The Justice Department was frustrated, for example, when the Manufacturers Trust Company and the Hanover Bank merged and became the nation's fourth largest bank in 1961. Despite Justice Department warnings, the two banks consummated their merger and co-mingled their funds. After much litigation, a federal judge in March 1965 ruled that the merger was illegal. Says Attorney General Katzenbach, mulling over the difficulties in disentangling the banks' affairs after nearly four years, "You almost wish to hell you hadn't won."

Many businessmen worry about the line that competition should not cross. Irwin Miller, who is president of several corporations, a member of AT&T's board of directors and a church lay leader, asks: What should a businessman do when his competitor offers one of his big customers a price cut? If the businessman decides he has to meet the competitor's price, is he then morally required to offer the lower price to his other customers, so they can compete too? If he does not make the price cut general, he may be acting immorally; if he does, he may go broke.

Supermarket trading stamps raise moral questions about competition. A woman shopper may not be interested in collecting stamps to get a bridge table, but the stamps force her to pay more for food. Supermarket experts figure they must increase their volume of business by 16 percent to pay for the stamps. Says a King Korn stamp promotion booklet: "The basic pattern for a stamp program within a community calls for nothing less than complete mobilization with one goal in mind. . . . a captive market." When one New York supermarket chain dropped the stamps, it promised "drastic price reductions."

Deceptive packaging also hurts the consumer. Companies are under attack for keeping box sizes and prices the same while they reduce contents, put false bottoms in bottles or conceal the amount of the contents in tiny, hidden type. Objections are also raised against retailers who advertise products as "10 percent off"—without saying "off" what. One retailer asks whether he should advertise a phonograph record as "$2.98—down from $3.98" when nobody is selling it for $3.98.

Some companies try to beat the competition by treating buyers to everything from bribes to prostitutes. Others make illegal agreements among themselves to share the market. Some executives have come to believe "rig we must," despite the higher cost to the consumer. They argue that this collusion "stabilizes prices" and prevents competitors from cutting each other below the point of profitability. Actually, these business executives agree on prices that will guarantee them handsome and often excessive profits.

Most notorious of such agreements was the conspiracy in which 29 companies of the giant electrical industry were judged guilty in 1961 of price-fixing and bid-rigging in heavy equipment, resulting in excessive profits. They were fined a total of more than $1.9 million; seven executives went to jail and 23 received suspended sentences. In addition, the companies have had to pay the federal government $8.6 million in damages (General Electric alone paid $7.4 million) and face some 1,900 private damage suits. In announcing payment of $75 million in settlements, partly charged against 1962 earnings, GE executives at the end of 1963 reported that the damages would not hurt earnings "substantially." By September 30, 1964, GE had paid out a total of $178 million to settle damages suits. And the company still had millions more to pay. Ralph J. Cordiner, then head of GE, was not implicated by the government and denied knowledge of what had been going on. He was quoted as saying the affair was only a matter of "individual business ethics and morality." *Fortune* magazine called the case one of "cynicism, arrogance and irresponsibility."

The vast steel industry has faced at least seven major anti-trust suits since the beginning of 1962. In January of that year four steel companies selling $100 million worth of steel forgings a year were indicted for fixing prices and rigging bids. In July, 1963, a grand jury indicted eight steel companies for conspiring to fix prices in the $75-million-a-year heavy steel castings industry. This was followed in April, 1964, by a federal grand jury indictment against eight steel firms for price-fixing in a basic consumer-goods product—carbon sheet steel—which resulted in higher prices for washing machines, refrigerators and automobiles. The grand jury charged that the conspiracy had taken place from 1955 until 1961, and that prices were fixed in hotel-room meetings at which no minutes were kept. This suit involved companies doing $2 million in carbon sheet steel sales. In July, 1965, both the steel-forgings case and the carbon-steel case were settled when the companies were allowed to plead "no contest" and were fined from $35,000 to $50,000 each—the latter being the puny maximum allowed under the anti-trust laws.

In still another industry, prices are fixed and sales territories divided by "pilot-room agreements." By "coincidence," from time to time, top executives in this industry all find themselves and their private planes at the same airport waiting for fuel or repairs. While they wait, they sit in the pilots' ready room and talk business.

Justice Department officials tell of one company that was indicted in 1961 for price-rigging and fined $10,000. The company claimed such a fine would force it out of business, so the judge reduced it to $2,000. Two years later the company was indicted again for price-rigging. Katzenbach regards penalties for anti-trust offenses, like price-fixing, as too weak. He says of the large companies: "If they did it as a cold business risk, and I don't think they do, it's worth it. The fine in the General Electric case should have been $10 million. Something that would hurt enough so they wouldn't do it."

Katzenbach says, "I think there's been less price-fixing since the General Electric case"—price-fixing by executives sitting around a table and agreeing on prices and bids. He is concerned now "about fixing of prices by means other than agreement." He challenges the concept of "administered prices," in which one company sets a price and all its competitors follow. He explains, "In pure economic theory, people will have to sell at the same price, but there is little pure economic theory operating." He believes the Justice Department should investigate situations in which several companies charge identical prices. "The purpose," he says, "is to create as much price competition as possible. It's important to the economy as a whole."

Another common practice that raises moral questions is the technique used by some manufacturers competing for large government contracts. They submit bids so low that they will lose money on them, and then they jack up their prices on re-orders and spare parts. Says a manufacturer of military hardware, "That's where the big profits are." It also helps to have on the payroll a retired general or admiral armed with an expense account with which he can keep in touch with his hand-picked successors and other former Pentagon buddies.

Senate investigators early in 1964 accused Douglas Aircraft of netting profits of 36,000 percent on a contract, and accused Western Electric of making $77 million on Nike missile contracts for work done by subcontractors. They called this "profit pyramiding." Western Electric said it only took a profit of 3.5 percent and this was proper because of the responsibility the company assumed.

Talking of his own experience, a hotel man says, "Who can tell what is moral and immoral in competition? We do anything to get business. A competitor got a girl for a guy, and we lost the convention. I sit at home at night and realize they just outsmarted us." He draws a line for himself: "You drop out of competition when the dollars don't work out."

Many businessmen are repeatedly torn between their responsibility to make a profit and their loyalty to their business associates. One prominent businessman says his worst moral dilemma came when he had to decide whether to fire the aging executive who years before had brought him into the company. (He did.) Preston R. Tisch, president of Loew's Hotels, says, "You have a tremendous responsibility to your stockholders, your company and your employees. You're affecting their lives." And another top executive, with a certain false bravado, says, "The nice guys I want to have lunch with are the guys I fire."

Labor leader Walter Reuther believes that business' greatest moral problem is created by the emphasis on "pure economic efficiency." He says, "We have always made man sovereign over the machine. The individual human being is the central consideration of our society." He adds, "We have to convince management the most efficient way to run a plant is to include the human equation."

An example of this problem is demonstrated by the company that finally air-conditioned its plant after it bought a computer that needed constant temperatures. Before that, the company would never spend the money to air-condition for the benefit of its human personnel.

The executive world is filled with distrust, says Yale's

Professor Chris Argyris, a specialist on business ethics. Executive politicking costs one company he studied $186,000 every year. Argyris, the author of thirteen volumes on business ethics, says, "At the moment, we have a world that has the cards stacked against the morally behaving man." Of most businessmen, he says, "If you observe their behavior, you find they are Sunday Christians, but they want something better, a more meaningful life."

Professor Argyris sees three important values which make it difficult for a man to act morally in business:

The first is the idea that the only important human relationships in business are those that get the job done. "This leads," he says, "to the sale without regard for how the sale is made. You are a hero if you accomplish the end result. You are not asked how the sale was made." This leads to executives collaborating, in self-defense, on the kind of price fixing exposed in the electrical industry.

Second is the idea that in business people ought not to act emotionally. Argyris explains: "They learn to suppress their feelings. When a man suppresses his feelings, he begins to mistrust himself. Then he will begin to mistrust others because he will always wonder if they are behaving to him as he is to them. Thus, we are living in a world where conformity makes sense. If we can't trust, we'd better play it safe." Such distrust is costly. In one company Argyris found second-level executives keeping a "JIC file"—just-in-case the president asked. The president had adopted a practice of asking unimportant questions to see if his subordinates were on their toes. So they wasted time and money developing JIC files to protect themselves against his lack of trust.

The third value that increases business immorality is the idea that only rewards and penalties get people to work.

Argyris says, "That leads to conformity. In time you are going to have to increase the rewards and penalties to get the same output. It is like increasing the dosage of a drug from one cc. to two cc.'s. The way the worker reacts is through apathy, indifference, goldbricking, cheating on quality. He de-emphasizes morality and emphasizes money."

Professor Argyris believes, "The challenge is not to destroy institutions but to make them viable." He adds, "The logic that the free-enterprise system has used to run its plants has led to workers being dependent on management. This way of life translated into the political sphere is socialism. What a manager wants inside his plant, he fights outside."

Argyris asserts that workers must be given greater responsibility, and management must start taking risks in the open: "Morality comes from self-esteem which comes from making decisions which require risk."

But even our greatest corporations fail to see the value of such an attitude. In the summer of 1964 the American Telephone and Telegraph Company asked its employees to take a pledge upholding a new nine-page "code of business conduct" that prohibited the giving away of confidential business information, having a financial interest in any of the corporation's suppliers and loafing on company time. The company's pride in not permitting employees to accept even calendars as gifts contrasted with its own lobbying activities and the revelation that an investigator for the New York Telephone Company, a subsidiary, had been selling information about gamblers' telephones to policemen who would then shake down the gamblers.

Amusingly, AT&T's new code of conduct warned employees to limit personal telephone calls at the telephone company's expense. This, of course, was the same giant corporation that hid automatic cameras in an employees' washroom to catch someone who had been scribbling obscenities on the walls. When a strike was threatened over this invasion of privacy, AT&T withdrew its cameras.

If in business "bigness" has crippled the personal loyalties that curtail selfish ambitions in simpler societies, bigness also affects other organized sections of our society. Universities and labor unions, for example, encounter much the same moral problems as big business. Professors are the first to decry the vicious backbiting and infighting that go on among educated, and supposedly principled, faculty members for status, promotion and recognition.

As the newest of our powerful institutions with moral responsibilities, the labor unions have agonized through the evolution of their moral problems. In the beginning, many Americans thought collective bargaining and the workers' refusal to work (the strike) were not only economically dangerous but immoral: the demand for a decent wage and an eight-hour day would undermine the moral fabric of the nation. But that stage has passed (in the lifetime of many of us) and only the antediluvian can any longer insist that labor unions be wiped from the American scene.

By now the moral problems of the leaders of big unions are surprisingly similar to those of leaders of big business. Industrial unions with tens and hundreds of thousands of members cannot retain the fraternal character or the crusading spirit of the early days, any more than big industrial companies with vast numbers of employees can keep up personal relationships in their plant.

The big unions have become vulnerable to the ambitions of men who seek power and wealth. They sometimes become corrupt as the distance widens between the leaders up on the platform and the members down in the pit. Labor leaders will often let their members and the public suffer as they battle among themselves for jurisdiction and power.

Governor Romney, an ex-businessman, says of labor leaders: "Some are out to win, regardless of what it takes. Many take economic measures that are immoral. Other labor unions shape their policies along more moral lines. To the extent the labor leader is under the same temptation as the politician to make demagogic victory his prime consideration, there is a tendency to use union power for selfish and pressure reasons. There are exceptions; I want to stress this."

Walter Reuther detests the labor leader who grows greedy. "He gets that way by little compromises. 'Why can't I get mine and still be respectable?' He can't."

What a union becomes, in moral terms, is often the result of how its leaders utilize the opportunity that size and strength give them. They can gain the freedom to make responsible decisions as size weakens the members' effective demand for narrow and immediate gains, or they can manipulate the power that results from size for their own profit. One of America's most powerful union leaders, Dave Beck, president of the International Brotherhood of Teamsters, had virtually total freedom to stick a hand in his union's treasury. He lived handsomely and exercised vast power until a Senate investigation and a series of court trials resulted in a five-year jail sentence. Beck escaped a charge of income-tax evasion by arguing that if he had stolen the money from the union, he was not required to pay taxes on it. When he was released after thirty months in federal prison, he had the security of a $50,000-a-year Teamster pension to fall back on.

In the past, unions represented the exploited underdog; today, organized labor, strengthened by the barriers against immigration, more and more belongs to America's middle class—sharing the nation's prosperity and comforts. This fact is reflected in the growing affluence of many labor leaders, in the corruptness of some and in the dying-out of the crusade for better working conditions and a living wage that lit the emotional fires of the labor movement during the 1930's and earlier. "My own personal conclusion," says Professor Argyris, "is that the unions do not presently have a viable mission, except to ask for more."

Today the unions must find moral answers in two new situations: Their own role is changing as a result of gaining strength, prestige and material benefits. And the creation of enough jobs has almost superseded the urgency of putting more money in the pay envelope.

Unions have tried to meet technological advances by demanding protection against layoffs, reduction of work time to spread the work, and protection of workers who have been laid off. The unions have negotiated to give companies a free hand to modernize in return for a share in the benefits from increased productivity.

Reuther is one of many labor leaders who believe that the unions must do much more than just "ask for more." The 1964 automotive industry negotiations demonstrated that agreement could be reached relatively easily on wages but that the real struggle was over who was to control working conditions. The companies were making enough money to absorb increased labor costs—or they could if necessary, pass them along to the consumer. But they were much more sticky over the control of working rules.

For labor, working conditions and the pressures of the

assembly line have become insistent issues. Reuther asks, "How would you like it if you couldn't get out of your chair to go to the john until your relief man came along and tapped you on the shoulder? What if you had to go an hour earlier?"

Although a leader like the Teamsters' James R. Hoffa sees the world as a "jungle" where each must grab for himself, Reuther says, "We want to make progress with the community, not at the expense of the community."

He asserts, "In the period ahead, the labor movement has to change its character from an economic organization to a social movement. The labor movement is the only entity with economic power and moral purpose. The church has moral purpose but no economic power. Business has economic power, but people forget General Motors Corporation was organized to make money—it makes cars on the side."

Reuther continues: "Economic power is not the purpose of the labor movement. Jimmy Hoffa has economic power. General Motors has economic power. The labor movement is about people—about their hopes and aspirations —their dreams." To Reuther, the unions' job is incomplete as long as "in the richest country of the world between 30 and 50 million people live in the sub-basement of our society—they are the have-not people of America."

Reuther denounces the big union salaries and the corruption and authoritarianism that permeate some unions. But Professor John T. Dunlop, chairman of Harvard University's economics department, asks, "What do you expect of union leaders?" Of those large salaries, expense accounts and carpeted offices, he points out, "If you want a Spartan labor leadership that is austere, puritanical in behavior, then you are going to have a radical leadership. If you want labor leadership that is conservative and businesslike, they are going to act like businessmen. You can't have it both ways. Stop kidding me about the kind of labor movement you want."

Dunlop sees in America "a tradition of business unionism." And he asks: If we accept corruption among some businessmen, why are we more shocked to find it among some labor leaders? "Why is it that what we call corruption in the labor movement occurs in the trucking industry, parts of the garment industry, longshoring and almost nowhere else? It is not a matter of personal morality. Why isn't there corruption in steel and autos?" Dunlop feels the key ingredient is the nature of those industries—undesirables can get work in trucking, on the docks and in the garment industry, which are broken up into small units invisible to public scrutiny. He adds, "Labor organizations in national public view are more scrupulous."

The UAW deals with large employers. It has established a seven-man Public Review Board, a kind of Supreme Court, which can declare unconstitutional any act of the union executives who run the UAW between its national conventions. Any member of the union can appeal to the Review Board, and this opportunity, the union's executives believe, encourages fair settlement of internal union disputes. Says UAW President Reuther, "This is the way you keep a union clean and democratic. A union goes bad by a whole series of little compromises that erode standards. I hoped other unions would follow but they haven't dared to."

Professor Dunlop believes one of labor's most worrisome problems is the morally questionable practice of featherbedding, keeping men employed after their jobs have disappeared. Says Reuther, "Featherbedding is a defense mechanism just like the 35-hour-week demand. I don't think it is morally right, but as long as there is not full employment, you will have workers trying to protect their jobs." He adds, "It is the law of survival. It's not a very good law, but men have been using it for a long time."

The labor leader also faces the difficult job of arriving at compromises that will allow the economy to function. Reuther says, "The basic problem a labor leader has to wrestle with is the area where you have to draw a line between the interest of your members as a group and the interest of the community as a group." The labor leader must not only get management to make compromises at the bargaining table, but he must achieve compromises among various factions, interests and ideas within the union membership. "The real skill of a labor negotiator," says Reuther, "is to persuade his troops the settlement reflects their equity. A labor leader always negotiates in both directions—with his own members and the company —at the same time. It takes skill."

Dunlop emphasizes the complexity of the labor leader's job: "It is one of the most difficult jobs in our society and society doesn't appreciate its difficulty. The principle of negotiation is to settle disputes within the group. This is a tremendously difficult job. It requires real imagination and the highest diplomacy. How do you persuade guys they ought to be laid off from their jobs because of new machines—and like it?"

The working out of compromises raises moral questions about devices such as the so-called "fixed arbitration." This occurs when labor and management, fearing the reactions of union members and stockholders, cannot openly agree to a compromise. The leaders on both sides of the bargaining table then secretly arrange a settlement and ask an arbitrator to impose it on them. This solves the immediate conflict by deceiving those to whom both union leaders and managers are responsible. The workers are led to believe, falsely, that their spokesmen did not agree to the solution voluntarily, that it was forced on them. One labor lawyer, who regards such "fixed arbitrations" as immoral, tells of a mill owner in a small Southern community who said he would be run out of town if he had openly accepted a settlement which he believed was right and proper.

Professor Argyris sees hope for solutions to the moral problems of the business world: "Management, to trust themselves, have to start to take risks with self-esteem in the open." He cites the case of an executive in one company who would not risk proposing a radically new product and then saw a competitor come out with the very same idea. "In some companies," Argyris says, "the guy who will be the next president will be the guy who takes the most risks."

In business, he adds, morality can most easily be shown to be not only right but profitable. All that is necessary, he suggests, is to include the costs of executive distrust and worker apathy and resentment in a business' accounting system. If these attitudes, which drain profits from virtually every large company every year, were figured in, the business world would become aware of the real price it is paying for failing to solve its moral problems. Argyris thinks businessmen are learning this. "There is an increasing number of executives who have put their money where their mouth is. If we can make trust, openness and concern for human beings viable in the business world, we might be able to help the churches."

Edwin Etherington believes businessmen who want to act morally need guidance: "The complexity of society tends to make it harder for the individual to behave morally, especially in business. He may not know the ground rules or may lose respect for them. When we get to the corner, we have to know when the light is red or green." He cites the example of his five-year-old child, who points a water pistol at his head. Etherington raises his hands and he is shot anyway. The child, he says, does not know the rule that if you raise your hands, you don't get shot. But once told, the child obeys the rule.

"There is a need for a network of rules, and we need to see the reason for the rule. If we don't see the reason, it's blind obedience," Etherington adds. He says highway signs in Maine read "Safe Speed 60 M.P.H.," and this he believes is better than imposing a speed limit. "We need to have everybody retain his own initiative about deciding what is moral—and doing it."

Newton N. Minow, former chairman of the Federal Communications Commission, sees this change already occurring: "I think you have a growing corporate conscience in business all the time. Better education, a greater sense of responsibility, greater awareness of public opinion."

Irwin Miller, businessman and church lay leader, suggests: "In no other age would an electrical vice-president go to jail. We are holding business to higher standards of morality." Speaking from his own business experience, Miller says the crucial moral question in business is: "What is fair, what is right, what do you do? You take this problem to your preacher and he takes to the hills. The church belongs in this field. Maybe the church says, 'How can I expect to be competent in pricing, employment, retiring?' The church has to be competent in these things, or it will be irrelevant."

Mortimer Caplin believes that many businessmen are looking for guidance. He urges business leaders to articulate rules of conduct. "The leaders must appear at all levels. The big cry is for the responsible people to make themselves heard."

The important fact is that the world in which businessmen must make their decisions has changed radically from the heyday of the "robber barons" and the sweatshop. There are more restrictions on greed and there is more profit in seeking moral decisions. As a result, businessmen's dilemmas are all the more acute and all the more puzzling.

«« *10.*

The Press—A Scarcity of Courage

The press supplies the mortar for our pluralistic society; it enables more than 190 million Americans to share, to an important extent, the same experiences. As Philip Hauser says, "The mass media of communication are the chief means by which people in a mass society can acquire intelligence—information to govern their behavior." Without a free press, the American people could not rule themselves.

The problem of cohesion is acute in a vast, diverse nation like ours. Harvard historian Oscar Handlin says, "We are probably less clear in our understanding of ourselves than at any time in history. What people in Texas are thinking has almost nothing in common with what people in New York and Massachusetts are thinking. . . . This must reveal some failures in both political leadership and in the effectiveness of education media—in the broadest sense."

Our press meets its moral responsibilites no better than the other major institutions of our society. Because of the nature of the press, its examples of moral courage and leadership are more visible than those of other institutions. But the press' failures are also more visible. As Louis M. Lyons, for twenty-six years curator of the Nieman Foundation of Journalism at Harvard University, puts it, "A doctor buries his mistakes; a newspaper publishes its mistakes."

How responsibly did the press behave during the McCarthy era? How boldly did the press report the medical community's concern over the relationship between cigarette smoking and lung cancer? How many newspapers covered adequately the electrical industry's price-fixing scandals? How thoroughly has the press reported the activities, habits and morality of the Establishment—the powerful men and women of government, business and the professions? How responsibly did the press report the Negroes' plight in America as seen against the standard of our Fourth-of-July ideal of equality for all? The list of questions can be extended indefinitely and the answer to each one would have to be that a great part of the press has failed to meet its moral responsibility.

This responsibility is to find enough courage to inform the people of the realities of their changing world. James Reston of *The New York Times* said in an address at Columbia University: "Change is the biggest story in the world today, and we are not covering it adequately. . . . In my view too many newspapers are not only failing to report change on their news pages, but are deploring change, inciting opposition to change, and perpetuating rather than destroying popular illusion on their editorial pages."

The saving grace of the American press is, of course, its variety. Both responsibility and irresponsibility exist within every branch of the press and even within an individual newspaper or television station. The presence of mediocrity and incompetence is the price we pay—and must pay willingly—for having a press that is free from dictation. Too often a newspaper merely reflects the mores of its community or the prejudices of its owners—when, for example, it beats the drums for the radical right or waves the bloody shirt for racial segregation. All too commonly the press lacks the courage to buck the holders of economic, political or religious power.

Louis Lyons says, "The business community is the part of the community the publisher is most conscious of and dependent on." He says that the publisher generally belongs to this part of the community; he is "a big employer and a big taxpayer. It is difficult to ask or assume that such a publisher will operate his paper in conflict with that part of the community." What is surprising, Lyons adds, is that so many do keep their news columns open, but "you don't get it everywhere and you don't get it enough."

The tendency to temper opposition and skirt controversy is particularly widespread in the broadcasting media, which carry the added burden of government regulation. John Horn, writing in the *New York Herald Tribune*, refers to "the networks and their sponsors, who queue up to buy TV entertainment but make themselves scarce at the mention of news and public affairs. . . ." He notes that on television, entertainment gets all the prime viewing time. This timidity is strange when one reflects on the power of the mass media. Says Newton Minow, who as chairman of the Federal Communications Commission made the public aware of some defects of television programming, "Many people who run the television industry say the medium is just a mirror of society. This is where I fall off the ship.

The presidents of the three networks have, in some ways, more power than the President of the United States. They decide what millions of Americans will do in the evening. They decide what people will see."

He adds, "The mass media should have higher standards. Their responsibility is greater. Their real question is: I am a trustee for millions of people. Am I doing the best I can? They aren't." Yet Minow is hopeful about TV; he thinks it is beginning to deal with "tough, hard social issues," thinks it is "growing up."

Timidity prevails even among the most powerful press lords. For example, many press and broadcast managers in New York fear that criticism of Republican, Catholic or Jewish views will offend men who make decisions in the advertising agencies along Madison Avenue. Throughout the country, timidity is one reason to deplore the compression of newspaper ownership. Today hardly twenty communities have more than one newspaper owner. Says Louis Lyons, "Nobody but the local media can keep an eye on City Hall and local utility rates. If you don't have competition, there is no incentive to be vigorous and alert."

A passage in Pope John XXIII's *Pacem in Terris* states the need well: "By the natural law every human being has the right to respect for his person, to his good reputation, the right to freedom in searching for truth and in expressing and communicating his opinions, and in pursuit of art, within the limits laid down by the moral order and the common good. And he has the right to be informed truthfully about public events."

Speaking of his own medium, films, and of the others too, John Huston says that the responsibility is "to keep our nerve up, not to be afraid to say what we believe is the truth, not to be intimidated into silence." Gardner Cowles warned a Sigma Delta Chi convention, when he was the journalistic society's honorary national president: "Don't try to be an editor if you lack a spine or have to be loved all the time. You will fail. The only really successful editors I know have guts and are not afraid to be unpopular. Respected you can be; fair you must be; but you can't edit vigorously and provocatively and still win a popularity contest."

The press' problem with courage occurs in three areas: courage to report change, despite the objections of those who have a vested interest in the status quo; courage to meet the problems caused by the existence of so many media; and, finally, the courage to withstand the pressures of monstrously powerful government.

The first moral dilemma for the leaders of the American press is that they have both a business and an editorial responsibility. When the two clash, the press' leaders face their moment of truth. Sometimes the press sensationalizes to attract a larger audience and sometimes it compromises its independence of judgment to appease its advertisers. The tendency to sensationalize can be damaging. Walter Reuther says, "When the press commercialized on McCarthy, it was equally guilty." The tendency to bow to the advertiser takes the form of publishing hand-out news, accepting gifts and junkets, and omitting news unfavorable to business.

The reality that a bankrupt newspaper can perform no editorial function at all must be considered along with the principle that one way to bankruptcy—as well as a way to fail to serve the public—is to lack editorial integrity. If the editor who feels pressured will recognize that the advertiser needs, most of all, an environment of believability, he will realize that stopping the truth at the advertiser's door destroys both of them.

There was a legend in the city room of *The Newark*

(New Jersey) *News*, where I first worked full time, that the owner of a large local department store had come to the publisher's office and demanded that a certain story be retracted or he would pull out his advertising. The publisher called for the department store's advertising contract, tore it up and dropped it into the wastebasket. His newspaper, he explained, did not accept threats, and the store could not advertise in the *News* for a year. When the year was up, the department store owner, having learned that he needed the newspaper too, was back with his ads.

I don't know whether this story is apocryphal; it really doesn't matter (and I suspect its equivalent is told in other city rooms). What does matter is that the story set a level of moral responsibility and deeply impressed young reporters seeking support of their own ideals.

Such pressures are not limited to big cities and big businesses. When I became the editor of a weekly newspaper in Westport, Connecticut, years ago, I assumed my duties in the spring, just as the business of renting homes to summer visitors from New York City reached its climax. I interviewed the leading local real estate dealers and discovered that, during this particular season, business was bad. My story reporting this fact brought a torrent of protest, and accusations that I was stimulating a decline in rental prices and had betrayed the community by reporting the truth. A few real estate dealers withdrew their advertising (temporarily) to persuade the newspaper's owner to veto future stories that might hurt their incomes. (He didn't.) Their concept of the moral responsibility of the press was that it should be a propaganda weapon for local business which, through its advertising, made the newspaper possible. They thought, wrongly, that buying space should give them some control over the paper's editorial content.

More recently, as a magazine editor, I was assigned to develop a story on one of America's greatest business companies. My report included an interview during which the powerful man who ran that corporation criticized the qualifications of the Kennedy Administration. When he saw a copy of the magazine just before the issue went on sale, he tried with great energy to have the presses stopped and his quotations deleted. I took pride in the fact that, although his company was an important and respected advertiser, the men responsible for *Look*'s integrity would not brook such interference.

In these three instances, the people responsible for these publications stood up to pressure. But all too often, leaders of the press, because they are in weaker economic positions or because they lack courage, do knuckle under. For one example, a prize-winning reporter on a Southern newspaper told me that his publisher had killed a story on the death of several Negro residents who had been turned away from the emergency room of the local segregated white hospital. And the executive editor of *The Louisville Courier-Journal* criticized "the lax practices of a large segment of the American press" when 250 reporters took a freeloading junket to Hollywood as part of a movie's publicity campaign. Apparently, only five of these reporters had their expenses paid by their newspapers. Many of the others were open to the suspicion of being willing to exchange a favorable story for a free trip to California.

To report the problems of the American economy with objectivity can require courage. Few parts of the American story are told so badly; much economic reporting today is just puffery buried in jargon. It is no longer good enough to cover the American economy with rewrites of company annual reports and with press agentry. The stories of our unused production capacity, the problems of our foreign trade, the coming of automation, the development of investment overseas and unemployment at home, all bear vitally on our lives. The American press is faced with the moral challenge to tell these stories despite fears of retaliation.

The second moral dilemma is how the press can deal responsibly with its own proliferation. The hordes of reporters and photographers who cover a Presidential news conference or jam up any major news event are exasperating evidence of the press' problem with its own size. At the 1964 Republican National Convention, newsmen outnumbered delegates. One solution is "pooling," the self-defeating device by which a very few reporters and/or photographers are permitted to cover an event and must allow their material to be used by all. This is self-defeating because it destroys the press' variety—its lifeblood in a democracy. Without variety the press would, as it has in so many other societies, become merely the tool of a few.

The press was made urgently aware of the problem of its numbers by the Warren Commission report on the assassination of President Kennedy. The Commission placed the blame for Jack Ruby's shooting of Lee Harvey Oswald on both the police and the press: "The Commission believes that the news media, as well as the police authorities, who failed to impose conditions more in keeping with the orderly process of justice, must share responsibility for the failure of law enforcement which occurred in connection with the death of Oswald." Even if the mass of newsmen did display, as the Commission charged, "a regrettable lack of self-discipline," Ruby's presence near Oswald cannot be blamed on the press.

The press' third moral dilemma is that it must withstand

government efforts to undercut and limit the public's right to know what is going on. In March, 1964, the United States Supreme Court strengthened the freedom and usefulness of the press when it unanimously found that a newspaper cannot libel a public official by criticizing his performance of his public duties, even when the criticism is partially untrue. The Court said that the newspaper can be punished only if deliberate malice is proved. It threw out a $500,000 libel judgment against *The New York Times*, which had been upheld in the Alabama state courts.

In this ruling, the Supreme Court asserted that there is "a profound national commitment to the principle that debate on public issues should be uninhibited, robust and wide-open, and that it may well include vehement, caustic, and sometimes unpleasantly sharp attacks on government and public officials." The requirement that the truth of critical statements must be proved, the Court said, would impose a "pall of fear and timidity."

In concurring opinions, Justices Hugo L. Black, William O. Douglas and Arthur J. Goldberg said that even malicious statements against public officials should be permitted. Justice Black said that the Constitution grants the press "an absolute immunity for criticism of the way public officials do their public duty." Justice Goldberg added, "In my view, the First and Fourteenth Amendments to the Constitution afford to the citizen and to the press an absolute, unconditional privilege to criticize official conduct despite the harm which may flow from excesses and abuses."

In America the single acceptable exception to the people's right to know what their public servants are doing is in the very narrow area of specific military security. This means that no local school board has the right to make decisions in private, no state legislature has the right to wheel and deal in secret, no federal bureau or representative has the right to conduct the public's business in private. But throughout the United States, government officials get away with such secrecy every day.

This means the local reporter must pry open the police blotter and the closed-door sessions of his town's governing board. It means he must fight the efforts of the judiciary and the legal profession to keep the press' nose out of the court-room. In Washington it means the press cannot permit federal agencies to hide error, malpractice and corruption under the stamp of national security.

The Pentagon, for example, tries to gag newsmen for reasons of "policy" far beyond legitimate military security. The line between the communists' need-not-to-know and the American public's need-to-know becomes a fog-covered battlefield where both government and press grope blindly. I have spent an entire day clearing one sentence that the Navy insisted was classified but finally conceded had already been made available to the world. In his effort to impose civilian control on the giant military establishment, Secretary of Defense Robert S. McNamara consistently tightened the Department of Defense's grip on news. He did cut down the services' use of publicity to further inter-service rivalry, but he made legitimate news more difficult to get. Our lives depend on the decisions of the people in that oversized block-house. Except where specific military security is involved, the activities of the Pentagon are simply too important to be kept under wraps.

During World War II the press limited its freedom for the duration. But today we are in a new kind of struggle that cannot be ended by riding up the Kremlin steps on a white horse. The limitations we permit today will handcuff the free press for the rest of our lives and our children's lives. We have to figure out with care the solutions we want for the problems in what Douglass Cater in *The Reporter* magazine described as "the no-man's land where news and national security are in conflict."

The newsman's desire to map this "no-man's land" is too often frustrated by those who seek to manipulate the press. They leak information to win support for some pet project or to squelch a competing program. They hide error and incompetence under the stamp of SECRET. After the disaster at Cuba's Bay of Pigs, the *St. Louis Post-Dispatch* editorialized: "What Government officials seem to want the press to hide is not so much official secrets as official blunders." And James Reston wrote in *The New York Times*, "There is nothing in the Government's handling of the Cuban affair to suggest that the press should just look the other way and let officials do what they like in this field. Likewise, the handling of the U-2 spy plane case is not exactly a recommendation for the infinite wisdom of the bureaucracy. . . ."

What the public has been permitted to know about the progress of the war in Vietnam has been erratic. In July, 1964, the *Times* said editorially: "Until now the Government's negative—indeed, repressive and distorted—news policies obscured both the purposes and progress of the war. The public was not only misinformed by Government spokesmen but unpalatable facts were withheld and the truth subverted." Senator Fulbright made quite similar accusations on the Senate floor on September 15, 1965, when he criticized our intervention in the Dominican Republic: "U.S. policy was marred by a lack of candor and by misinformation." He charged that the American people were given the wrong reason to explain the intervention and he even accused President Johnson of making a statement about massacres for which there was, he said, "no evidence to support [his] statement."

War can be a closed-shop business as far as news is concerned. It is difficult to cover a shooting war over the opposition of the commanders involved. During the 1962 Cuban missile crisis, newsmen were not permitted to cover our blockading fleet or our Guantanamo naval base. And in 1964, when Castro cut off Guantanamo's water supply, the Pentagon barred the base to reporters for a week. There was absolutely no basis for claiming military security; this restriction had little if any American precedent even during wartime. There was no question of keeping information from the Soviets; they knew what was going on. The American people were kept in the dark and told only what the Pentagon wanted them to know.

Fortunately, the military's instinct toward secrecy is usually limited by its need for public support—men, money, materials and the position of command. This has become increasingly true as the tight little peacetime military establishment that existed before World War II ballooned into today's massiveness. For example, the Pentagon actively solicited newsmen to go along in military aircraft when it wanted to publicize its demonstrations of how fast it could get troops to Europe.

Every administration tries to control and manipulate the press. None was more effective than the Kennedy Administration which used skill to get its story told and energetically sought to restrain the reporting of news it did not want out. President Kennedy himself sent the FBI gumshoeing through the Pentagon after *Newsweek* reported on some of our preparations to hold West Berlin. Reporters were shadowed; their phones apparently tapped. Once he personally telephoned a top military PIO after reading a *New York Times* article he did not like. These things were done not when military security was endangered but when politicians were embarrassed.

Secretary McNamara put his foot in his mouth when he proposed that the press should report that the Army's Nike-Zeus anti-missile missile was invincible. He said, according to the *Times*, "What we ought to be saying is that we have the most perfect anti-ICBM system that the human mind will ever devise. Instead the public domain is already full of statements that the Zeus may not be satisfactory, that it has deficiencies. . . . It is absurd to release that kind of information for the public."

The next day, the Department of Defense explained that the Secretary did not want to mislead the American people —only the Russians. How we fool the Soviets without misleading ourselves was not explained. Concluded *The Baltimore Sun*, "Secretary McNamara thinks the press, in the interest of national security, ought to print a lie."

Virgil M. Newton, managing editor of the *Tampa Tribune* and former chairman of Sigma Delta Chi's national freedom-of-information committee, has charged that censored documents in the Pentagon would measure, if stretched in files, 575 miles. He said, "It is utterly ridiculous that a free government should have 575 miles of secret defense documents. If any government should have even one mile of legitimate defense secrets, it would be able to dominate not only the earth but the universe."

Until 1960, power to classify and bury information was held by such non-military federal agenies as the Civil War

Centennial Commission and the Federal Home Loan Bank Board. And in 1962 this power to censor was extended to the Agency for International Development and even the Peace Corps.

Valid secrets do exist. Most newsmen would probably agree that the following represent legitimate areas in which they must limit full reporting: detailed capabilities of new weapons, specific war plans, crucial "fall back positions" to which our government is willing to retreat in diplomatic negotiations, and facts that will reveal to our enemies how we gain our intelligence about them. Turner Catledge, executive editor of *The New York Times*, has decried the trend to "ultra-secrecy" and he said in a speech, "Our responsibility is to tell as much of the truth as possible within, of course, the limits of the actual physical security of this country. This does not mean political security; it means the physical security of ourselves and our families."

Catledge added, "Secrecy and security are by no means necessarily synonymous, no matter how closely allied they may seem to some of those in military or government authority. If secrecy operates to deprive the public of facts which it needs for balanced judgments, if security leads the citizens of our country to feel smug and complacent when they should be aroused and alarmed, then secrecy really damages our security." There is no justification for excluding the people from the process of decision-making.

If the American people duck their responsibility and decide that they need not know whatever the government does not want to tell them, they must accept the fact that the people's decisions will be made by "the insiders." Then, to preserve our democratic way of life, we will have surrendered it. As Turner Catledge said, secrecy threatens to divide the United States, as it does the Soviet Union, "into an informed elite on the one hand and an ignorant mass on the other." Today we depend more and more on experts, technicians and scientists, but we cannot afford to let them dictate our political and ethical decisions.

Chairman Glenn Seaborg of the Atomic Energy Commission is concerned about this growing gap between the public and the scientific elite. "We have to counteract it with more and better education," he warns. "Otherwise we won't have a democracy." He worries about the people having to take a position on matters they do not understand, and he denies that security is a valid excuse. "Nothing is very secret very long. We don't keep large areas of policy determination secret—we can't. It's in the public domain very quickly." He urges that non-science majors in our colleges receive more scientific education so that they will be able to participate in the decisions of society. He says, "The colleges haven't met the challenge yet."

In his remarkable telecast before leaving the White House in 1961, President Eisenhower made this same point: "The potential for the disastrous rise of misplaced power exists and will persist. We must never let the weight of this combination ['the military-industrial complex'] endanger our liberties or democratic processes. We should take nothing for granted. Only an alert and knowledgeable citizenry can compel the proper meshing of the huge industrial and military machinery of defense with our peaceful methods and goals, so that security and liberty may prosper together."

In our mass, democratic society, the people cannot rule themselves by sitting together in a town meeting. They can do so only through their elected representatives and through the mass media of communication which keep them informed of failure and folly. This involves risks that no closed society need face. There is no simple solution.

Pericles in ancient Athens said in his funeral oration commemorating the death of those killed in the first year of the war with Sparta: "If we turn to our military policy, there also we differ from our antagonists. We throw open our city to the world and never by alien acts exclude foreigners from any opportunity of learning or observing, although the eyes of an enemy may occasionally profit by our liberality; trusting less in system and policy than in the native spirit of our citizens . . . and yet [we] are just as ready to encounter every legitimate danger."

In our world, where each side is able to destroy the other totally, few secrets are meaningful. As Pericles suggested, we cannot survive with sorcery and secrecy, only with courage based on our knowledge of the facts. But across the country one hears increasingly the accusation that newsmen tell the communists too much—that they chase scoops and headlines and forget that the nation's survival is at stake. A surprising number of Americans are ready to surrender some of our traditional freedom of the press in their panic to save their skins.

How far this attitude has metastasized was made clear at the 1964 Republican National Convention, when those assembled cheered an attack by ex-President Eisenhower on "sensation-seeking columnists and commentators." Many in the hall shook their fists at working newsmen. These reactions, which seemed to startle even Eisenhower, demonstrated that some Americans who cry loudest for individual freedom and free enterprise do not really want a free press. Responsible newsmen came away from the GOP convention convinced that many there wanted the press suppressed. The convention had barely adjourned when Presidential candidate Goldwater asserted that the Columbia Broadcasting System had been wrong in reporting that he had been in communication with pro-Nazi right-wing groups in West Germany and CBS should not be permitted to function. He said in a TV interview: "I don't think these people should even be allowed to broadcast." It may be expected that politicians will try to make the press a scapegoat; what is disturbing is the readiness with which many Americans, under the pressure of the existence of communism, are prepared to destroy one of the foundations of democratic freedom.

A free press, unfortunately, must be free to be irresponsible. The question is: Who shall judge what is vital or interesting enough to be printed or broadcast? Those who do not understand the job of a free press feel that some "responsible" person or group should make this judgment. They prefer that it be made by a government czar or a council of "lords of the press" rather than by the separate and fallible judgments of thousands of editors from Midlothian, Texas, to Manchester, New Hampshire, and New York City in between.

Perhaps the most important force that operates against the press' doing its job courageously comes not from outside pressure but from bad reporting, bad editing and the failure of the press itself to act. An important example of our press' failure to fight government manipulation with courage was its acceptance of the original State Department prohibition (later rescinded) against allowing U.S. reporters to cover the tremendous story of Communist China, where 20 percent of the world's population lives. The willingness of the American press to accept this denial of its freedom and responsibility to report the world's events to the American people will go down as one of the blackest marks in its history.

On a day-by-day level, the lazy reporter who is satisfied that the whole truth is given in a government briefing, a company press release or a self-interested interview is simply not doing the job. The hand-out has become the most sophisticated means of "keeping" the press. For example, James McCartney of the *Chicago Daily News*, writing in the December 1963 *Nieman Reports*, said, "the White House press tends to be the most docile in town. . . . The beat produces so much front page news without critical reporting that a sycophant can stay in business for years." He also accused the Capitol Hill press of having protected Bobby Baker from publicity although many knew of his dealings. The sad fact is that reporters can develop a vested interest in their beats. That is why responsible editors never send the police reporter to expose the police department.

"The journalist is really the fellow on the first line of this terribly complex situation [in the world]," says Louis Lyons. "He has a tremendously responsible job and it is not reasonable to expect he will always be up to it."

The reporter who sees the world in terms of angels fighting devils denies the American people the insight they need to meet the changes of today and the challenges of tomorrow. This kind of reporting—and the editing that accepts it—is as damaging as that which bows to outside interests. We should be concerned when the press fails to use its freedom with courage.

Clark R. Mollenhoff of the Washington bureau of the Cowles publications stated the principle in the fifteenth annual William Allen White lecture at the University of

Kansas in 1964: "Democracy is contingent upon an informed public with the means to learn what the government is doing, the right to criticize what the government is doing, and the mechanism for effectively expressing opposition by voting to oust our highest officials from office."

It takes courage to report a war—almost as much as it takes to fight one—if you do it as did men like Ernie Pyle, George Polk, Robert Capa and Henry Taylor, Jr. But today we need other kinds of courage at least as much. We need the kind of courage Edward R. Murrow had when he reported the McCarthy story. We need the kind of courage with which Ed Reid covered police corruption in New York City in the 1950's; with which Anthony Lewis exposed the mistreatment of Abraham Chasanow; with which Pierre Salinger and Clark Mollenhoff investigated the Teamsters Union; with which Ed Stevens, Phil Harrington and William Worthy went to Communist China; with which men like Harry Ashmore and Ralph McGill stayed home and put out newspapers in Little Rock and Atlanta.

Examples of this kind of courage can also be found among the editors of weekly newspapers in localities where publication of the truth can mean physical danger as well as economic disaster: weekly editors like Hazel Brannon Smith in Lexington and Jackson, Mississippi, whose paper was bombed; Penn Jones, Jr., in Midlothian, Texas, whose shop was bombed; Wilcox Dunn who was beaten up in Virginia Beach, Virginia; Samuel Woodring who was attacked in North Augusta, South Carolina, and Gene Wirges who was shot at in Morrilton, Arkansas.

We need the courage of honesty—to see things as they are. We need the courage of doggedness—to ask the next question when the chips are down. We need the courage of responsibility—to offend the powerful if necessary to make public the truth. And these kinds of courage must be welcomed—in fact, demanded—by everyone up the line. Any reporter knows that what he does find will only see the light of day if those above him have the courage to put it into print. The ad manager must recognize that without editorial courage the space or time he is selling sinks into the morass of the undistinguished. The publishers, and the stockholders, must recognize that without this courage they are only in the entertainment business. And above all, the people must respect and treasure the courageous act performed for them, because without it they cannot survive.

Theodore H. White put it well when he wrote: "Our profession is like the medical profession. News and truth, like healing and medicine, are things that must be provided our people, at no matter what cost. Our society cannot survive without good medicine and without truthful information."

The press has a responsibility not to pervert the truth for profit or partisanship and not to knuckle under to the pressure of any of those forces that want the facts suppressed. Men and women who have no other interest than to report the truth as they see it can affect the fate of us all.

«« *11.*

The Failure of the Churches

If the moral problem of the American press is to find courage, the problem of the churches in America—our fourth institution with a moral responsibility—is to find relevance. The churches too have failed to provide moral leadership, and because their responsibility is the greatest, their failure is the worst.

Harvard Divinity School's Dean Samuel Miller says: "The church simply does not have a cutting edge. It has taken the culture of our time and absorbed it. Most churches are floored that there is any difference between Christian faith and prosperity. It's ghastly that the church is run not to serve the reality of human beings but to conserve institutions." He adds that, for the most part, the minister has become "a big operator."

Asked if he felt the churches were meeting their responsibility, theologian Paul Tillich replied, "Simply, No! But I know the struggle of many ministers who try it and are defeated and almost go to pieces by this defeat."

The failure of the churches to supply moral leadership is widely agreed upon. Says the Archbishop of Canterbury, "The churches aren't reaching people as much as they ought to." In the idiom of his field, industrial administration, Professor Argyris says, "The marketing division of the Lord is pretty ineffective."

As the Reverend John A. T. Robinson, the Bishop of Woolwich, England, wrote in his book *Honest To God*: "The sanctions of Sinai have lost their terrors, and people no longer accept the authority of Jesus even as a great moral teacher. Robbed of its supranatural supports, men find it difficult to take seriously a code of living that confessedly depended on them. 'Why shouldn't I?' or 'What's wrong with it?' are questions which in our generation press for an answer. And supranaturalist reasons—that God or Christ has pronounced it 'a sin'—have force, and even meaning, for none but a diminishing religious remnant."

Yale's Chaplain William S. Coffin, Jr., says, "Christianity has not been tried and found wanting. It's been tried and found difficult and watered down and perverted over and over again. We churchmen are gifted at changing wine into water—watering down religion. The problem of the church today is ineffectiveness. We've never had attendance so high and influence so low, and maybe the two are not unrelated."

It is not surprising that at a time of the failure of religious leaders to lead, those who lean heavily on the churches grasp at straws. Since 1961 they have printed "In God We Trust" on paper money (rather a strange place). They inject God into the national Pledge of Allegiance, and they struggle to keep children saying prayers in the public schools. "As long as we had the prayer," says Dean Miller, "people thought we had religion and morality. Maybe getting rid of the prayer is the first step to getting religion and morality."

When the U.S. Supreme Court declared, in 1962 and 1963, that officially prepared prayers and devotional Bible reading in the public schools are unconstitutional, 37 states had laws either requiring or allowing religious exercises in their public schools. After the Court's decisions, some 167 congressmen and at least 30 senators rushed to save God and country by advocating an amendment to the Constitution to promote praying and Bible reading for worship in the public schools. They did this despite the opposition to such a violation of the separation of church and state by spokesmen of the Baptist, Methodist, Lutheran, Presbyterian and Episcopalian denominations. The National Council of Churches opposed the proposed amendment; so did some Catholic authorities and most Jewish leaders. Both Catholic President Kennedy and Protestant President Johnson spoke against it. But the congressmen insisted the mail from their people back home forced them to support the amendment. Even when their religious leaders spoke out on the subject of prayer, many people would not listen.

The build-up for such a Constitutional amendment was a clear sign of the failure of our religious institutions. The furor suggested that many people were truly distressed about the moral training of their children. Having found their churches inadequate or unlistened-to, they sought to transfer some of this responsibility of home and church to the public schools. Among the organizations supporting the amendment were the American Legion, Lions, Kiwanis, Catholic War Veterans and others, plus a sprinkling of "hate groups." In some quarters, even in some responsible quarters, the public schools were attacked for leaving a moral vacuum in our children's educational development. Catholic Bishop Fulton Sheen, supporting the amendment, said the wall of separation between church and state in the United

States is a myth. One Lutheran minister, receiving a 1964 Americanism award from the Westchester County (N.Y.) American Legion, damned UNESCO and the National Education Association as "seedbeds of atheism" and said, "One sometimes wonders whether the Supreme Court members have been appointed by the Kremlin in Moscow." The Legionnaires gave him a standing ovation.

The demand for school prayers is always preoccupied with personal morality and an allegiance to the idea of God. Social concern is not involved, and among the communities most reluctant to give up prayers and religious observances in their schools will be those with segregated all-white public schools of the Bible-Belt South.

The high-pitched emotionalism in this desperate attempt to keep prayers and Bible reading in the schools points to another moral problem ahead of us: In the near future we will have to re-examine the ability of our various denominations to live together in a pluralistic society. Much of the churches' leadership has already demonstrated its awareness and concern by its moves toward ecumenicalism and by its widespread support of the Supreme Court decisions. But many people still fail to grasp the problem—perhaps the most serious religious problem on the road ahead.

Pressures against the American doctrine of the separation of church and state have been growing. Although many of our early colonists came here to escape an established church and to worship as they wished, in our colonial period, church and state were usually firmly linked. Many of our early colonies were exclusive and conforming theocracies and adhered to one of the many quarreling sects. But when the Founding Fathers created a nation, they appreciated that the only way to avoid the interdenominational strife and at the same time to preserve the diversity of faiths was to separate church and state. They did this, despite the arguments made today, not to eradicate religion but to strengthen religious faith. And in those days no Americans agreed more strongly with separation than the Catholics.

In our present surge of religiosity, many have lost sight of this heritage of separation. They attack the wall between church and state from two directions: First, they would introduce religious declarations, prayers and teaching into our official and public institutions. Here the main drive is to introduce prayer and religious instruction into the public schools, despite the simple fact that in America government has no right to tell anyone—especially a child—what he must believe about God.

The second attack on separation is the increasingly successful effort to gain public tax money for denominational schools. The possessors of denominational schools, pressed by rising costs and teacher salaries, want a piece of the government hand-out pie that so many people share in today. They want either straight-out subsidies, payments to parents who send their children to denominational schools or the right for denominational school students to use expensive facilities, such as shops and laboratories, in nearby public schools. The cost of denominational schools is becoming too burdensome; in some communities, churches have already had to cut back their school programs. In the final analysis, the fight for aid for denominational schools is an effort on the part of some religious leaders in a number of denominations to get public tax money. They have succumbed to mammonish temptation. And they have already won the right to acquire tax money to pay for text books and school transportation as well as the passage of the 1965 federal aid-to-education law. One study says that nearly half the states now subsidize denominational schools to some degree with public tax money. These are holes already knocked in our traditional wall of separation between church and state.

Dr. James B. Conant, former Harvard University president who has studied American education intensively, has made the additional point that federal money given to any private schools will multiply the number of these schools and endanger the power of the public schools as, what he has called, "an enormously important instrument for forwarding the ideals of our society."

"Since Constantine gave the church official status, we have no longer been persecuted and have inherited special privileges that have reduced our capacity to criticize society. Or we have been sold out to the state and tend to make it a bought church," declares the Reverend John Morris, executive director of the Episcopal Society for Cultural and Racial Unity.

Church leaders blame three problems for their failure to create what Irwin Miller calls "the church relevant." First is the concept that moral leadership should concern itself only with private actions, and oppose drinking, dancing, smoking, etc. "Negative piety" this has been called. Says the Reverend John Usry, a young Congregationalist minister in Deerfield, Illinois, a comfortable suburb north of Chicago, "People enjoy hearing about family morality. They say, 'You sure tread on our toes today.' But stay away from those other concerns. The cardinal sin in the church is to be involved in controversy." This concept of Christianity, says Dean Samuel Miller, is "inadequate" in our world.

"Ministers feel they are relevant to personal problems but not to the larger sphere," explains the Reverend Gibson

Winter, associate professor of ethics and society at the University of Chicago Divinity School.

Second is the material competition among denominations. "Episcopals are still fighting with Baptists over infant versus adult baptism," says the Reverend Michael Allen, rector of St. Mark's-in-the-Bouwerie Protestant Episcopal Church in New York City. "Who the hell cares? These are not relevant issues. If we are going to have divisions, let them be realistic."

Ralph McGill, the courageous publisher of the *Atlanta Constitution*, says, "There's been a lot of intellectual dishonesty on the part of the church. They have big building debts and unhappily 85 percent of the big givers want to keep the status quo." Adds the Reverend Usry, "It's so easy to see people in terms of pledge units, rather than people to minister."

"What we have sold out to is a success pattern and financial strength and a successful career for the clergyman, the rising executive," says the Reverend Morris.

Irwin Miller points out that there are more than two hundred denominations of Christians. At least 21 have memberships of more than one million; the Roman Catholic Church with 44.8 million American members is by far the largest single denomination. And with the Catholic population reportedly growing at three times the rate of the Protestant population, historian Will Durant says, "The birth rate is probably making America a Catholic country."

Of the competition among denominations, Irwin Miller warns: "This tarnishes the example. If they won't lose their lives, how can they preach to you to lose your life. A church that cannot solve its own split personality isn't going to put together many split personalities in the world." Miller sees hope that the ecumenical movement will at least bring Protestant denominations together. "This," he says, "could loom as important in the twentieth century as the Reformation did in the sixteenth century—and as radical."

The third reason for the lack of relevance is the concept that the church must hold fast to positions out of the past. Says Michigan State scientist Leroy Augenstein, "As a Christian layman, I've condemned many ministers for not bringing the Christian church up to date. I can't believe the God who can make an electron and a proton and put them together to make atoms would really give us one set of rules in the form of the Bible and expect us not to use our intelligence to go further."

Historian Arnold Toynbee comments on religion today: "Lots of its doctrine are very out of date, and religions said either swallow our doctrines whole or be an outsider. So people rejected the whole thing."

University of Chicago sociologist Philip Hauser asserts, "The more fundamentalist the religion, the more intolerant it is—the more absolute it is. Determine what's right and stick to it—you are bound to be wrong as the world changes." The old moral leadership, Hauser charges, is "so covered over and encrusted with piety and irrelevance as to be lost."

The tragedy of the churches' failure stands out sharply in America's suburbs, which have grown so fantastically since World War II. The churches' responsibility in suburbia, said Dr. Tillich, is "to undercut the false security in a well-to-do society." He added, many suburbanites believe: "We are better than these masses in the city. We are better than other nations. We are what mankind should be. Who doesn't follow without controversy the pattern is bad." Pride, concludes Dean Samuel Miller, is "the cardinal *virtue* of our time."

Tillich went on: "I'm afraid the suburban church is one of the many social agents that give some social cohesion to the people. This is not always evil but it's not what the church is supposed to do. But who is the minister who would attack fundamentally the system? They would dismiss him the next Monday."

Deerfield, Illinois, where the Reverend Usry preaches and ministers to the suburbanites, has since World War II tried to keep out Jews (unsuccessfully) and Negroes (successfully—so far). When an attempt was made to build an integrated development in Deerfield, the effort was beaten by turning the prospective site into a public park. There were local ministers on both sides of that issue. Says Usry, "There is probably more danger of a minister losing his soul in the suburbs than in the inner city."

As the Reverend Gibson Winter puts it: "The church finds itself allocating its ministry on the power to pay. We are completely dominated by the norms of society. Where we are most needed, we cannot sustain the enterprise." He believes that Christianity has done so badly with the race problem because it is so closely tied to residential morality. "The total impact of the residential mind on the public morality," he says, "seems to be the establishment of a separate morality." Integration may be acceptable in the factory but "in the residence they would throw bombs."

Winter advocates that the church undertake a "metropolitan mission" that will free it from its residential shackles and allow it to minister to an entire metropolitan area. Then, he feels, it could explore "what it means to be human in a metropolis." Because of the way it is now organized, he says, "the church has been captivated by the middle-class society."

Dean Samuel Miller agrees: "The ministry too often has become something that lives on the yes-yes man or yes-yes woman." The minister too often does what is popular with the congregation. "This leaves you no fulcrum to pry people loose from their prejudices."

What worries the Reverend Usry most about his suburban parishoners is not their private morals but their lack of concern about other people. He says, "We have been trying to save the souls of men too long. The good man is the man who is going to succeed. He feels no guilt about excluding—because those who are good succeed and come to Deerfield. When churches are held captive in this kind of morality, they can't be relevant to the kind of morality involved in Birmingham. As soon as you start challenging, people are not too anxious to get involved."

Irwin Miller speaks of Americans' "split morality": "Because I'm a fine fellow and go to church, everything goes." And Tillich has written that those who are not believers during the week, but only on Sunday, are "practical atheists."

The Reverend Michael Allen deals with morality on the other side of the tracks, in New York City's slums. He has turned down opportunities to minister in the suburbs in order to stay in the slums. He says, "The communists have a real vision and they will work, bleed and die for that vision. They've stolen our thunder. That's what Christianity is supposed to do also. The Kingdom of Heaven is not out there, it is here. It means you fight for a new school or to keep the social welfare program afloat. Jesus was not born in a nice German barn. He was born in a tenement with the rain coming in.

"If you start off believing men are evil—lost in their

selfishness and greed—then you believe this need not be so. Bread is the symbol of greed. Wine is the symbol of drunkenness and escape. In Christian worship you start with these two manufactured things because God is in the midst of teeming slums and horrendous social problems. But our society believes you can find salvation through caviar and champagne."

The failure of the churches to be relevant to our changing world is one important reason why Americans are faced with the burden of solving their own moral problems. As a result, says Yale's Chaplain Coffin, "We have in this country more conscientiousness than religiousness—[people] depending more on conscience than on their religious faith."

But the religious faith is there, perhaps waiting to be shown its relevance. John Cogley says, "The classical doctrines of religion have a tremendous effect on the American character. Even our atheists are Christian atheists; the God they are denying is a Judaic-Christian God. Just kick a dog and see what happens. You can go to some cultures and nobody will care."

And Hauser adds, "As a social scientist, I'd say there is a God because he's believed in by millions of people. And I know who invented him—man invented him in his own image."

Bishop Robinson has written in *Honest to God* that the knowledge that the earth was not flat destroyed the concept of the "three-decker" universe with hell below, the earth in the middle and God "*up* there." Similarly, the space age has destroyed the idea of God being "*out* there." He says that scientific advances have made us wonder where God is and ultimately whether He exists at all. Bishop Robinson sums up his own view: "Belief in God is the trust, the well-nigh incredible trust, that to give ourselves to the uttermost in love is not to be confounded but to be 'accepted,' that Love is the ground of our being, to which ultimately we 'come home.' " He asserts that the way to a knowledge of God is "by unconditional love of the neighbour."

Irwin Miller is more optimistic than most about the future of the churches. He says, "It is becoming relevant. It is stepping on some toes. This means it's moving in some areas where it is needed." Certainly nothing has awakened the churches in America like the struggles over civil rights. But Miller warns: "The church says do right and don't do wrong. But this is no help. The problem is to choose between two evils. Times are changing more swiftly than the church. This could be its downfall—or at least cause it to fail to serve. Our society could become unglued because of it."

⫷ 12.

The American Vice

"I see institutions that are supposedly the custodians of our moral values and see that they are corrupt—the church, the educators," says Dr. Kenneth B. Clark, professor of psychology at The City College of New York and a prominent Negro leader. "The moral institutions have defaulted. They are captive of the moral dry rot. The idea of a white church is so preposterous that it must reflect moral and intellectual bankruptcy. It is hopeless if the only cure is a moral revolution."

Among all the failures of America's religious institutions, the most destructive is their inability to sell the basic religious idea that prejudice is immoral. At the heart of all religions is concern for man's fellow man—belief in brotherhood. But common also to our Western Judaic-Christian denominations is a contradictory principle of exclusivity and superiority, which says a human being must belong to a particular faith to be right and to be "saved." As one Lutheran service reads, "He that believeth, and is baptized, shall be saved." This means your "brother" must believe as you do to be your brother—and to some it means not only his mind but his accent and his skin must also be like yours. This teaching of superiority nutures the hate and prejudice we live with—the very evil our Western faiths preach against. If it is true that most ministers, priests and rabbis do not preach hate, it is more emphatically true that they have failed to bury it.

The principle of exclusivity and superiority is an old idea and has led to death and destruction. In the West, it caused the Crucifixion, the Crusades, the Inquisition, the murder of uncounted pagan unbelievers and the extermination of six million Jews—in our time alone. In our country, it has opened the door to violence, prejudice and segregation.

In a bygone age when human beings banded together in small, isolated communities, religion could preach exclusivity and superiority—and pay the price. Then the Pilgrims could escape across the ocean, Roger Williams could flee to exile and safety in Rhode Island, the Mormons could trek westward, fighting a rear-guard action. But the world has changed; the growth of population, the industrial revolution, the modernization of non-Western societies have thrown men together in pluralistic communities in a pluralistic world.

Most of our churches throughout the country passively accept the social norms of discrimination and lend them prestige, the semblance of righteousness and even the support of the Bible. Without the seal of approval of the "respectable" citizens of Bronxville, New York, the extremists of Birmingham, Alabama, could not exist.

Today anti-Semitism is our quiet prejudice. It sits there, waiting, while Jewish Americans hope that their Christian fellow citizens will live by their Christian and American principles. The Roman Catholic Church, even now, found it necessary to debate whether today's Jews are responsible for the death of Jesus in Jerusalem nineteen centuries ago. According to the Anti-Defamation League, 45 percent of the members of American Protestant congregations who were polled believe that Jews can never be forgiven for the Crucifixion. One recent study of anti-Semitism in the United States concluded, "Religious bigotry is still widespread and deeply embedded."

In the fight against anti-Semitism, Benjamin R. Epstein, national director of the Anti-Defamation League, says, "I genuinely believe there has been tremendous progress." But according to ADL studies, 10 or 11 percent of Americans are still "hard-core bigots" and roughly one in four Americans dislikes Jews. "Our job is not to convince the 25 percent at the bottom, but to contain them," says Epstein. He is more concerned with trying to reach the apathetic 50 percent of Americans who "just don't give a damn—don't know and don't care."

A study of the automobile industry disclosed that of 51,000 white-collar, professional and executive employees of the "Big Three" manufacturers in Detroit, only 328 were Jewish. Prejudice in the medical and legal professions has also been exposed. A 1964 survey by the *Yale Law Journal* stated that Jewish law school students find jobs more difficult to get and have less chance for promotions and partnerships than their Christian classmates. But anti-Semitism is covert, the *Journal* said, because "the demands of the commercial world compel businessmen with prejudices to suppress them during the working day."

ADL studies of discrimination against Jews at the executive level of American big business show, Epstein says, that Jews are "just not there." ADL has examined banking in New York City; Epstein says, "Aside from those few banks that are Jewish, it is almost '*Judenrein.*'" And, he adds, insurance company "executive offices are like a Christian country club." But Epstein is optimistic: "The most effective pattern against anti-Semitism is that it is just not fashionable. The climate is so much better now. I think we have come a long way."

An ADL survey shows that, although substantial improvement has been made in the last six years, almost one in ten resort hotels in the United States still discriminates against Jews. Some of the most discriminatory resort areas are Arizona: 22 percent; North Carolina and Virginia: 20 percent; Michigan, Minnesota and Wisconsin: 16 percent; Maine, Vermont and New Hampshire: 15 percent; and Florida: 12 percent.

The Reverend Coffin, who participated in the Freedom Rides and was jailed, says, "We are not taking up crosses. We are putting crosses aside in this country. The weakness of the churches is that they have lost their capacity to suffer. On this racial thing nobody wants to pay a price. Jesus boasted a few enemies, and it's dangerous theology to try to improve on Jesus. The pursuit of happiness means a willingness to undertake suffering. If you're not suffering for some good cause, you ought to re-examine yourself. After all, Jesus died at thirty-three.

"When a man feels guilty, to protect himself he projects guilt on someone else. The anti-Semite hates the Jew not because he was the Christ-killer but the Christ-bearer. What does the Negro hater see in his hatred but the projection of his own guilty fears."

And Coffin adds, "Some say, when in Rome do as the Romans do. Others say, When in Rome do as the Christians do, if you are a Christian."

Pressed by the revolt of the Negro American against discrimination and segregation, churches of the Bible-Belt, religious South are only slowly and painfully bringing into the open the immorality of the Negro's plight. It was mid-1963 before the National Council of Churches, which has long opposed segregation, set up an Emergency Commission on Religion and Race to make its Christian principles felt more effectively and to re-enforce its Department of Racial and Cultural Relations, which was established in 1950. At the end of 1963, almost 90 percent of the 32,892 churches in the Southern Baptist Convention, one of the largest Protestant denominations in the nation, refused to admit Negroes. In July, 1963, the two-million-member United Church of Christ voted, after long debate, to cut off funds from segregated churches. In 1964, 82 Methodist bishops called for the immediate abolition of their church's all-Negro division called the Central Jurisdiction, but the church decided to stretch out the integration of the Jurisdiction over four more years. And although the Mormon Church admits Negroes, it prohibits them from becoming priests.

In August, 1965, the First Baptist Church and First Methodist Church of Americus, Georgia, turned Negro civil rights workers away from its door on Sunday morning. At the Methodist Church an official told the would-be worshipers, "We don't have room for you."

"The worst of all failures of the church," says Ralph McGill, is the acceptance of segregation. "Of the major groups, the Baptists are the worst of all. They're largely rural and people from rural areas. They bring their prejudices with them. But there are a lot of decent people in the Baptist Church too."

McGill is equally critical of his own church and the Episcopal Cathedral in Atlanta at which he worships. The cathedral's leadership a couple of years ago wrestled with the possibility of desegregating its affiliated school, the Lovett School, which had turned away the son of the Reverend Martin Luther King, Jr. One well-to-do citizen of Atlanta reportedly said that if the board was afraid to keep the school segregated because it might lose tuition money from displeased white parents, he would repay the school's losses, and if the school would also exclude Jewish children, he would replace their tuition too.

Of the Lovett School problem, an Episcopal clergyman wrote me from Atlanta: "It seems to me that this local situation offers one of the most vivid and tragic examples of the failure of the church in the area of race relations, but also goes deeper to the heart of the matter of the church and its loyalties to the power structure and money of the community." When Ralph McGill, in an Episcopal publication, objected to the policies of the Lovett School, he was censored by the office of the Atlanta bishop.

At the same time, outside a Methodist church in a white section of Atlanta, a sign proclaimed: "Kind words are the music of the world."

Mrs. Ruby Hurley, Southeastern Regional Director of the NAACP, who has worked in the South since 1951, says, "To live in a section that claims to be the Bible Belt, it's hard for me to see how we can claim to be Christians with any morality. How can we expect our youth to have any regard for law and order, for the Ten Commandments, for truth, when everything around them points in another direction?" She says Negro children recite the Pledge of Allegiance in their segregated schools, but "our young people know it isn't justice and liberty for all, it's justice and liberty for all white people. We're living a lie."

Although the Catholic Church has been, incredibly, debating who should be blamed for the Crucifixion and has been seriously attacked for papal silence in the face of Hitler's murder of six million Jews, its record in the American South has been cautious but better than many Protestant denominations. The American bishops have spoken out ever since the end of World War II. The Catholic limitation is usually in terms of belief, not race.

"If you are a Catholic, you have to be color-blind," explains Archbishop Paul J. Hallinan of Atlanta. "You have to accept the universality of the Church."

Archbishop Hallinan and Joseph Cardinal Ritter of St. Louis were the only two Americans appointed by Pope Paul VI to an expanded liturgical commission in March, 1964. Cardinal Ritter is the Indiana-born prelate who integrated the parochial schools of Indianapolis in the 1930's, when the Ku Klux Klan was still powerful in Indiana. After he became archbishop of St. Louis, he integrated the parochial schools there in 1947, seven years before the Supreme Court decision on school segregation. He was made a cardinal by Pope John XXIII in 1961. Catholic authorities desegregated their schools in Alabama and northwest Florida in 1964, and only in Louisiana have such moves provoked serious trouble. The Catholic Church in October, 1965, courageously appointed a Negro bishop in New Orleans.

When he came to Atlanta from Charleston, South Carolina, Archbishop Hallinan found fear within the Church that if Negroes were admitted to the parochial schools, enough

Protestants would withdraw their children to force the closing of the schools. "I am perfectly willing to take a moral
stand," he says, "but I can't take the risk of closing some of
these schools. Morality is made up of cases where we choose
between a lesser and a greater evil."

Since the Atlanta public schools had already begun
gradual desegregation, Archbishop Hallinan felt it was safe
to follow suit. "When I appealed to the Catholic people on
the basis of loyalty to the Church, they responded magnifi-
cently. Now the vast majority of Catholics in the South are
aware that Christian teaching on racial justice is very clear—
that segregation is wrong. The Catholic is willing to make
an intellectual acceptance of this and to make practical acceptance and to act on it. On the part of some Catholics,
undoubtedly, their lack of emotional acceptance of this
they share with other whites in the South."

In 1962 Archbishop Hallinan—whose office is, ironically,
in a one-time Ku Klux Klan headquarters—integrated all
the schools in his archdiocese and then began integrating
the Catholic hospitals. In May, 1963, he ordained the archdiocese's first Negro priest.

Of his dilemma between compromising principles of
human equality and risking the destruction of church
schools, he says, "We were concerned with doing the best
we could for both white and Negro. You might say we
tolerated segregation." But the Archbishop sums up his view
firmly: "Christ's law is love thy neighbor as thyself. He
didn't say your white neighbor."

Some priests have outspokenly criticized the Church for
moving too slowly against racial discrimination. And some
parishioners—like James Chaney, the local Negro civil
rights worker who was beaten and murdered in Philadel-

phia, Mississippi—have moved on ahead of the clergy. The tightrope a Catholic bishop sometimes walks was visible when the bishop in Mississippi during the summer of 1964 sent home priests who came from outside the state to work in the civil rights movement. Finally, after the passage of the Civil Rights Act of 1964, the bishop began slowly to integrate parochial schools.

Clergymen of all faiths who want to break down segregation have often found themselves opposed by their superiors, who are responsible for their denomination as a viable institution. Jewish rabbis in the South also face the dilemma between pragmatism and principle.

The Catholic Church, when it desires to move effectively against segregation, has an advantage over most Protestant denominations: No priest has to worry about a parishioner saying, as a Baptist woman said to Ralph McGill, "The preacher is just a hired man. If we don't like what he preaches, we'll fire him."

Protestant ministers in the South have had to choose among three difficult positions. First, they can speak boldly about the immorality of segregation and resign, as did a young white Baptist minister in Linden, Alabama, or be kicked out, as were eight Methodist ministers in Mississippi. In January, 1963, twenty-eight young white Methodist ministers, all native Mississippians, proclaimed their opposition to racial discrimination; by June only nine remained with their original church. Some had been threatened with violence; others had had their salaries cut off. According to *The New York Times*, their bishop said only that integration is a voluntary idea in the Methodist Church.

The Protestant minister in the South has a second choice: to keep silent and support the system. Or, finally, he can try to find some middle ground, hoping to lead the prejudiced back to the beliefs of their church and give voice to the moderates. One Atlanta minister, for example, searching for such middle ground, decided to discuss the race issue with individual members of the congregation and with youth groups, but not from the pulpit.

Hallinan understands the Protestant minister's problem. He says, "A minister going to a cannibalistic society tries to preach against cannibalism. How long will he last? He'll probably be in the next pot. There are times that call for martyrdom by blood and times that call for martyrdom by collaboration."

Harvard's Dean Samuel Miller, a Baptist, says, "We live by compromise. We don't live pure lives anywhere. The minister's job is to lead the people. It's up to him to make clear the contemporary mores are not the church's mores. His job is to play Job and Jeremiah and be an eternal disturber of the peace."

Many young ministers are deeply troubled by their responsibility on the race issue. This moral question dominates their minds and lives. The failure of them and other responsible moderate leaders to meet the moral challenge leaves the command of the racial situation to the extremists, who will teach their children to pour ketchup over a Negro girl's head at a lunch counter, who will order police dogs to attack Negro demonstrators, who will bomb a Negro Sunday school and kill four children and will permit Southern police to kill, beat and rape prisoners whose only offense is that, although their skins are dark, they stood up for their rights as American citizens. The man suspected of killing Medgar Evers was an Episcopal Sunday-school teacher. Many people in Philadelphia, Mississippi, where three civil rights workers were murdered in July, 1964, and buried in an earthern dam, were more critical of the "Judas" who betrayed the murderers than of those who did the killing.

In Atlanta, the Reverend Morris says, "Most of us are not strong enough to preach this objectionable world and take a position that will offend people." And he adds, "To maintain an effective role in the South, you can't resign from the white race. It's my concern that I stay in the white community as long as is necessary to bring the white community along. To be effective, this is where I must remain."

The Negro, rising in revolt, is at last forcing the churches to face the immorality of his plight. Discrimination against a human being whose skin is dark is not a Southern problem alone; it is an American problem. It is not the Negro's problem; it is the white man's problem. As James Baldwin, the eloquent writer who grew up in a Harlem tenement, says, "White America has to face the question, why do you need the 'nigger' you invented?"

"I think there is a latent racism underlying the whole country—in fact, all of Western civilization," says the Reverend Morris. Discrimination is a stain on every ideal that Americans profess to have about man's equality and equal opportunity. The discrimination against the Negro began in human slavery long before the nation was born and has been swept under the rug by most Americans since the Emancipation Proclamation, a century ago. It is America's most horrendous example of social immorality.

Every society has people who are ablaze with prejudice and hate. But in Germany and in Mississippi, they came to absolute power. The preservation of the old gods, the insistence on racial purity, the subjugation of a minority who regard themselves as part of the nation, the brutality of the authorities and of the mob—all these have happened in Nazi Germany and in the United States.

Disaster overtakes society when men of prejudice and hate—supported by the cynical who can profit from such extremists—win control, as they did in Germany in the early 1930's. The Nazis, who never commanded more than 44 percent of the vote, came to power with the support of reactionary politicians and unprincipled big-money men who thought they could control Hitler.

Extremists still control some of our Southern communities, and only the U. S. Supreme Court and opposition of the majority in the nation prevent them from achieving the power to go as far as did the Nazis. Or it may be more accurate to say that they would go as far as the Nazis if the intensity and urgency of the Negro revolt had not aroused a counterforce that seeks to wrest from die-hard segregationists some of their vicious power.

The Negro revolt started in the South, where oppression was worst and where white extremists knew that the law would not often be enforced against their violence and terror. The record of murders, beatings and shootings is staggering. Police harassed, threatened and beat up American citizens who had broken no law, been given no trial. They permitted and even encouraged hoodlums to attack and injure Americans, whites and Negroes. The story of the attempts to crush the Negro revolt in the gallant, romanticized state of Mississippi is as brutal as the record of the street-brawling days of the Nazi Storm Troopers.

The revolt began there, despite the enormous odds and very real dangers, for a variety of reasons: During World War II and in the northward migration that continued afterward, Southern Negroes became increasingly aware of what their lives should be like; the Supreme Court school-desegregation decision affected the South primarily; and in the South the Negroes' goals were the most concrete and visible.

As Negroes across the country have fought, peaceably and violently, for their rights, it has been embarrassing to watch white public leaders suddenly find it impossible, as they say, to keep silent any longer about outrages that they have permitted for a very long time. The lesson is that even in our country human lives are little valued when people do not have a voice in their governments and their fate. The disenfranchised despair unless, through benevolence or guilt, someone holds out a hand of charity. And the lesson is also that when someone shoves our faces into the horrors of racial discrimination, Americans of principle and moral commitment cannot turn away.

The advent of effective federal legislation, especially the Civil Rights Act of 1964 and the voting rights law of 1965, provided underpinnings for many who have wished to honor the principle of equality but lacked the courage or the power to live up to their convictions. The effect of these laws was evident in Mississippi where politicians and businessmen, faced with federal law enforcement, a growing Negro electorate and the loss of federal funds, have—willingly in some cases, reluctantly in others—begun to speak for the Constitutional rights of Negroes. Some have acted because their pocketbooks conflicted with their principles, but a surprising number have found the backbone to take a stand on moral grounds.

Dr. Oppenheimer points out that Pope John XXIII reminded us all, in his last encyclical, that "evil is the monop-

oly of no people." When I talked with him, Dr. Oppenheimer gave me a written statement of his view:

> "The encyclical *Pacem in Terris* is for us a very great
> event of our time. It has brought encouragement and re-
> newed hope to uncounted millions; I am one of them. It has
> reminded us that evil is the monopoly of no people; it has
> reminded us of the immanent brotherhood of all men, and of
> the need, in radically altered circumstances, to recreate hu-
> man institutions to embody this ideal of brotherhood; it has
> reminded us of the evil, the orgy, the brutality, the inhu-
> manity of war; it has restored the hope, to whose fulfillment
> it invites our dedication, that our tradition, coming to us from
> our past and that of others, and from the prophets and the
> Gospels, refined by accumulated knowledge and wisdom,
> may enable us not only to survive, but deserve to survive.
> We have reason to be grateful."

To hate all Germans for the extermination of six million
European Jews merely represents another search for a rational explanation of the irrational. The Germans who
turned their souls over to the Nazis were not some strange
tribe from another planet. Their incredible evil is evidence
that the possibility of such deeds exists within all of us.
"The illness was not one limited to Germany. The symptoms existed elsewhere," says Mayor Willy Brandt. "What
is overlooked is that the Germans went through something
that lay there in many other lands. Because the Germans
went through it, and have learned their lesson, I hope,
maybe other people will not have to go through it."

Historians will agree that there has always been a streak
of prejudice, violence and hate in the United States too: the
"witch" killings in early New England, the lucrative slave
trade, the brutal extermination of the Indians, Millard Fill-
more's support of the bigoted Know-Nothing party, the

persecution of the Mormons, the signs of "NINA"—No Irish Need Apply—which were current a century ago—or Father Coughlan, the Ku Klux Klan, the concentration camps for Japanese-Americans during World War II or the treatment of our migrant laborers. Discrimination has been in America for a long time.

Goldwater, who voted against the Civil Rights Bill of 1964, is pessimistic about the end of discrimination: "Frankly, I don't think this is going to come in your time or mine. It hasn't in seven thousand years. Immorality begins with discrimination."

It is equally true—and more hopeful—that there has been a moral streak too in our history and that this has usually been dominant. Professor McCloskey says of the 1954 Supreme Court justices: "They did not come out of the woodwork. They came out of the intellectual and moral context of their times. In important respects, we are more moral than we were."

In 1883 the Supreme Court in a series of decisions said that the Fourteenth Amendment applied only to governmental discrimination and did not restrict private discrimination within a state. The Court has now decided that local and state laws establishing and supporting segregation are invalid. Since 1954 the Court has struck down local laws requiring segregated buses, parks, swimming pools, libraries and transportation terminals. The 1954 ruling climaxed a long series of decisions protecting civil liberties, but it was crucial. From the Negro's point of view, Mrs. Hurley says, "Before 1954 we were playing the music of freedom by ear."

Dean Erwin Griswold of the Harvard Law School says, "Many of us thought *Plessy v. Ferguson* had been a great mistake all along." Under that decision, which created the separate-but-equal standard in 1896, the Negro has had separate but never equal education in the South. Griswold feels that for twenty years the Supreme Court had "undermined" *Plessy* by decisions dealing with unfair jury trials, voting, unequal education—until, he says, "There just wasn't any ground to stand on—nor was there in the first place. By 1954 it had become clear this had been a grievous mistake."

In 1954 the Court said, "We come then to the question presented: 'Does segregation of children in public schools solely on the basis of race, even though the physical facilities and other "tangible" factors may be equal, deprive the children of the minority group of equal educational opportunities?' We believe that it does." It decided, "Separate educational facilities are inherently unequal. . . . Such segregation is a denial of the equal protection of the laws."

The "grievous mistake" was corrected, at least in theory. Certainly white Americans are less apathetic and more openly concerned about the Negro's rights than ever before, since the Negro himself has forced us to decide where we stand. This present concern represents honest morality, terribly late and terribly compromised, but still alive. A growing number of white Americans are displaying the physical and moral courage that this revolution in our midst demands.

But ten years after the Supreme Court ordered public schools desegregated, only 1.18 percent of 2.8 million Negro school children in the eleven states of the Confederacy were going to school with whites. Mississippi had no Negroes in desegregated schools; South Carolina, 10; Alabama, 21, and Georgia, 177. U.S. Attorney General Katzenbach says, "Some of the school plans in the South have been absolutely preposterous. Twenty-four-year plans. The only plan that makes sense is to start at the lower grades. It's got to go much faster than it has."

Many hoped that the federal aid-to-education bill would speed up desegregation by holding out cash money as bait to the school systems' directors. And many school districts did pledge compliance with the civil rights law. But at best this was the spread of tokenism. In the 1964–65 school year, only 75,400 Negroes, of a total of 2.9 million in the eleven states, were in classes with whites. By the fall of 1965 the number of Negroes in school with whites in those states was estimated to have tripled under the pressure of Title Six of the Civil Rights Act. But this was still only 217,000, a token of desegregation in the Deep South. The prime Southern tactic seemed to be to switch from local-law-imposed segregation to de facto segregation based on residence, as exists in many Northern communities.

The Reverend Coffin warns: "It is not enough to show compassion for the individual Negro. You must show concern for the institutions of society that make him an object of compassion—poor housing, poor education and lack of opportunity for upgrading himself in employment. Some people don't see this as a moral problem. A Christian must be concerned with politics, with economics. All human society is a package deal."

Seeing the Negro's plight as a moral issue—not an economic, political, sexual, competitive, cultural one—is difficult for many whites brought up in the hammered-home tradition that there is something inherently inferior about a man whose lineage goes back to the slave ship of labor-short America rather than to the steerage of an immigrant-laden steamer or the hold of the *Mayflower*. Of the South,

Dean Griswold says, "Many people down there don't get to the moral issue. I had hoped there would be more people in the South who would speak up." And he adds, "In the long run, it is wrong to look to the courts. People should do it because it is right to do it."

Integration is being recognized more and more as a moral problem that must be faced in terms of the ideals and principles we profess. In Michigan, to which many Southern Negroes have moved to look for jobs and an even break, Governor Romney says of the race issue: "It's a tremendously urgent problem. It affects almost every aspect of life. It's a moral, human problem. I think it's our most urgent specific problem.

"There is no justification under our system for anything other than equal civil rights and equal opportunity regardless of race, color or creed. The vast difference between our principle and our practice encourages people to question our conviction."

The Mormon Church, to which Romney belongs, has been criticized for its attitude toward Negroes, but he says, "There isn't anything we believe that the Caucasian world can attain in this world or the world beyond that they cannot attain too. It's equally clear that different people are at different places at any one time." After making that point, Romney adds, "We believe literally in the fatherhood of God and the brotherhood of man—as an actual belief, a real thing."

The most renowned leader of the Negro's current fight for equal treatment in America, the Reverend Martin Luther King, Jr., president of the Southern Christian Leadership Conference, preaches that the Negro must win his struggle through nonviolent resistance to discrimination. He says,

"While the race question has economic and sociological and political factors, it is at bottom a moral issue—a question of the dignity of man. Segregation is morally wrong because it relegates persons to the status of things. It will ultimately have to have a moral solution. If we are going to have a totally integrated society, it will boil down to every man respecting the dignity of others. A totally integrated society is a society where an individual is able to develop socially, intellectually and morally with no distinction of race. I think this is a real possibility in this century.

"In five years from now *legal* segregation will be broken down all over this country—education, public facilities. The job of real integration will be something else. It will take longer. I think in five years we'll have a desegregated South. In the North we'll have more integration in housing, which will break down segregation in education."

King adds, "The only way you can solve a moral problem is for the individuals involved to communicate. One of the tragedies of the South is there has been a monologue, not a dialogue." When a Northern delegation visited Atlanta to see how it was handling race relations, the mayor advised them that the first thing they should do was to meet with the Negro leadership in their city. The visitors confessed that they did not know the Negro leadership back home.

"There is a new moral awareness among many white people—including the white South," says King. "Many people have a nagging conscience about this, but they fear 'their' Negroes are no longer acting like 'their' Negroes. Down deep, I believe, there is a sense of shame. I'm convinced that many white people in the South have a great sense of guilt about how the Negro has been treated." He feels this guilt stirs strong reactions of either shame or hate.

For the Reverend King, the moral question a white American must ask himself is: "Are Negroes being treated like you would like to be treated?" He says, "The Golden Rule must be universally applied."

Ralph McGill, who has helped lead his community to a degree of slow, painful desegregation and has given the South's moderates a voice and dignity, has had his house shot at and is barraged daily with violent, obscene mail from respected businessmen and near-illiterates alike. One Mobile, Alabama, banker addressed McGill as "a paunchy glutton" and wrote: "You racists, black, white and pink, have set the Southern negro back a generation." He added, "I want no part of federal subsidization of the negro race just to buy his vote, or to improve our image abroad."

But McGill is hopeful: "We've never met the Negro here. We've known a cook or a yardman or maid. We entrusted our children—our most precious possessions—to them, but we've never seen the preposterousness of not sitting down on a bus with the same maid we entrust our children to. As they begin to come into the restaurant and people see them, they lose the old myth. I think in the long haul people are changing."

McGill realizes that such change has only begun. He says, "The idiots are loose more than they were. I always blame the Virginians for it. The Talmadges and the Eastlands, Marvin Griffin—those Southern demagogues—were not so popular at the moment. Then these fellows were made respectable by the Virginians. For Virginia to be the one to tilt the scales!" His point is the crucial one that keeps recurring. The extremists, the demagogues, the rabble rousers, the hate mongers, the paranoiacs can win only if the respectable and responsible "gentry," out of fear or greed, make them respectable. He says, "The White Citizens' Council is the country club Ku Klux Klan."

Says McGill of the demagogues: "They know the ball game is in the seventh inning. They know they're licked, and they can't take it. They are getting more vulgar and obscene. What you have today is the combination of the redneck and the man of substance, the banker—'the white-neck.' "

McGill estimates that perhaps 14 million of America's 19 million Negroes have white blood. They share the genes of some of the best families in the Old South. McGill says of the whites: "They say they're afraid of intermarriage. When I ask: Are you afraid of yourself or your children? —they get awfully mad."

Thanks greatly to McGill, Atlanta is regarded as the most liberal city in the Deep South. But its problem is certainly not solved. An Atlanta workman expressed the redneck's feelings: "It's just communism—forcing people to do what they don't want to do. We got nothing against the niggers, but we don't want to eat with them, sleep with them, marry them, like they want us to do."

There are clear signs that things are changing. One clue: A white cab driver, given an address by a white visitor to Atlanta, said, "That's in the nigger section, isn't it?"; but he was troubled enough to volunteer that he had been in the U.S. Army in the Korean War, and, once he got used to it, had not felt too upset about living with Negroes. He expected that his daughter would start school in the fall, and there might be Negroes in the school. That didn't seem to frighten him. A straw of hope?

Another clue: Atlanta's Mayor Ivan Allen, Jr., testified in favor of the Civil Rights Bill in 1963. He called segregation "slavery's stepchild" and spoke especially for the public accommodations section of the law. He told the Senate committee: "I beg of you not to let this issue of discrimination drown in legalistic waters. I am firmly convinced that the Supreme Court insists that the same fundamental rights must be held by every American citizen."

The pain a Negro feels today can be glimpsed in simple everyday situations:

A highly educated, well-dressed woman enters a Southern airport, with a suitcase in each hand. With Southern courtesy, a white man starts to hold open the door for her, sees she is a Negro and lets the door slam in her face.

A Negro, driving from Atlanta to Cleveland to attend a family funeral, has to drive straight through the night. He feels he can find no place to sleep until he reaches Ohio.

A Negro woman, Miss Mary Hamilton from Cedar Rapids, Iowa, is given a five-day jail sentence in Gadsden, Alabama, because the prosecutor insists on calling her "Mary" and she refuses to answer to her first name. Her contempt conviction was eventually reversed by the United States Supreme Court, and all Negroes won the right to be addressed with ordinary courtesy in all American courts.

The Negro in the South must live not only with violence, death and terror, but with daily indignities and the ever-dominant power of the white man to fire him from his job, to take away the mortgage on his home, to stop his credit in the white-owned store. Negroes who have had the temerity to register to vote found that their contracts as tenant farmers have not been renewed. Mechanical cotton pickers are being brought into some areas as fast as possible to "hunger out" the Negroes, in the hope that they will move away and not become local voters.

Yale's Chaplain Coffin describes the "redneck and white-neck" alliance as he has seen it: "You buy off the redneck by letting them stomp on the Negro. That's the deal the rich white has made with the poor white."

He says people often seem more upset by disorder than by injustice. The Negro revolt has stressed the principle of nonviolent resistance, a technique which, in another sense, the Negro has been practicing for a very long time. Hubert Humphrey, a leader in the fight for a civil rights act in Congress, observes, "When the Negroes use Gandhi-like demonstrations, they are very effective. The day they pick up a rock, they've lost public support. The segregationist seeks to provoke the Negro into violence. Then he loses."

How close a Negro leader who is deeply dedicated to nonviolence can be driven to provocation is expressed by the Reverend Andrew J. Young, who left a comfortable job and home in the North to work with the Reverend King. As a leader in Birmingham during the demonstrations there, Young remembers the segregationists: "I said these people are savages and nothing but a machine gun is going to deal with them. But then you cool down. . . . You get the feeling the whole system is against you: the courts; the press doesn't understand. You wonder if this whole social order can be redeemed. You want to be a John Brown. You get the impression that nobody really understands that the Negro is being crushed."

After we talked, the Reverend Young wrote me a letter in which he expanded on his thoughts and said, "These same violent and almost savage white people are really confused, afraid and sick people who really need to get therapy more than retaliatory violence. Sometimes even, a spark of humanity will peep through and you realize that these are God's children too."

Dean Griswold tells of a Harvard Law School student, a young Negro man from Toledo, Ohio, who spent the summer of 1963 working for a Negro lawyer in Richmond, Virginia. The lawyer was active in the demonstrations against segregation in Prince Edward County, and at one point he sent the law student to the courthouse with a message for the judge. A deputy sheriff threw him out and arrested him. Griswold says the young man was clearly entitled to be there. The student was indicted for assault with intent to do grievous harm, a felony that makes one liable to six to twenty years in prison. But no white lawyer in the area would defend him. It was purely the young Northern Negro's word against that of six local white deputy sheriffs. Asks Griswold, "What can any court, including the Supreme Court, do about it?"

Of the young men and women who have gone South to work for equal civil rights, Griswold adds, "This is not child's play. The risks to them are very considerable, not only violence but framed cases. These people can be caught in the meat grinder and be badly hurt." Even knowing this, many went. They made a mockery of the claim that the present young generation is "lost" or "silent."

Those who "went South" risked their lives. The Alabama murder of an Episcopal seminary student in August 1965 and the triple murder at Philadelphia, Mississippi, the summer before were brutal proof of that. A resident of that Philadelphia told a reporter after the killings: "Our people as a whole cannot be held accountable for what happened any more than Dallas can for the assassination of President Kennedy." A local Baptist minister criticized "those who come as disturbers among us."

These young people went to help teach Negro children

and to try to bring the simple democratic right to vote to the Negro American in the South. And they performed another function too; however well the young people understood it, the leaders who sent them did: the function of martyrdom. Some civil rights leaders felt that the "closed society" of Mississippi could never be changed from within. It could be pried open only by the action of the rest of the nation. To achieve this, they need some way of overcoming the apathy so many Americans have displayed to the fate of Mississippi Negroes who have been shot, beaten and cowed. They decided to create a confrontation between young white people from the North and the whites of Mississippi. If young whites from back home became the targets of the hate and violence, perhaps Northern apathy would be pierced and all white Americans would realize that their ox was being gored in Mississippi.

When searchers, looking for the bodies of three civil rights workers near Philadelphia, turned up bodies of local Negroes, the only newsworthy, attention-getting value was that these were not the bodies of the civil rights workers, two of whom were white. The murder of Southern Negroes no longer had any impact.

"I never know when my phone is going to ring and I'm going to learn that one or the other person has been killed," says Mrs. Hurley. "After a few years in the South, I had to work on not being anti-white. There's never been any love for white people in the South, but now active discontent borders on hatred." She tells of a Negro war veteran who shot a white storekeeper for not leaving his wife alone. He had warned the storekeeper, but to no avail. When the police tried to catch him, he killed several people before they shot him.

And in Mississippi you can hear of the courageous Negro farmer who, when his house was attacked in the night by Ku Klux Klanners, went out the back door, circled around and shot his gun repeatedly into the white crowd, which immediately fled.

On June 12, 1963, thirty-seven-year-old Medgar W. Evers, Mississippi field secretary for the NAACP, a World War II veteran who had received two battle stars in Europe and father of three, was shot and killed outside his Jackson, Mississippi, home. He was buried in Arlington National Cemetery. Evers was Mrs. Hurley's deputy in Mississippi, and of his murder (for which no one has yet been convicted), the Reverend Young says, "This was the first thing that shocked this country to understand the moral implications of the race issue. Negroes are killed in Mississippi all the time, but this is a good man doing what he thought was right."

Equally tragic was the story of Clyde Kennard, a Negro ex-GI who had tried unsuccessfully to enroll in Mississippi Southern University in 1959. He was sentenced to the state penitentiary for seven years, as an accessory to the theft of twenty-five dollars' worth of chicken feed. For calling Kennard's conviction "a mockery of justice," Medgar Evers had been sentenced to thirty day in jail. Kennard was released five months before he died of cancer at the age of thirty-six—one month after Evers' murder. The barrier in Mississippi higher education was not breached until James Meredith entered the University of Mississippi with the help of federal marshals.

Mississippi is an anachronism as immoral as South Africa and most Americans have been unaware of its horrors. Names like Medgar Evers, Emmett Till, Mack Parker have flashed out in the headlines, but few have understood that these headlines represent only the peak of an ugly un-American iceberg. In a state with less than two million people, more than 900,000 have been disenfranchised because their skins are dark. With the support of law-enforcement officials and with the use of terror, physical violence and murder, they have been denied the basic American right to vote. Civil rights leaders also charge that 75 percent of Mississippi's Negro citizens live in housing without toilets, washbasins or bath—not because they want to, but because they are held in the chains of poverty and ignorance. The average annual income of a Mississippi Negro is reported to be $600—one fourth of the white average in the state. And any Negro Mississippian who wants to stay in his home state, yet tries to break out of this servitude and achieve his rights to vote, send his children to a decent school or bargain collectively for a living wage is chopped down brutally.

One Negro youth who tried was killed and his body thrown into the Mississippi River. The sheriff came to his parents' house and told them that their son had gone away and if they raised any fuss or made any inquiry, another member of the family would also go away—permanently. It is hard to imagine the fear that can prevent a mother from protesting when her son has been murdered.

Dr. Kenneth Clark is discouraged: "I don't put any trust in the goodness of mankind. Mankind must be controlled. I expect from my government not that people understand and love me but that my government prevent them from letting their feelings out. You can't count on love in the mass. I want only that the government control people. I don't ask that it change people's minds and hearts."

This is echoed by Mrs. Hurley: "I don't care whether

they love me—get their feet off my neck! Let me move as a human being." The courage and resolve of Autherine Lucy at the University of Alabama, James Meredith at Mississippi University, Medgar Evers and Martin Luther King —and of thousands of men, women and children whose names we shall never know—have helped lift that foot off the Southern Negro's neck.

Too many whites in the South have refused to accept the abolition of slavery and the fact that the United States Constitution does apply to all. This was supposed to have been settled a century ago at Appomattox Courthouse, Virginia, a dozen miles from Price Edward County where, in June, 1959, the white powers-that-be closed the schools and left 1,700 Negro children without education. John Hersey described the results: ". . . after four abandoned years the children were half-starved, their clothes were ragged, their teeth were rotting, their souls were set away from the world; many of them were apathetic, silent, cowed, sullen, uncommunicative—and little wonder." More than five years after the schools were closed the U. S. Supreme Court ordered them reopened, saying, "The time for mere 'deliberate speed' has run out. . . ." Even so, the scars would remain; no one can give those children back their lost years.

The whole Negro effort came to a massive climax in the spring and summer of 1963, when the brutal suppression of demonstrations in Birmingham, Alabama, shocked and enraged the world. That spring the morality of the Kennedy Administration came under heavy attack. The apex of that attack came from a meeting Attorney General Robert F. Kennedy held with a group of Negro intellectuals and leaders in New York City on May 24.

The Negroes left the meeting stunned, angry and despairing. They were convinced that the Administration saw the race problem only in terms of votes, not morality. They felt that the only thing that had moved the Attorney General had been when a bone-broken young Negro named Jerome Smith, who had been beaten up repeatedly by police in the South, pointed his finger and said, "I was nonviolent but I'm not any more." Immediately after the meeting, James Baldwin, who had helped organize it, said bitterly, "The cat wasn't listening. Where do we go from here? We're in the streets. We know this."

Looking back on the commentary of those spring days, it is clear that some thoughtful observers felt the Kennedy Administration was failing to display leadership on the race issue. On June 4, Walter Lippmann wrote: "It is the unhappy truth that the right national policy is being adopted not because it is right, not because it is wise to do justice, not because those in authority and the responsible leaders of opinion understood the growing desperation of the younger Negroes, but because the Negroes have gone into the streets to face the fire hoses and the dogs and the clubs." He called for "unambiguous, unweaseled national leadership." And on June 9, in a column about the racial crisis, James Reston wrote of President Kennedy, "There is something wrong with his leadership on the home front. . . . He plays touch-government, he seems to touch everything and tackle nothing."

President Kennedy's civil rights speech on June 11 showed the despairing and the desperately impatient that they had been heard. The President referred to "the growing moral crisis" and said, "No one has been barred on account of his race from fighting or dying for America—there are no 'white' or 'colored' signs on the foxholes or graveyards of battle." Benjamin Epstein called that speech historic and said, "He is the first President who has said this is a moral issue."

The great March on Washington in that summer of 1963 spoke for the depth of feeling and determination among those people, as Baldwin says, whose "only crime is color." What the Negro had expected—to go into the streets— did not happen during the heat of that summer: the widely anticipated and feared race riots did not break out. Instead, the Negro movement ran head-on into apathy. The March on Washington seemed to drain away any feeling of guilt, and many white Americans turned from a problem that so many did not want to see in any case.

A year later, in May, 1964, Attorney General Robert Kennedy spoke to the students of West Georgia College in Carrollton, Georgia, and dared ask, referring to the status of the Negro: "How would any of us like it if we were in that situation?" He told the students that six Negroes had been killed in Vietnam and he said that the wife of an Alabama Negro soldier could have her husband buried in Arlington National Cemetery, but then she would have to travel home with her children—never knowing if the children could use a bathroom, eat a decent meal or stop in a decent motel. Said Kennedy, "It is a continuous insult." He was applauded, and the *Atlanta Constitution* reported the next day: "It wasn't polite hand-clapping. It was ringing, rolling applause—so solid it was startling. . . . It means that the bigotry of the father is not being handed down to the son."

But it was also in that summer of 1964 that the outbursting hate, which is a price of the Negro revolution, struck the North with the slugging impact of race riots. In the

North, where goals were more elusive, the previously successful tactic of nonviolence gave way to violence. First
hit was Harlem—the New York ghetto where some 300,000
Negroes are contained, often existing in rat-infested tene-
ments, sending their children to crowded, antiquated schools
and despairing of ever breaking out of their black world.

In the muggy heat of July, an off-duty white police
officer shot and killed a fifteen-year-old Negro boy who, it
was said, had come at him with a knife. Then Harlem's
social dynamite exploded. Steel-helmeted police responded
with guns and billies and Negroes looted and hurled bricks
at the police from rooftops. If the March on Washington
had been a safety valve in the summer of 1963, there was no
such diversion this time. The rioting flashed over to Brook-
lyn's Negro section and to Rochester at the western end of
New York state, and to New Jersey. The surging violence
was crushed by brute strength; many were injured, hundreds arrested, though fortunately there were few deaths.

The next summer the death toll was higher. Rioting
broke out on Chicago's turbulent west side, where the expansion of the Negro population had been met with hatred
and small-scale violence for years. And then on August 11
the savagery ripped open the Negro section of Los Angeles
called Watts. It took only a minor incident between a white
policeman and a drunken Negro driver to set off five days
of brutal, bitter fighting in which 36 were killed, nearly
900 injured and $46 million worth of property destroyed.
Before the Watts violence was over, 13,000 National
Guardsmen used tear gas, bayonets and gunfire to suppress
the racial warfare.

In the South, Negro protests can aim nonviolent tactics
at specific and visible targets—the right to send children to

a school, the right to eat in a restaurant, swim in a municipal pool or register and vote. Nearly half of all Negro Americans live outside the South, in areas where there are no local ordinances to overthrow, no clear-cut goals to win. The protest against the more subtle but equally brutalizing Northern segregation thrashed out in wild anger.

Attempts to pin the blame on communists or other "outside agitators," whether or not they did in fact exploit the situation, merely avoided the issue. And official proclamations that law and order would be maintained, necessary as they were, made some feel that the restoration of order would close the matter. But the real problems remained. Hundreds of thousands of colored Americans live in filthy slums, fear beatings by the police and are frustrated by the hopeless knowledge that job opportunities are scarce for a Negro who wants to get out of his trap and enter the stream of the nation's fluid social structure. One civil rights leader asserts that 25 percent of the Negro labor force is unemployed. The persistent effort of so many Negroes to live decent lives and rear their children well is truly amazing, given the barriers erected against them.

And although mayors and police chiefs called for peace and order, those who really dominated the power structure —most of the bishops, the publishers, the wealthy, the business leaders—sat silent. And many middle-class whites who had moved out to New York's suburbs rode the commuter trains from Connecticut and Westchester buried in their newspapers or busy playing bridge; they never saw the misery of the Harlem they passed through. During the height of the rioting some trains did not even stop at the 125th Street Station; it was as though Harlem simply did not exist. Too many of the responsible and the respectable seemed to hope the whole dangerous affair would blow away. It was easier to contribute to a fund for civil rights in Mississippi.

Slums exist because they are profitable and ghettos exist because of fear, and even the riots did not communicate to the white leaders that the Negro wanted his world changed and that suppression is neither a moral nor a final answer. To face the basic problems that create places like Harlem and Watts seemed still too much to attempt or expect. It required morality to rise above economic interest. Even thoughtful Negro leaders like Dr. Kenneth Clark felt that when the surge of violence subsided, everything would return to "normal"—at least until next time. And the Negro would still be locked in his black world—at least until next time. It seemed inevitable that, if rioting in Harlem and Watts could not stir the silent Establishment, someone would seek a terrible confrontation—not of black citizen against white police (who are paid for that sort of thing) or even against National Guardsmen—but of black citizen against white citizen. It came close in Los Angeles.

The implications of Birmingham, Alabama, and Oxford, Mississippi, and Cambridge, Maryland, and Harlem and Watts are worldwide. They point up for all to see— friends and enemies alike—the ugly gap between what America preaches and what it lives. Georgia-born Secretary of State Dean Rusk puts the issue plainly: "The first and overriding reason for settling this problem correctly has to do with our own society and our own ideals of freedom. Secondarily, it affects our foreign relations. We must solve this problem. We carry a special burden of responsibility because we are called on to be the leader [in the world]."

United Nations Secretary-General U Thant adds that

the race issue has hurt U.S. moral leadership abroad. He says, "These developments have tarnished the American image. Governor Wallace should realize his activities are watched all over the world in terms of the United States of America, which has been regarded as a torchbearer of freedom and human dignity."

As Walter Reuther puts it, "You cannot defend freedom in Berlin as long as you deny it in Birmingham."

And Dr. Kenneth Clark says, "This country can't have moral leadership in the world and its garden-variety racial barbarity and cruelty and tokenism at the same time. There is no closet to keep the skeleton in any more.

"I'm not sure America has the capacity to survive—that a nation with the pictures with the dogs in Birmingham on the first page has the strength to meet the challenges in the world today."

The Reverend King contrasts Africa's freedom, coming at "jetlike speed, while we were moving at horse-and-buggy speed to get a hamburger and a cup of coffee at a lunch stand." The failure to stand up and initiate a moral attack on the Negro's chains in America is the failure of the organized leadership of our society.

The official elimination of segregation in the armed forces was proclaimed in July, 1948, but fifteen years later, just after the Civil Rights Bill was introduced in 1963, a Presidential study group reported that racial distinctions in promotions and assignments were still evident: 20 percent of the Navy's Negroes were still food workers; there were no Negro generals in the Army and only one in the Air Force; the Navy had no Negro officers above the rank of lieutenant commander. And in addition, reports filtered back to United States that overseas integration stopped at camp boundaries. Fights between white and colored American soldiers were reported in West Germany and Berlin; whites and Negroes would each stick to their own taverns; German camp followers had to choose one group or the other, and racial fights followed.

Educators have been little better than these soldiers. The National Education Association did not support the 1954 Supreme Court ruling until seven years later, and not until 1964 did it finally pass a resolution desegregating itself. Even then the initiative came not from the association's leadership but from its membership. And the doctors have been even more tardy. The AMA continues to permit lily-white local medical societies within its federation.

The racial attitudes and practices of business and union leaders are also condemned by civil rights leaders for the damage they have done to all Americans. Martin Luther King says, "I feel the economic phase of this problem is tied to the moral aspect. There are those who seek to perpetuate human values that came into being in a slave plantation society. This leaders to economic injustice, exploitation, refusal to allow labor to really organize, cheaper labor. These industries often move South because they want cheap labor." A Northern businessman who recently was searching for a textile plant site in Alabama said he was avoiding all towns that had "a race problem."

The Reverend King states his position clearly: "Business is not only a right but also a privilege and responsibility. A man does not have a right to refuse to serve a person of a different race."

Ralph McGill says, "Ninety-seven percent of them in steel and textile have a vested interest in retaining segregation and work at it—lend private and public support for it." And Mrs. Hurley, whose headquarters was in Birmingham for five years, adds, "The Tennessee Coal and Iron subsidiary of U. S. Steel in Birmingham did nothing to alleviate race in that city. Neither did the unions. From all I could ascertain when I was there, TCI was a supporter of 'Bull' Connor." Police Commissioner Connor's bitter opposition caused President Kennedy to say wryly that he should receive as much credit for the Negro's progress as Abraham Lincoln. And Sheriff James G. Clark, Jr., at the bridge in Selma, Alabama, on March 7, 1965, certainly helped get the voting rights bill passed.

Walter Reuther, who organized his first picket line to oppose a segregated swimming pool in Detroit back in 1932, tells of the problems he has had with union locals wanting to hold on to segregation. In one Southern plant his United Automobile Workers trained several Negro welders and, with management's co-operation, prepared to put them to work with the white welders. The white welders fought the move, and finally Reuther told them, "You don't have to work with Negroes, but if you want to work in this plant you will."

A UAW local in Memphis wanted to build a new union headquarters. The plans called for segregated washrooms, and when UAW headquarters objected, the local said they could not get a building permit unless they planned separate toilets for Negroes and whites. Reuther allowed them to be built, but he asserted that they would not be used. They were built, and segregation signs were erected; the UAW ordered the signs removed. The local put them back up. When Reuther threatened disciplinary action, the local took the case to court and the judge ruled that the UAW could dictate to the local but not to the separate building corporation through which the local had put up the building. Reuther's response was immediate; he moved the local out of the new building. After a short time playing landlord to an empty building, the local's officials capitulated and integrated the restrooms.

Such expressions of prejudice by unions are not confined to the South. In July, 1963, the president of the New York Building and Construction Trades Council, which coordinates 122 unions, turned down the ideas of a board appointed by the mayor suggesting ways the member unions could accept more Negroes and Puerto Ricans. The council president said the unions did not discriminate and would not permit "dictation by any outside group." In the spring of 1964 the same plumbers' local in New York City which produced George Meany, president of the AFL-CIO, made headlines by resisting integration with Negroes and Puerto Ricans. "The building trades unfortunately did not do their homework. Now history is catching up with them," says Reuther. "The area in which the least progress has been made is where there are apprenticeable trades. The average Negro coming out of a slum school can't compete."

Finally, the National Labor Relations Board, on July 2, 1964, for the first time declared that a union which discriminated racially was guilty of unfair labor practices under federal law. The key vote on the board was 3 to 2. Negro leaders called it "a significant breakthrough."

Large-scale Negro migration to the North had been encouraged during and after World War II, when unskilled labor was in short supply because of the war effort and our discriminatory immigration laws. In the North, some businessmen expressed their prejudices through their economic power, at least until recent pressures from the Negro started a change. A Negro civil rights leader tells of a large super-market chain that had until recently only four full-time Negro employees. He cites another company which took a nondiscrimination pledge back in 1925—and has still never hired a Negro secretary. And he tells of meeting with the head of a New York company and listening to the man explain at length how open his company's hiring policies were. The Negro leader had done his homework, and he knew the facts: Negroes held only the seven lowest jobs in the entire company. A 1964 Labor Department study stated that a Negro teen-ager had less chance of finding a job than he had ten years before. Because Negroes have found it almost impossible to enter many union apprentice-training programs, they are restricted to non-skilled jobs. Says Reuther, "Employment and jobs are the key to civil rights."

Business and unions have generally passed the buck, each blaming the other for the scarcity of job opportunities for Negroes. And many union workers fear the Negro competition would threaten their incomes. Paul Tillich noted, "The lower middle class is always a pillar of totalitarianism. They have a morality very close to that of Hitler."

A Maryland realtor who, after searching his conscience, announced that his company would represent any home owner who desired to sell his house on an open-occupancy basis, wrote me: "And so we have taken the final and only step we could take, and the most surprising result to me has been that all the fears that so many of us seem to have really are without foundation, because there has been no marked difference in our volume of business in either list-ings or sales, and our declaration of policy was really well received in the community. Especially the fear of going it alone and facing economic suicide has turned out to be purely a myth; and now I can really live with myself and know that we are really on the right track."

But in November, 1964, California's voters decided by better than 2 to 1 to nullify all state legislation aimed at eradicating racial discrimination in housing. The California Real Estate Association is credited with drafting the proposition and collecting more than one million signatures to get it on the ballot. Previously, similar action had been taken on a local scale in Berkeley, Seattle, Tacoma, Detroit and Akron.

The price that both white and Negro Americans have had to pay for racial discrimination is high. Hubert Humphrey says, "People are beginning to see what's happening to us. It's like the mentally ill. We used to lock them up. When we opened the institutions, it was a revolting sight." The Negro is at last forcing open the doors of his ghettos and making the white man look inside. The reaction of many Americans is horror.

There is an often-quoted statement from the German pastor Martin Niemoller that sums up the lesson: "In Germany they first came for the Communists, and I didn't speak up because I wasn't a Communist. Then they came for the Jews, and I didn't speak up because I wasn't a Jew. Then they came for the trade unionists, and I didn't speak up because I wasn't a trade unionist. Then they came for the Catholics, and I didn't speak up because I was a Protestant. Then they came for me—and by that time no one was left to speak up."

Perhaps the most immoral price that the Negro has had to pay has been the crippling injury to the Negro family. Says sociologist Philip Hauser, "With slavery we completely destroyed the Negro family. After Emancipation the Negro has remained for one hundred years an underprivileged, segregated sub-culture in the South. The majority of Negroes in the North had their origins in the slum South."

An expert on the Negro family, Mrs. Helen Harris Perlman, professor of social work at the University of Chicago, says, "One of the most serious problems in our society is the poor Negro unmarried mother." That 63 percent of the 224,000 illegitimate children born in 1960 were Negro, she says, is the result of inadequate knowledge of contraception, inability to afford abortions; also, she adds, "They absolutely have so little that sex is a way of escaping from the black pocket they're in."

Professor Perlman emphasizes: "The problem of Negro illegitimacy is looked on as a race problem when it's actually a class problem affecting an economic group with the lowest opportunities for employment and education. This economically deprived group is largely Negro. Until opportunities are opened up, apathy and hostility will be the results.

"I never knew a family, Negro or otherwise, who didn't know what they are supposed to be and act like—that you were supposed to have a family. Proof of this is that nobody is more conforming than the middle-class Negro family. The ones that come up North don't want to live by plantation morality." She adds, "We've got to give the Negro the idea somehow that society sees him as someone going somewhere. Otherwise, we'll have violence or the apathy that might just as well be dope addiction."

The destruction of Negroes' self-respect has left us with social problems that reach far beyond the boundaries of their ghettos. Professor Perlman explains, "Unemployed

Negroes make many of these babies. I'm sure some of these men would not want to work, but most would want to work. Many of them don't know they are living unless they blot things out with drugs or alcohol or using the momentary vitality of sex." She believes this is one of the central attractions of the Black Muslims: They give the unemployed, hopeless Negro a sense of identity, a purpose and even a sense of superiority.

The distortion of family and home life is one price the victim of prejudice pays, but each American pays also within himself. "If one is saturated with racial bigotry, his whole personality is warped," warns the Reverend King. "If one is a bigot in reference to Negroes, pretty soon he's going to be a bigot where Catholics are concerned, where Jews are concerned. Pretty soon he will come to the point where he will not see people as human beings."

Prejudice, says James Baldwin, "is a human characteristic but an American vice."

Paul Tillich agreed that prejudice is human, and explained: "Prejudice is inherent because we are finite and cannot have empathy with everything. These are our finite limitations. If it become prejudice, it is evil.

"In the South, it is the continued experience. I have not sympathy but empathy for the feeling of the South. We must have more understanding. It's wrong, but we must understand the right and the wrong."

This parallels the thinking of Secretary-General U Thant: "We have to understand the Southern white and the Negro point of view. Critics have to understand the Negro attitude. There is only one application of morality. Basically, it is to understand the other man's view. The philosophy of live and let live should be our aim."

The Reverend Michael Allen makes the point another way: "You hate Negroes or Jews really because this is a transferred hatred of your own condition as a man, which ultimately means your hatred of God. God is the one who put you in this condition. How are you going to love God or hate God? The only conceivable way to hate God is by hating his children, as it is impossible to love God except by loving his other children. Like a kid who hates his father beats up other kids; he can't beat up his father."

Dr. Clark sums up his feeling about the racial issue on an ironic note: "The presence of the Negro in America is one of the best things that ever happened to America. If every Negro in America disappeared tomorrow, then America would have to face what its problems are. The Negro is the real enemy of the American white because he has been used so successfully to hide his problem—the basic problem of injustice, status, cruelties—the lives of quiet desperation."

The tragedy of the race problem is that neither the ideals of our Judaic-Christian tradition nor the incantations of our American creed have been able to convince all Americans to do the moral thing. Some of those who pray the loudest and wave the flag the highest are the least willing to face up to the gap between their principles and their practices. Says Martin Luther King, "A man has a moral obligation to keep his mind open, to be intelligent." James Baldwin emphasizes that the moral problem is a white problem, and he states the reality clearly: "I'm an American. That's a fact."

Anyone who would not accept a Negro or a Jew or a Catholic or a Puerto Rican living next door is a bigot, because he is judging people not on their individual worth and merit but because they belong to a group. There is no rational reason to reject a human being because his skin is dark or he thinks differently about God.

The possibility that attitudes are changing offers the greatest hope. "Decent people don't want violence, and most of the people in the South are decent," says Attorney General Katzenbach. "Darn few people in Alabama are going to say its okay to go out on the road and shoot a woman because she's a civil rights worker. You have hundreds of Alabamans sick to death with the race problem." He believes more and more Southern segregationists realize they have no alternative to the national decision to end discrimination. And he believes that as the Southern Negro electorate increases, change will be accelerated.

In the end, this moral dilemma, as it must, comes back to the individual American. He must figure out, as Baldwin said, why he invented the "nigger." He must crawl out of the fortress of his apathy and realize that he can no longer hide in Birmingham or Bronxville from the moral question. The Negro has served him well by making him face prejudice. When he would rather turn away and put it out of mind, the Negro revolt has pulled his face around and made him look. For many Americans, white and black, Christian and Jew, Southerner and Northerner, the immorality of prejudice has become the most pressing agony of our time. And it is not going to go away quietly.

««13.

Suburbia—

The Self-Satisfied Society

Hordes of middle-class Americans have swarmed to the bedroom suburbs that surround our cities. In a mobile, frenetic nation, these suburbanites try to "belong" by a ritual of joinings and meeting-aattending. They try hard to convert these commuter communities into hometowns.

One need only fly between Washington and New York to see the patterns suburbia has stenciled on the land. From the air, the tight mosaic of the mass developments and the more spacious repetition of house-driveway-lawn in the higher-priced communities give a misleading impression of permanence.

Inside, the suburban cosmos seethes with motion. There is eager, hard-pressing movement "upward" from a Levittown development to a higher-status community—status, of course, being measured in dollars. Development families dream of the day when they can move up, and those who grow too impatient plunge into a sea of debt to reach the place in life they think is important. Ask the suburban merchants: They will tell you that often the family with the big cars and the big house is the last to pay its bills.

There is also a zigzag movement between suburbs of approximately equal rank, as corporations shuffle their executives and young hopefuls across the country—or as a job is lost or debts pile too high and tumble. The 1960 census shows that 45 percent of the population of New York's suburbs were living in houses they did not occupy five years earlier. In New Canaan, Connecticut, the five-year turnover was 53.5 percent. In one Westchester, New York, suburban neighborhood of some 500 families, a recent count showed that one in every ten families had moved out in the preceding eighteen months. Although some had lived there from fifteen to thirty years, this turnover meant the disappearance of about fifty families and the introduction of fifty families of strangers. None of the older residents could hope to be neighborly with and intimately concerned about that many new families every eighteen months.

In our industrialized society not only machine parts but people are interchangeable. Many couples sit in their "den" late into the night and agonize over the next move, which may offer a short step up the corporate ladder but means dragging the children from one school to another and giving up home and friends. It is a rare family that will put their suburb above success.

Finally, there is also movement from suburbia back to the city. This usually occurs after the children have grown and left home, or after the man in the family has suffered a heart attack, the most common physical damage that results from adding the strain of commuting to the business-world rat race. The reverse migration may also represent a wish to return to the stimulating, heterogeneous city from the sterility of suburbia. "I don't think the suburbs are all bad," says John Cogley. "There is a case to be made for grass and space." But, he adds of the suburbs: "They are just such bloody bores."

The extent to which suburbia has flowered and dominates so much of American life is one of the fascinating socio-logical developments since World War II. It raises two moral questions: Why have people flooded into suburbia and what is the character of the communities they have formed?

The essential reason for the migration has been the desire for flight from the central city. In the suburbs, the grass is greener, the trees more plentiful, the schools usually superior and a house is more homelike than an apartment.

The more questionable motivation for the exodus has been to seek out neighbors like oneself and to get away from those who are different: the poor, the immigrant and the minorities. If one drives through the Tuscan country-side of Italy today, one can still see the walled towns in which groups of people of past centuries huddled together with some hope of security. On the suburban countryside of America, the walls are invisible, but they are there. And what may appear to be a grand expanse of neighborliness is, in fact, a checkerboard of jealous self-interest and mirage-like security.

On the pavilion at Jamestown island, Virginia, the site of the first permanent English settlement in the New World, is lettered this quotation from John Donne, dated 1622: "You have made this Island, which is but a suburb of the Old World, a bridge and gallery of the New." Apparently, the idea of suburbia is a very old one in the American story. But it was a different concept then and has been completely turned around today. Donne saw Jamestown as an outpost of an Old World—an adventurous extension. Our suburbia is not an adventure but a womb.

Suburbia is the part of our society that contains the greatest self-satisfaction, the greatest sense of superiority, the greatest sense of pride in itself. Many suburbanites think of themselves as too smart for the farm, too good for the city. Somehow they feel they have been granted wondrous gifts which they deserve and which they should enjoy. They are a self-tranquilized society.

"What worries me in our society is the sense of self-satisfaction," says Hubert Humphrey. "Because so many people are doing well, people forget there is still poverty in the United States today. People know more about poverty in Iran than in South Chicago or Olson Avenue in North Minneapolis."

The suburbanites flee the city to mix with the "right" people, to live in the right neighborhood, to enable their children to go to the right high schools, to meet the right members of the opposite sex and to make the right contacts. They want to use suburbia as a launching pad for their children. They know they are better than some other people, with whom it doesn't make much sense to mix.

Suburban society is organized to perpetuate these goals. Zoning regulations keep out the poor. The country clubs and the social and youth activities centered about churches and temples are divisive. Children's dancing classes openly discriminate and even Boy Scout troops accept the de facto segregation created by residential discrimination and church-sponsorship. Some civic organizations are "restricted," and even some of the hospitals do not want Jewish or Negro volunteer workers. Of one respected community, an expert says, "No other community in America has so consistently maintained such highly rigid residential restrictions, to the extent that Bronxville has now become a national symbol of total exclusion." The suburban world is the end product of the Judaic-Christian principle of exclusivity.

The Reverend Gibson Winter of the University of Chicago, in his book called *The Suburban Captivity of the Churches*, points out that our religious lives are centered in our residential communities, and for an increasing number of better-off Americans these communities are suburban. As a result, the churches have failed to meet the problems of modern society. They are captured by the pride and exclusiveness of suburbia, when in Tillich's phrase, their responsibility in suburbia is "to undercut the false security in a well-to-do society."

In another book, *The Creation as Metropolis*, the Reverend Winter writes, "We verge now on the creation of two cultures in the metropolitan areas: a culture on the periphery which enjoys affluence and privilege; a culture in the central city which suffers discrimination, under-employment and deprivation."

Here is the heart of the suburbanite's moral dilemma: Is he going to renounce all he has achieved and declare that those stupid, shiftless people in the city's slums are just as good as he is? He knows they are not. Says the Reverend Coffin, "Rascals are easy to deal with, compared to the pious and the pompous."

This cleavage between city and suburbia was driven home for me some months ago on a visit to Cook County Hospital, a tremendous, overcrowded hospital that treats so many of Chicago's poor. One patient had been knifed in the street. The police had first taken him to a fashionable private hospital which had turned the man away because there was no evidence that he could pay for treatment. So the police carried him to Cook County, where he was operated on and his life saved. Cook County Hospital, struggling along with insufficient funds and then threatened with losing its accreditation because of overcrowding, cannot turn anyone away. But the people of Chicago are not putting up enough money for their hospital, and the more prosperous Chicagoans have fled to suburbia and feel no responsibility.

As the more prosperous people leak out of the central cities to suburbia, they leave behind those least able to take care of themselves. This is why the rejuvenation of the decaying city requires massive injections of state and federal funds. For example, Dr. James B. Conant feels strongly that educational facilities in our city slums must be improved if the urban poor are not to become perpetually impoverished and left without all hope. Dr. Conant, who has written a book called *Slums and Suburbs*, says there is something wrong when New York City spends little more than $600 per pupil for education while some suburban towns spend more than $1,000 per pupil. He suggests as a solution that the states collect all school taxes and distribute them equally on a per-student basis, rather than in relationship to the income of the children's parents. Such a plan would disrupt suburbia, but it brings into focus a basic moral question about the suburbanites' responsibility in a democratic society.

The Reverend John Usry said to me of his people in Deerfield, Illinois: "In their own eyes they are very moral. There are no wife-beaters. But they live in isolation and are not in contact with problems of a metropolitan area. When I say our critics refer to the Congregational Church as the Republican Party at prayer, some of our laymen thought it was a great idea.

"If we think we can go into the Loop and earn our money

and come back here and barbecue and be happy, this is immoral. The fact that they had everything stacked in their favor never enters their heads. This is the thing that burns me about the complacent kind of attitude in suburbia." He feels the suburbanite's greatest moral problem is to learn "just to doubt the premise that the best ways are his own ways and to listen to the fellow who is different."

Suburbia's sense of superiority leads to discrimination. It is only relatively easier to fight discrimination in the comfortable "Wasp" (white Anglo-Saxon Protestant) suburbs of the North than in the South. Usry explains, "Even if a Negro had attained the status by which he could come to Deerfield, no realtor would sell him a house, no lending agency would lend him money to buy the house." In suburban America, the realtor and the banker wield greater power over morality than the minister.

It was no accident that during the prolonged Senate debate in the spring of 1964, the powerful National Association of Real Estate Boards announced its opposition to the Civil Rights Bill, because it might limit the right of property owners to dispose of their real estate as they preferred. The Association's president carefully pointed out that his group was not against civil rights.

Suburban discrimination fences out and injures not only Negroes. Benjamin Epstein of the Anti-Defamation League says of the relations between Christians and Jews in suburbia, "In too many places, I'm afraid, separate islands have been established that perpetuate differences. There has not been enough intermingling on the individual family level. The only place they come together is in a drive for a new school or recreation center." To a great extent, there is a Five O'Clock Barrier; Christians and Jews who work together in the city go their separate ways in suburbia.

A 1965 Anti-Defamation League study reported that 13 percent of the real estate listings in 13 of Chicago's North Shore suburbs excluded Jews. In Kenilworth 60 percent of the homes for sale were not available to Jews; in Lake Bluff, 32 percent; Winnetka, 30 percent; Lake Forest, 29 percent; Northfield, 24 percent. Parallel discrimination will be found in the suburbs surrounding most of our large cities. As an ad for a suburban New York house said carefully, "the character and quality of this property will appeal to the discriminating buyer."

Epstein sees discrimination against Jews as different today from discrimination against Negroes: "The Negro is seeking basic rights—jobs and freedom. The Negro has to worry about sending his son to college, finding work as skilled labor. Jews may be concerned about discrimination in country clubs and discrimination of employment at the executive level."

In Scarsdale, New York, a few years ago, the directors of an annual debutante Christmas ball at the all-Christian Scarsdale Country Club prohibited a girl from bringing an escort who, although born of Jewish parents, was a member of the local Episcopal Church. The Episcopal priest refused communion to those who had made this decision. He at least achieved some open discussion of the problem of exclusiveness—but today he no longer ministers in Scarsdale.

William K. Wolfe, executive director of the Urban League of suburban Westchester County, New York, says bluntly: "I trust the culture of the city. I don't trust the culture of the suburbs. . . . In the city, power has to be fought directly, but in suburbia, there are boards and wives and clubs, and everyone keeps smiling. This suburbia is more like a foreign country than anything you can find."

There are 60,000 Negroes in Westchester's total popula-

tion of 800,000, and most of the Negroes are congregated in
some communities and virtually excluded from others. According to Wolfe, the only Negroes living in fashionable
Chappaqua are domestic workers and perhaps some sanita-
tion-department employees. In Scarsdale, there is not a single
Negro policeman or fireman, and few Negro residents.
Wolfe says that in Greenburgh, in one neighborhood of
seventy-two homes, four Negro families moved in and
everyone panicked, tried to sell their homes and move out.
He adds, "Most Negroes live in ghettos in Westchester."

In a very important way, suburbia's seething mobility
fans the fear that builds ghettos—mobility plus a morality
that measures so much in terms of dollars. For many
suburbanites, their house is their largest investment, and
some day the house will have to be sold. Any morality that
even vaguely threatens the value of their property threatens
them directly. They find it too risky to believe the "do-
gooders," the advocates of open-housing policies, who assure
them that neighbors from minority groups will not lower
their property values.

American Stock Exchange president Edwin Etherington
is a suburbanite who has given thought to this dilemma:
"Each person's greatest moral problem is to work out a fair
balance between his own comfort and his own rights, and
the comforts and rights of others. I don't say to a person,
You shouldn't worry about the value of your house, and at
the same time I can't condone the concept of any solution
that would preclude the Negroes' right to live in the house
next door. This is a moral issue.

"You do this in a happy marriage. Dad wants to play golf.
Mother wants to go to the movies. The kids want somebody
to read to them. You work out some kind of compromise.

You have a moral obligation to try to balance out your comforts and rights against those of others. If you recognize this obligation and try to act on it—do your best—you are a moral man."

As Dean Miller of the Harvard Divinity School sees it, "It is the choice between the reality of being human and its very many substitutes—between being and appearance, and between self and all the current disguises and masks that the self wears. This is a moral choice."

Since so much of suburbia is ruled by a money morality, it is almost a truism that the more well-to-do a suburb, the less democratic will be its local government. Our wealthiest suburbs, such as Winnetka, Illinois, and Scarsdale, New York, have long been run like corporate board rooms—in secret and by agreement among caucuses of like-thinking friends. Not until 1964, after 60 years, did The Town Club, Scarsdale's most influential civic organization, open its general meetings to the press and then only by a vote of 98 to 94.

I have watched closely the political power structure at work in two suburban communities. Some years ago, when I was the editor of a weekly newspaper in Westport, Connecticut, the community was governed by an old-fashioned New England town meeting: A meeting was called and everyone interested turned out and spoke and voted. That was traditional American democracy. As Westport became too large for this system, it moved one step to a Representative Town Meeting. Each small neighborhood elected representatives and sent them to the town meeting. This was the next best thing—for a community grounded in the principles of democracy.

In Scarsdale, New York, however, political power was

rooted neither in a town meeting nor in the people of the village. For a long time political power had been held by a small group of people who controlled the village's two major civic organizations, one of men and the other of women. The local government was dominated by an elite of "Old Timers"—an Establishment that has only reluctantly been giving up its tightly held power, adjusting itself step by step as the village's population grew and newcomers discovered they had little say in civic affairs. Scarsdale's Establishment had created a community with superior schools and high property values, but without representative government. Power did not come up from the people, but down from the few. This seemed strange, because few communities are better fit to govern themselves.

Suburban morality is also conditioned by the fact that each suburb is a residential entity in which children are reared, educated and in which they often find partners for marriage. To admit a boy with Jewish antecedents to an all-Christian debutante ball, the purpose of which is to place young women on the marriage market, is to open the social door—just a crack—to people whom the parents of some debutantes do not want their daughters to marry. Those who seek racial, ethnic and religious purity even in our pluralistic society insist on keeping this door shut. When a Fair Housing Committee was formed in Scarsdale, the local Ministers Council refused at first even to meet with it, and one church denied the committee permission to meet in its building.

Suburbia not only isolates children from the real world but also presents them with pressures for achievement almost from the moment they are born. Parental pressures demand that they make "nice" friends and do well in school to win admission to the best colleges. Peer pressures demand that they participate in a plethora of activities from Cub Scouts and Brownies to competitive sports, dancing class, instrumental music lessons and, later on, "drop-dead" dates and flashy Mustangs and Thunderbirds. In the view of one suburban psychiatrist, suburban children most often develop the same lopsided values their parents hold. Middle-aged delinquency has its effects, and many a suburban child discovers that not performing up to expected standards or even breaking the rules is a wonderful way to gain the attention of otherwise busy and preoccupied parents.

The suburban psychiatrist adds, "The hothouse suburb has many disadvantages as well as advantages. When we deny children cross-cultural experiences, we are denying them a great deal, especially when we are going to ask them to live in a democratic society."

William Wolfe believes suburbia's moral problem is one of class as much as race. He says, "Ask some of your friends what they don't like about Negroes. It's not about race. They say they are dirty, loud and so on. This is class." Perhaps deep inside, the people who have fled to suburbia are afraid of the poor.

Wolfe forecasts that the Negroes who will, in time, move into our almost-pure-white commuter communities will be middle-class people seeking to live out the same dream that brought the white residents from the city to the suburb. He worries about the children of upper-class Negroes and what he calls "the hell they live through."

Think of the questions that the wife of a Negro doctor or lawyer or businessman who moves into an all-white neighborhood must ask herself: Who will her children play with? What will happen when they get into the social life of the high school? It takes a great deal of courage to be a mother and pioneer like that.

Without the prejudice that suburbanites harbor and pass on to their children, bigotry's base of respectability would collapse. White-collar prejudice leads to redneck prejudice. It is possible that the moral failure of the "respectable" citizens of Bronxville and Darien is even greater than the immoralities of the extremists in Birmingham and Jackson and Dallas. For there is something we might call The Moral Responsibility of the Respectable. Being faithful to one's spouse, paying bills on time, giving to the Community Fund —even all these moral acts are not enough in this world we now live in.

Our greatest moral challenge, said Paul Tillich, is "to break through the surface of our ordinary existence to the depth of the ultimate question of the meaning of our lives. In our case, the superficiality is stronger than in other ages. In our age the main demand is to ask again meaningfully the question of the meaning of our life. I'm not so afraid of juvenile delinquency as of superficiality—always looking ahead but never standing and looking down and up."

ᚼ 14.

Is Money Our God?

How we shall overcome prejudice is the most dramatic and urgent question of our moral crisis today, but equally difficult for the individual American is how he will deal with money honestly. In our society, money is worshiped as the root of all happiness; to many, it is more godlike than God.

Says one hard-driving young executive, "Making $40,000 a year will be like getting an 'A' on your report card."

Only an altruist can totally condemn using money as an incentive. The real question is: How far will you go to win your "A"? Many an American will connive, lie and stomp over friends and competitors. In a society which holds money in such high esteem, the American consensus is that one can both be good and cheat a little. A *Look* magazine survey, in which reporters talked with people across the nation, concluded that Americans believe they have a "freedom to chisel." Says the Reverend Coffin, "Even if you win a rat race, you are still a rat."

The Reverend Gibson Winter says, "America is preoccupied with success in measurable terms. This is a self-defeating goal. We can't communicate with our children because they suspect it. We can't communicate with each other because we would give ourselves away. We can't risk the church getting involved in the city because we know it would be a failure." In the end, we are afraid of being found out.

"If we would stop and look at our values, maybe we wouldn't have to press so hard," says Professor Kirkendall of Oregon State University. "We have to ask ourselves what are the moral values for which we are living."

To exhibit our material "worth" (as we call it), American consumers are in hock for nearly $70 billion. They buy 65 percent of new cars, 75 percent of used cars and 85 percent of furniture and appliances on credit. Many families pay out 25 percent of their after-tax income for installment payments. "This is what bugs us," says Irwin Miller. "We really want to have more than our neighbor across the street." Credit checking has become big business. "A good part of the country lives on credit," says hotel executive Preston R. Tisch. "People feel they are not expected to pay right away. It's something we in business are instilling in people's minds. Buy now and pay later."

With a bigger home, a longer car and more TV sets than he can afford, the American who hasn't won his "A" sits at his desk facing mortgage notices, overdue bills and the dread that his unearned luxuries will be taken away. At work he finds it safer to be a "Yes!" man; at home he neglects his family to run on the status treadmill. Perhaps he finds consolation in the fact that if he (and all the Joneses he is trying to keep up with) suddenly reverted to the old morality of buying only what one can afford, the entire economy would cave in.

How far a man will go was demonstrated by Texas' Billie Sol Estes—a lay preacher who did not swear or smoke or allow mixed bathing in his swimming pool but who perpetrated a multimillion-dollar swindle on his neighbors and a dozen finance companies. It put him in the three-Cadillac, private-airplane class—which must rate an A-plus. Estes could have pulled off his schemes only by exploiting the greed for the quick buck of hundreds of farmers and businessmen. "We have a society," says Walter Reuther, "in which the main motivation is the acquisition of material wealth." And Harvard College's Dean John U. Monro says sardonically, "The ability to make money excuses everything else."

Money-as-God creates dilemmas for and distorts the lives of people much less notorious than Billie Sol Estes. A theological student in Connecticut, who had to leave school because he could not pay his way, told his roommate that his father had just bought a $12,000 boat. The president of a large company threatened by a stockholders' revolt said to an associate: "I won't give up this company. The president of a corporation lives better than a Louis of France. I have at my disposal a car and chauffeur, a yacht, an airplane, a hotel suite in New York and all the entertaining I want."

Barry Goldwater lays the blame for our compromise of morality to gain money squarely on the income tax: "I go back to the income tax as the first signpost in America. This took property away from the people with due process of the law, but not in people's minds. Thousands of lawyers make their living teaching people to beat the government. I don't say 'cheat' but 'beat.' It might be legal, but it's not moral. This is the biggest factor leading to immorality in this country. Slowly—drip by drip by drip—he becomes immune to other laws."

Goldwater also blames Prohibition: "I saw people change from law-abiding citizens to sneaking out to buy liquor. The kids saw the old man bring home whiskey. They knew it was illegal. It created the most immoral generation in our history. We're paying for it today."

Another moral dilemma about money results from the current idea that cheating a big impersonal company is not really stealing at all. A dedicated churchgoer recently handed a $5 bill back to a small-town drugstore clerk who had given him too much change. But when he completed a long-distance phone call from a pay booth and the unseen operator returned his five quarters by mistake, he kept the money without a qualm. "The phone company's so darn big," he said. "They won't miss it."

This is so typical of our money morality that when a ten-year-old girl in Madison, New Jersey, found $6.30 in the coin-return slot of a public telephone and gave it back to the operator, the New Jersey Telephone Company made a big fuss over her, put her picture in the newspapers and treated her to lunch. The company was trying frantically to say that when a person faces a machine with a moral question, his answer should be the same as when he faces a human being.

It doesn't work that way. A man in a telephone booth is a clear-cut example of the confrontation between the ordinary human and the ordinary machine. One need not be a professional crook to try to beat the machine—just stick a hopeful finger into the coin-return slot. The Bell System, which owns most of the telephones in the country, has had to wage a counterattack against ordinary men to give the ordinary machine an even break. People use slugs, coins on a thread, ice cubes and spinning pennies to get a free phone call. (College students taking engineering courses are the cleverest offenders.) When bookies who knew tricks to get their coins back were caught and brought to trial, the judge insisted that the prosecution explain how they did it. Rather than spread the know-how, the telephone company dropped the case. Other people, more ambitious, steal whole coin boxes. The telephone companies have had to devise a box that their own employees cannot tamper with when it needs to be emptied. In their coin-counting rooms, the phone companies have found girls stuffing their bras and panties with nickels, dimes and quarters. Says a Bell System authority, "In the early days we believed in people—before we found we were wrong."

Scientist and writer C. P. Snow says, "We are more dishonest about money than our grandfathers were." In New Haven recently, an automobile-insurance broker advised a client who had been in a collision to pretend his back had been injured. When the client protested, the broker explained, "But everybody does it. The insurance company expects it. That's why the rates are so high." Insurance experts estimate that 75 percent of all claims are tainted with fraud.

The insurance companies see repeatedly how the apparent impersonality of big companies encourages the individual to act without moral restraint. In Massachusetts, insurance executives assert, the compulsory insurance required by law only covers bodily injury, so accident victims dream up or exaggerate personal injuries to cover the cost of their property damage. Even more widespread are repetitive claims. Insurance companies have records of one individual who made twenty-five automobile claims in ten years, at an average of $200 each. Another individual filed nineteen claims in three years; another twenty in eight years. Says one insurance investigator, "They are not crooks, but they take advantage of everything that happens."

Such moral schizophrenia afflicts the Texas oilmen who stole, by slant-well digging, some $50 million worth of oil, chiefly from the lands of big oil companies. It has encouraged policemen from Denver to Long Island to raid stores at night. It inspired guests during the first ten months at the New York's Americana Hotel to swipe (among other things) 38,000 demitasse spoons, 18,000 towels, 355 silver coffee pots, 15,000 silver finger bowls and 100 Bibles.

Personal morals often surrender to the worship of money. One New York hotel manager says he does not care if an unmarried couple sign the register as man and wife. But he is angered if a man takes a room at the single rate and brings a woman in—that is cheating the hotel.

Supermarkets are especially vulnerable to "amateur" thieves, 80 percent of whom are women. One example: 500,000 supermarket shopping carts disappeared in one recent year; at an average cost of $30 per cart this comes to $15 million. An expert estimates that 15 percent of your food bill goes to cover what customers and employees take, salving their consciences with the thought that the big company can afford it. (The more accurate economic question is: Can *you* afford it?)

Department store executives know that on a rainy day someone will usually walk out wearing a raincoat unpaid for. Fashionable suburban stores are plagued with teen-agers who leave the premises wearing stolen sportswear. When the store complains, the teen-agers' parents are likely to explode with indignation at the store. Amateurs pick up portable TV sets, radios, even rugs. To battle theft, stores have had to hire detectives, use walkie-talkies, install monitoring television cameras.

Even more costly is the immorality of American business' faithful employees. One department store, which does $100 million worth of business a year, figures it loses, mainly from customer and employee thefts, more than $1 million annually. Retailers estimate that supermarket employees steal the equivalent of $300,000 every working day. Across the country, employee thefts of money and merchandise are estimated at $2 billion a year. Such pilferage has destroyed companies.

Pilferage is often in such innocent-appearing quantities that it hardly seems evil at all. Secretaries go home with pencils and carbon paper. Employees use the telephone for personal calls that add up to big money in a large company. (Says one executive, "If you asked a girl to put down a dime, she'd think you were crazy. She regards this as one of the benefits of working here.") Bartenders and waiters pocket cash or leave charges off a customer's bill to get a bigger tip for themselves. Clerks damage goods intentionally so they can take them home. At the other end of the hierarchy, a New York department store executive has a crew from the store go up to Connecticut each spring on company time and paint his home—free.

Our third dilemma over money is the result of the feeling that whatever is customary is ethical. In the television-quiz scandals a few years back, a college instructor, a lawyer and a minister were among those who took thousands of dollars by letting themselves be convinced that they were doing what came naturally in the TV world. They did not regard themselves as dishonest. Those who went on to perjure themselves before a grand jury had to figure out some other rationalization. But the courts did not penalize them or even bring to trial the quiz-show executives who made the whole mess possible. Maybe there was no legal offense in what they did to gain larger audiences; there was a moral one.

The same moral question faces the traveler returning from abroad with false bills to show the customs inspector. Or the doctor who uses experimental drugs on a patient without telling him—especially when the doctor owns stock in the drug company. Or, again, the doctor who puts a patient in the hospital to make sure he gets his fee from Blue Shield. Or the financial writer who buys a stock, plugs it and, when it climbs in value, swiftly sells it at a profit. Or the tax lawyer who tells his client to add some phony deductions because the Internal Revenue agent needs something to cross out.

Mortimer M. Caplin, recently the chief of Internal Revenue, believes that no more than 3 percent of the people cheat on their income taxes. He says, "You hear that our income-tax laws are making us a nation of cheats. Our law cases say it's perfectly proper to minimize your taxes. I think most errors are errors of judgment. People will give themselves the benefit of the doubt in close cases. We get out of perspective. We see the wheelers and dealers in the headlines. This is a small percent of the population."

The fact is, however, that most taxpayers have no opportunity to cheat even if they want to. Their taxes are paid automatically from their wages. Caplin estimates that the IRS, which collects $100 billion annually in all taxes, would have collected an additional $5 billion if everyone were honest.

Caplin found it interesting that, as the Internal Revenue Service automated the checking of returns, people began to report taxes that should have been paid as long ago as 1918.

In six months, a thousand people sent in their contributions totalling $2.9 million, in amounts from $4 to $250,000. Automation has become important to the IRS because by 1962 there were 62 million individual income-tax returns filed, compared to only 7.9 million as recently as 1940. Government experts estimate that by 1980 they will have to process 135 million individual returns—more than twice as many as now. When the master file of all taxpayers (each reduced to a permanent identification number) is amassed and the electronic computers are whirring in the National Computer Center at Martinsburg, West Virginia, and in seventy-one subordinate centers across the land, fewer Americans will get away with tax evasion. Whether the big-time tax dodger and revenue-agent briber will also be caught electronically remains to be seen.

"The real enemy within our society," Caplin said in a speech, "is the man with contempt for democratic government—who would undermine our government by attempting to corrupt public officials. This man must be ferreted out, pursued, and brought to the bar of justice."

Some 20,000 trained people are employed to catch America's tax evaders. In one year alone (1961) 1,129 offenders were imprisoned for a total of 271 years and were fined $2.5 million, and additional probationary and suspended sentences were imposed by the courts totaling 2,274 years. These law breakers represented all parts of our population. Some were employers who withheld income taxes for their employees but failed to pass the money along to the government. A gambler was sentenced to three years in prison for failing to report his winnings, and a dentist was sentenced to fifteen months in prison after pleading guilty to not reporting all his earnings. (IRS officials point to the conclusion of the late Senator Estes Kefauver's special Senate committee that the gambling profits collected by organized criminals from many "two-dollar bettors" are the financial foundation on which are built empires of rackets, narcotics and prostitution.)

Of the federal government's effort to keep the lid on tax evasion, Caplin says, "I think the average person would like to be in full compliance. If there were greater assurance that there was a uniform level of high compliance, you'd get more compliance. You get this uncertainty about just what the rules of the game really are." But, he adds, "You know on a tax return if you've made a $500 lie or fraud."

Caplin believes this is particularly true in regard to expense accounts, which gained so much public attention when he tried to define "the rules of the game.'" He says, "There was a lot of fudging, and people gave themselves all kinds of wild benefit of the doubt. The law was fuzzy. What is it doing to the 90 percent of the public not claiming deductions when they see ostentatious spending?"

The desire to wriggle out from under the burden of paying taxes results not only in individual immorality but raises some perplexing questions about organized forms of escape. New Hampshire, for example, has neither a state income tax nor a sales tax. At the same time it spends little per student for educational purposes, ranking forty-eighth among the states in state and local public school revenue as a percent of personal income.

"What do we want to buy and how much are we willing to pay?" says Professor Augenstein. "That's a definition of morality." We are willing to be good if we don't have to pay too high a price.

Rather than raise some $20 million over two years to lift

their school systems to higher standards, the Yankees of New Hampshire launched a sweepstakes in 1963, in which residents and visitors from all over the country could buy a three-dollar ticket and gamble for the jackpot. Although those who supported the sweepstakes insisted there was nothing immoral about it, tickets can be purchased only in state liquor stores and at racetracks, and only by persons over twenty-one. Its critics refer to New Hampshire's system of taxation—which gains revenue from liquor, cigarettes and horse racing—as the "sin tax," collecting on "booze, butts and bets." Even more questionable in the eyes of the sweepstakes' opponents is the expectation that the approximately $2.5 million to be distributed from the sweepstakes each year will enable the state legislature to avoid raising the $20 million the state really needs for its schools. Some communities have actually used the sweepstakes booty to decrease their local school taxes.

Edward DeCourcy, the editor of the weekly *The Argus-Champion* of Newport, New Hampshire, and past president of the International Conference of Weekly Newspaper Editors, says of the sweepstakes: "New Hampshire displayed a deep decay of morality in adopting the gigantic fraud we euphemistically call the sweepstakes. It's an attempt to duck the state's responsibility to educate its kids by trying to get some money from out-of-staters. It's a fraud because it will be tried for several years before the failure to reach expected income and the certain growth of corruption finally disgust New Hampshiremen so much they'll throw it out, but in the meantime no legislature will pass any responsible measure for the support of education."

As a footnote, it is faintly amusing to hear some conservative New Englanders protest against federal taxation and then to drive through their states and see the new highways being built, with large signs proclaiming that the roads are being paid for by state funds, 10 percent, and federal funds, 90 percent.

All these are moral problems for the individual in our big-money society. His relationship to his fellow citizen, his government and the big corporate entities is increasingly distant and divorced from moral standards. In business, we have changed from a society of the handshake to a society of the fine print. In taxation, we have changed from a sense of communal responsibility to an eagerness to escape carrying our share of the load. In charity, we have changed from personal help between families who know and care about each other to massive fund-raising drives and writing a check. ("Writing a check," says Irwin Miller, "is a form of detachment—of wiping your guilt away.") In medical care, we have changed from the self-sacrificing family doctor to less personal group practice. Recently a Catholic bishop criticized doctors for rushing patients through their offices like IBM cards through a calculator. Many doctors use the technological advances of our day to increase their incomes at the sacrifice of personal attention to their patients.

Edward DeCourcy says, "We who cover the small-town police station see the immorality of the driver who purposely breaks the law, while urging his kids to keep an eye out for a possible police cruiser in the rear. This is the guy who brags about cheating on his income tax, lies about his kid's age so he can get him into the show at half price, brags about getting his ticket fixed, and then wonders why his kid cheats on exams.

"Personal morality has slipped. Too many of us today lack the self-discipline to do our work thoroughly, or to be punctual, or to meet our financial obligations by paying our debts on time.

"But there are also some diamonds shining brightly. The towns I know are filled with the people who have been called 'the obscure great.' These are the men and women of courage and conviction; their deeds of real gut heroism are never recorded. There are many of them."

Our mass society has reduced the individual's personal concern for his fellow man at the same time that it has given him greater freedom of choice about what his moral standards will be. Today a man can choose where he will live, where he will work and who will be his mate. Choices are burdens. Says Dean Samuel Miller, "This puts tremendous pressure on him. He has to be more humble and more daring than he has ever been before. When he gets scared of the burden, he falls back limp and tired and lets someone else tell him what to do, or he turns his back and turns to tranquilizers and racetracks and alcohol.

"If the world has become too ruthless, maybe it is time to stand up and make a decision not to be dictated to by the machine and to set a human pace. The question is whether man has the moral strength to stand up to this juggernaut. Does man have the moral strength to fire the retro-rockets? We are no doubt orbiting in this technological revolution. Shall we have more cloverleafs or more mental hospitals, more advertising or less built-in obsolescence? The question is: Do we have the guts really to make decisions?"

As an example of the kind of decisions we must face up to, sociologist Philip Hauser in Chicago says, "The reason you have organized prostitution and organized gambling in big cities is that the power structure wants them there—not only the police and politicians, but the pillars of society

—big business, big labor, big citizens. This is a 'concession to the convention trade'; it's important to business.

"There is hypocrisy. It's all right, to my mind, to say that Al Capone was a great benefactor of the human race. At some risk, he provided the American people with services they desired. He did it in an amazing way, by building up a subterranean 'outlawed' social order with sanctions (machine guns) and great rewards. Can anyone in his right mind believe this was really outlawed?"

The civil liberties lawyer Arthur Garfield Hays said half-seriously years ago that we should erect statues along our highways to the grafters and promoters who made fortunes out of them, because without these men the roads would never have been built.

Professor Hauser extends his idea that the individual must have the strength to make decisions that run counter to the practices of society. He develops what might be called "A Case For Sin." As an example, Hauser asserts that one of the ways for a young man to break out of a slum environment, walled in by poverty and prejudice, is through such illicit activities as vice and bootlegging. It is frequently the normal slum boy, Hauser says, who becomes a delinquent; the others are not bright nor strong enough to compete and break out. "Some of the kids I was in school with are in jail," says Hauser. "I am a professor and they are in jail for the same reason. We were both freed from the bonds of our [slum] culture and deviated from the norms of our culture. Without the ability to break out, you can't have either the criminal or the saint."

How can we help keep the balance in favor of the saint and against the criminal? The Reverend Michael Allen, who ministers to a slum area, warns, "You don't get morality by telling people to be good. Maybe he can't be, doesn't know how to be. You've got to help people have the strength, the guts, to be good." Professor Argyris says, "One way is to provide a meaningful challenge. To be a free person is to make decisions—to take risks."

This is not just a problem of the slums. If we are to re-examine our values about money, we face the risks of having to make choices. For any of us, it is difficult to break out of the immorality of our culture. Maybe our younger generations will see this and take the risks. As Robert Oppenheimer puts it, "The sure thing doesn't raise any problems. I'm interested in the beats, the young people. They are less concerned with literary and artistic forms than creating for themselves a life that has some aesthetic meaning. It is a moral, political movement. Our young people have something to revolt against—unction."

««15.

The Moral Confusion of Youth

"How do we transmit any moral ethos from one generation to another in America?" asks Dean Samuel Miller. "I see no sign of it being done in the home, where it can be done best, and what's being done in the church is extremely inadequate. Now we have a technological culture with no moral grounds; now if we want morals, we have to work at it. We have to teach children morals. There is something radically wrong with a society that does not know how to teach its children to behave in that society."

Father Walter Imbiorski, director of the Catholic Cana Conference of Chicago, points out: "Every culture teaches its young what it values. Sioux ride and endure hardships because the tribe needs hunters to survive. We don't value the hunter but people who can get along with others. 'It's not what you know, Buster, but who you know!'

"Lots of our children are brought up in cotton-wool, especially in the suburbs, and never see need. The very affluence of our society—the very confusion of our society

—deprives kids of the opportunity to see a need that has an impact on them. There is no confrontation, no involvement."

Professor Helen Perlman concurs: "There are just too many freedoms kids have and therefore too many temptations—cars, late hours, parents afraid to say 'Be home!'; parents pressing children to date earlier. The most important thing is the kids are not feeling inner-directed, not knowing who he is and where he's going."

Mrs. Katherine B. Oettinger, the chief of the United States Children's Bureau, says, "The greatest moral challenge is to build the kind of home that carries on the traditions of the past and is flexible enough to meet conditions of a changing world: standards and tolerance."

If an adult must make moral choices with little guidance, the problem is even tougher for today's youth. Says John Cogley, "The predominant note in our society is freedom of choice of personal conduct. It's increasing. This creates new problems. A girl who has a car and doesn't have to be in until two in the morning may have different attitudes toward necking and petting."

One expert tells of a girl who burst out: "No rules to break? How do you have any fun?" Part of the confusion of youth is illustrated by the licensing of sixteen- and eighteen-year-olds to drive cars without holding them legally responsible. In some states when they misuse their cars or break other laws, teen-agers are treated as "youthful offenders" and receive special kid-glove treatment. Without recommending any such solution, Harvard historian Crane Brinton points out, "You couldn't have juvenile delinquency in England in 1840 when children of nine worked twelve hours a day. They didn't have the energy."

Youthful freedom of choice is exploited by those who can profit from the manipulation of these choices. Business is often at fault. Much commercialism and high-pressure press agentry is aimed directly at teen-agers—from the Beatles to movies, records, TV programs. Teen-agers expect their desires and affluence to be catered to. In 1964, for example, the Ford Motor Company, at sizable expense, invited seventy college editors to Dearborn, Michigan, to help promote its brand-new Mustang car. Thirty-eight editors accepted and were brought free from universities as far away as Texas, Oregon and Connecticut. The company sponsored a "bash" at the staid Dearborn Inn and, as one Ford participant put it, the young people "drank up everything in sight." The company discussed promotion ideas with the students and then loaned each student who would accept it a bright-red Mustang to drive back to college and to keep until the end of the academic year, insurance and maintenance paid for. The student editors were supposed to inspire others on campus to desire similar flashy red cars by their example and perhaps through their newspaper columns. The student editors were also asked to allow themselves to be used in advertising (five refused).

In May the board of directors of Sigma Delta Chi, the national journalistic society that concerns itself with ethics and college journalism, unanimously passed a resolution condemning Ford's promotion. Editors, both student and adult, across the land debated the ethical questions involved. The *Des Moines Register* blamed the company less than the students and faculties, and suggested that the student editors should have asked themselves why they were selected rather than the top Phi Beta Kappa member on campus or other student leaders. *The National Observer* editorialized, "in

the profession of journalism, there's no such thing as something for nothing." A number of student publications
pointed to free-loading among professional newsmen as
justification for their free ride, but an editorial in the *Iowa
State Daily*, explaining why its student editors had turned
down the deal, said, "The *Daily* doesn't want to feel that it
can be bought."

This story of the Mustang and the students simply suggests the kinds of pressures that may pervert even bright and
able young people. The autombile company was teaching
these student editors morality (and journalistic ethics) from
the viewpoint of big-spending public relations. The student
editors who accepted did not find the whole dubious deal
outside their concept of moral conduct.

For young people especially, a world without guidance
can lead to disaster. Governor Romney says that in Michigan
65 percent of all major crimes (murder, rape, theft) are
committed by boys and girls twenty-one and under, and 35
percent by youngsters sixteen and under. Communities
from Fort Lauderdale, Florida, to Garnett, Kansas, have
seen massive juvenile riots. At Southhampton, Long Island,
after a society party, eighty to one hundred college students
wrecked a rented mansion and were eventually acquitted
"for lack of evidence." Suburban Deerfield, Illinois, had its
first teen-age rumble in the spring of 1963, and thirty youths
were arrested; teen-age drinking and wild parties while
parents are away are now problems there.

Drag races and broken school-windows are features of
many well-to-do suburbs. One suburban judge calls the
problem "auto-mania." A police justice said, "Some of these
kids feel they are big shots if they've had run-ins with the
law." Communities are building schools without windows to

avoid vandalism. Westchester County suburbs near New York City have suffered from teen-agers who force entrance at parties in private homes and even threaten the adults present. A Scarsdale, New York, judge tells of a high school sophomore who, fined $25 for speeding, pulled out his own checkbook, wrote a check and left.

In exclusive Darien, Connecticut, which has been described as "almost entirely white and Protestant," parents, who were worried about shoplifting and petty thievery by school children, made a study and reported in May, 1963, that the greatest trouble was stealing, but that vandalism, drinking (an estimated 85 percent of the teen-agers) and sex activity were all problems in their youngsters' behavior. The statement from a teen-age girl that "accepting a date to the drive-in movie is like accepting a date for sexual relations" received wide attention.

In June, Darien high school students replied, asserting that the majority of teen-agers in town were not involved in such activities. Still, they agreed that the community's youngsters had problems and charged that their parents were to blame for not supplying moral leadership. Said the students' report, "It is totally unrealistic to expect teen-agers to uphold standards that are abjured by their parents, who should be their moral leaders."

The following summer some Darien residents protested when the local weekly, after a rash of automobile accidents, began publishing the police blotter on its front page. The police commissioner said that teen-age drinking was one of his most serious problems. Then in September a judge demanded that the Darien police arrest all adults connected with two June parties at which liquor was served and which had been attended by two teen-agers who were later the same night in an automobile accident. The eighteen-year-old boy had been thrown clear of the crash but the seventeen-year-old girl with him was killed. Fourteen arrest warrants were made out for serving liquor to minors. The arrests shook the community, but its political leader said, "Darien is no different than any other community around. But the judge isn't a local, you know." Presumably if he had been "a local," the whole affair would have been hushed up as such things usually are in upper-bracket suburbia. Local clergymen, however, issued a statement saying, "We plead for a closer look at our accepted practices and for an increased sense of moral responsibility."

Perhaps the ultimate disaster in a world without guidance is that suicides among teen-agers are increasing. Dr. Milton J. E. Senn, director of the Yale University Child Study Center, is deeply concerned about the incidence of child suicide, by youths using aspirin, sleeping pills and their parents' tranquilizers. He says, "What we are now seeing in our pediatric department are more suicide attempts by young adolescents with a peak of fifteen years and as low as twelve and thirteen, both boys and girls."

He concludes, "I believe our children are under particular stresses and strains because of the swiftness of change. As someone said, our children have been precipitated into the twenty-fifth century. Children have a difficult time catching up."

And he warns parents: "In the home, talking about ethics and morals—like sex education—can be overdone and done prematurely. Some serious-minded parents talk about these issues so often that the children pick up the idea early that this is a rotten world, unusually guilty, overly conscious of every act. We often forget our young people are concerned too. I'd say, don't overdo it. We can make our children overly concerned so that they feel there is no justice, no happiness. Then they ask, why should I live in [this world]? We must give our children to understand that there is hope and faith and that there are wise people and ethical and moral people."

Dr. Mitchell Gratwick, principal of the Horace Mann School, a New York private boys' school, wrote in a special letter to parents: ". . . to love and to deal considerately with his neighbor, probably man's only hope of survival, is not a primal urge. To teach him to sublimate his brutal instincts and, contradicting his nature, to react compassionately is a hard job. The young must learn this lesson at an early age."

Parents are today accused of having one of two attitudes: The first resembles that of birds that feed their young even after they can fly, until the fledglings are big and strong and the parents worn to a frazzle. The other is that of parents who really do not want their children to interrupt their adult lives, careers and pleasures. And Dr. Dana L. Farnsworth, director of the Harvard University Health Services, told the New York Academy of Medicine: "Many parents are so busy trying to maintain a high standard of living for their families that they have too little time to invest in close companionship with their children, particularly in the adolescent period."

Parents who are bewildered by moral choices have trouble guiding their youngsters through stresses and strains. Although some child-development experts would like to save parents from the entire burden of responsibility for their children's misdeeds, most feel it is foolish to blame the child alone, and futile to blame "society."

John Cogley says, "The worst insecurity is to bring up a

child in a world in which good is not rewarded and evil is
not punished. This is an unreal world." But some authorities
believe that the traditional methods of reward and punishment cannot give children the kind of positive moral training
they need today. Parents should not, they say, imitate the
classic Ring Lardner line: " 'Shut up!' he explained."

Dr. Lawrence Kohlberg, assistant professor of psychology
and human development at the University of Chicago, has
studied how children learn moral values and says: "Reward
and punishment don't in themselves develop morality. There
is some suggestion it has the opposite effect. It focuses the
kid on what it does to him rather than the consequences to
other people or society. Delinquents seem to have been more
heavily punished. You can't stamp morality into people. All
you can do is guide children in some direction." Punishment,
he argues, teaches a child that you get punished for stealing
but not that it is not moral to steal. He adds, "Any civilized
society is one in which morality is an internal thing."

As a result of his studies, Dr. Kohlberg says, "I don't think
religious training has much effect. Religious educators seem
as confused as anyone about what they want to teach
morally."

Dr. Senn insists that religious education has a role to
develop: "I think there is a need to attack this in religious
education. My own feeling is that within the church and
school these questions should come up, not as sin and not-sin
but as human behavior. You don't slap the hand of the
children. You don't say, You are a thief. But it should be
discussed. Why do children steal? What do you do when
someone does? This is the kind of discussion that should
go on. To me this is good religious education, although it
is entirely without theology."

The central problem, Dr. Kohlberg believes, is: "Parents

want their kids to be morally good, but they want their kids to be successful." Dr. Senn agrees: "A parent who complains about spendthrift habits of a child often gives not of himself and his talent but his money."

Even if parents fail as teachers of morality, they are still models for their children. Dr. Senn recognizes that this creates a burden on many parents who fear that their own imperfections will be absorbed by their children. He says, "Parents introduce children to behavior by precept, by suggestion. Ideally, we should try to set up models in ourselves. We can be good enough models—human beings who try to be honest and fair. A parent who tries to be perfect would become so self-conscious he would be paralyzed."

At the same time, Dr. Senn is concerned about the moral example many parents present to their children. "I'm told pridefully how they teach their children to cut corners, how to get by without paying, without working. They would call me a liar if I say they are teaching their children to cheat. They say everyone expects this, the insurance man, the tax collector, the grocer. Parents say, 'You cheat where you can and you teach your child to be adept at this because this is the way the world is.' "

Says Harvard sociologist David Riesman, "The confusion of parents themselves is communicated to children like a contagious disease." (Our society is even confused over whether it is right or wrong to spank a child.)

Parents pile on pressures to make good grades, to get into a good college, to choose careers and mates early. In New York City, it has been recently reported, parents compete strenuously to get their children into the best private nursery schools and start them on the track to the best prep schools and colleges. At one nursery school 2,000 children were vying for 65 vacancies. As an educator put it, "The race to get into Harvard begins in the sandbox."

Dr. Mitchell Gratwick wrote to parents of his students: "The affluent of our society, with their worship of golden images, have established goals of their own for young people. . . . These people are not given to standing by and watching for the emergence of individual interests and aptitudes in their offspring. Material goals have been foreordained for those who would 'succeed' in their society, and they exhort their sons to get A's in school and, as the chief objective in life, to qualify for prestige colleges and to get to the top in business. Some of this enthusiasm for getting ahead is commendable and has unquestionably contributed to the growth of our economy; but some of it is not, especially when differences are not recognized and square pegs are pushed into round holes."

The U.S. Office of Education says that 45 percent of freshmen entering college drop out before getting a degree. Recently, Princeton University's admissions office received a letter from an able freshman candidate, asking them to turn him down and not to tell his parents about his letter. The boy's parents had forced him to apply. Princeton admissions director Alden Dunham says, "Parental ambitions are often tied more to concepts of social prestige than education." Such pressures result in college cheating, vandalism and promiscuity.

Many experts emphasize the failure of communication between today's parents and their children. "Parents themselves are quite confused," says Professor Perlman. "There is a bigger gap between parents and kids today because kids learn so much so fast. Parents' wisdom—or what was taken as parents' wisdom—disappears sooner." Says Professor Kirkendall, "The rapidity of change makes it difficult for the generations to interact. The kids can't extend back to the past; it was so different. On the other hand, we tell them, you can't count on what's going to happen five years from now. They can't extend in the future either. They try to live more for the moment. It again separates them from adults."

He thinks parents have found devices to free them from their children but at the same time have reduced the possibilities of communication. "Baby-sitting is perfectly designed to separate adults from children. Parents feel it isn't right to mix children with adults; children eat in the kitchen when company comes. You don't want to be bothered by the messiness and prattle of kids. I suspect adults and kids don't have very much in common. We are not actually engaged in much that provides interests in common."

Lady Snow, the novelist Pamela Hansford Johnson, also sees an "incredible gap" between today's parents and children. "A tremendous wedge has been driven between anyone under twenty and over twenty." She feels today's affluence has given youth more economic independence and reduced their parents' control over them. She says, "Parents must simply not feel that they are being driven underground by these children. How we shall go about it, I don't know."

Part of the problem comes from the changing nature of the American family. The old-fashioned, large, multi-generational family, living and working together, has been chopped down in our urban society to a "core" family of parents and children. Of the isolation of the older grandparent generation, Arnold Toynbee says, "It's gone to an extreme in the United States. They don't want to be in an institution. They want to be in a family. They've really been thrown out of the family."

Of the remaining "core," the Reverend Usry says, "These are people without roots, and the family has to carry a terrible burden. The immediate family has to provide all the protection against the blows from a hostile world. It's almost impossible for a family to provide." Comments Dr. Senn at Yale, "There is a feeling, justified or not, that the American family has gone to hell. I don't know whether it is decadent, but I am worried. We are concerned because of the nature of problems that come to us, problems of family breakdown."

Professor Kirkendall in Oregon agrees: "So many meaningful functions that tied a family together have disappeared. The result is the family is composed much more of separate individuals living under the same roof but each going his own way. Young people are left on their own and tend to work out their own codes."

The problem facing the child is summed up by Mrs. Oettinger of the U.S. Children's Bureau: "He has to be more on his own at an early age—more inner-directed in his own moral judgments and actions than at a time when he lived in a close-knit, family-centered, smaller community."

David Riesman recognizes the same problem: "It's important for parents in dealing with younger children to present them with family culture and have children conduct themselves not [according] to what neighbors think but what the family says."

Attorney General Katzenbach believes changes in the family have affected the rise in crime among youth. Where parents fail to take responsibility, he says, youngsters turn to "the adventure of breaking the law." He tells of visiting a federal institution and talking to a group of boys all of whom had been found guilty of stealing cars. They were asked how many of the cars were stolen from parking lots. Every hand went up. He asked them how many of the cars had keys in the ignition. Every hand went up again. Katzenbach says, "Hell, you've got the wrong person in jail. It doesn't seem right to put that much temptation in front of them."

He adds, "Lack of parental responsibility comes from the fact that we are more mobile—we have more divorce. I think kids who have parents who are around don't have as much of a problems as kids with one parent or none. In the suburbs, it's a matter of parents who are more interested in themselves than their children.

"If people care enough about the problem, it makes a difference. The kids who do it say, 'Nobody cares about me, you're on your own buddy.' The parents I'm critical of haven't given their kids anything to come home to."

Katzenbach offers a controversial solution to the failure of parental responsibility. He says, "Society is going to have to create substitute parents—institutions will have to do the jobs parents are unwilling to do. As a parent I hate all this, but I think it has to be done."

We have given young people the hope of rising as far as their abilities will take them. But Katzenbach warns, "Increased social mobility gives you more crime. If you don't make the grade, you have feelings of frustration, bitterness." He also points out "the unschooled can't get jobs, and there are a lot of unschooled people. . . . Kids who drop out of school have no jobs." He adds, "Youth employment is one of the biggest problems the country faces. We don't have educational facilities or jobs for them. . . . Young people are searching for things to do."

And the number of teen-agers is growing swiftly. We have about 75 million Americans 17 years of age and under. In 1974 four million Americans will reach their 17th birthday. High school enrollment will then be 30 percent higher than it is, rising from 12.7 million in 1964 to 16.3 million. And the boom stretches out as far as the eye can see: Four million children were born in 1964, six million births are predicted for 1975 and 6.5 million for 1980.

As the family becomes less meaningful and less controlling, the experts say, young people seek stronger attachments to a peer group. This leads to conformity. Explains Dr. Senn, "What they want is group acceptance and to qualify for peer membership. The child who doesn't agree with the behavior his peers prescribe has the choice of swaying the group or is thrown out or pulls out. If he is out, he thinks he is alone. He's lonely. To find another peer group is not easily done."

As to the future of these children, Toynbee comments: "It's rather a puzzle how the present generation of American children will turn into self-sacrificing parents."

Mrs. Oettinger reminds parents that there are many other influences on youth in our society. "I'm surprised," she says, "that people expect parents to take all the blame—the whole burden—for what happens to their children." Obviously, our educational institutions share the parents' obligation to teach moral standards. "In our educational system we have taught people to challenge and ask questions," Kirkendall points out. "This is sound, of course, but it has undermined our traditional authoritarian morals." Exactly what role our schools should play in teaching a sense of morality has long been debated within educational circles. So far we have not gone much beyond the teaching of patriotism.

Some teachers are extremely good moral models—dedicated, idealistic, concerned. But others can be rigid in their ideas, and fail to keep up with a changing world and to expose their students to the real moral problems of our times. Teachers have handicaps: Too often they are looked down on by their pupils' parents. They often prefer security and object vigorously to any system that will reward superior teaching. And many accept the standard that requires youngsters to make good marks rather than learn for learning's sake.

In the colleges, teachers often must "publish or perish," and spend more time in the library stacks than in the classroom. Says Professor Oscar Handlin, "More people go to college. I'm not sure more get educated." A recent survey of 6,000 students at 99 colleges found that 55 percent cheated their way to a degree; the study made the cheating scandals at the U.S. Military Academy in 1951 and the U.S. Air Force Academy in 1964 look mild.

Dean Monro of Harvard College is troubled about the moral values that colleges are projecting. For one example, he feels strongly that collegiate athletics, with pay-for-play scholarships and aroma of deceit, are teaching youth to be cynical. "The greatest hypocrisy we have is professional athletics being conducted in the colleges under the guise of amateurism—the prospective doctor or teacher who is compelled to play football and whose college program is a joke. The morality is awful and getting worse with the television profits. Newspapers are for it because sportswriters make a living off it. Colleges do it for money. It's as simple as that. I don't know how long the country is going to take this— that institutions assigned a good part of the moral education of the young are this cynical. This is a moral cancer in our country."

College athletics are big-time money. NBC bought the TV rights to the NCAA college football program in 1964

and 1965 for a total of $13 million. The traditional ex-
cuse that colleges need winning football teams to attract students no longer holds water when most colleges have a surplus of applicants. A good bit of the blame for professional
football in the colleges (and the national service academies)
must be placed on the Old Grad who keeps the pressure on
public universities through politicians and on the private
ones through his power to give or withhold gifts. Most colleges are unwilling to risk losing money to uphold what they
feel is morally right.

Despite such failures by parents and educators, Dean
Monro feels that young people today are increasingly concerned about moral issues, and that in this, many of them
are ahead of the older generation. Monro says, "What I've
got here is concern, and this is true of a lot of colleges. It's
important, it's growing, and it's intelligent."

Many college-age Americans are demonstrating their concern in the Freedom Schools, the Peace Corps, the work
many have done in the South and in the North's slums.
Their concern is also visible in the campus protests over the
war in Vietnam and in demonstrations against impersonal
college faculties. The keepers of these academic institutions
usually denounce the student revolts, such as the famous
one at Berkeley, as irresponsible, but some psychologists and
religious leaders see in them a meaningful rebellion against
the giant, cold universities that so accurately reflect our
society.

The Reverend Coffin sees concern at Yale: "The most
creative, sensitive students are deeply concerned with religious questions and skeptical of religious answers. If they
are skeptical out of love of the truth, not hate of the truth,
this is a good thing."

However, J. Edgar Hoover showed little faith in today's

youth and their loyalty, and little confidence in American democracy's ability to stand up under verbal attack, when he warned against allowing communists to speak on American campuses because they could, he said, "control the minds and win the allegiance of American youth."

Glenn Seaborg, former chancellor of the University of California, agrees that today's students are concerned: "I see an awful lot of them that are just brilliant. They know so much more than I did at the same age that it hardly seems like we are members of the same race." He even suggests that the atomic danger "probably increases their sense of responsibility." And he adds, "Now the kids really have a hard row to hoe—a lot to learn—and they know it."

As with almost every young generation, many in this one believe they are morally superior to their elders, but they are bewildered about how they can handle the same problems their elders have failed to solve. "Our problem is we don't have any confidence in [youth]. We should have," asserts Professor Kirkendall. "You have to be concerned about the kind of person you rear. The individual has to find fulfillment and worth in things he does for others."

Goldwater, who has spoken on many college campuses, sees the subject simply: "I have much more faith in America based on these young people's morals than I have in their parents'. I think this generation is better. I'd like to see us talk less about juvenile delinquency for a while and talk about juvenile good. Juvenile delinquency is the result of the unmoral home. It goes back to government—the man who beats the government, who cheats on his debts. What's a kid to think who believes in his father?"

Dean Samuel Miller tells of a friend whose son seemed irresponsible and only wanted to sing and play a guitar in coffee shops. Miller asked the boy to play for him, and discovered that his songs were about fall-out ("the rain on the prairies"), lynching ("the fruit of the tree"). "In every one," says Dean Miller, "there was a sense of moral judgment in what was happening. He was articulating the world, while the church was mumbling its old sacred formulas."

≪16.

Our New Ideas About Sex and Marriage

Sex is a subject of moral concern in our America. We cannot make valid comparisons between past sexual behavior patterns and today's because we do not really know how people behaved sexually in earlier years. Our knowledge of present patterns is also incomplete. But we do know that there is widespread anxiety that our traditional sexual morality is disappearing.

"American society is no longer accepting the Christian morality of sexual life—that sex should not be outside marriage," says French scholar Raymond Aron. "We are still living in a society where the main religious creed is Christian, and our private morality is primarily a revolt against Christian morality. Divorce is completely accepted, freedom of sexual intercourse between young men and young women is fully accepted. In sexuality, we are in revolt against Christianity."

As part of this revolt, almost everyone is more candid about sex. The facts of life are hushed up less. Some blame this candor on Dr. Alfred Kinsey and his studies of American sexual behavior, but the times were ripe for Dr. Kinsey. He may have made communication easier, but he did not create the change. Dr. Paul H. Gebhard of Indiana University, who is continuing Dr. Kinsey's work as executive director of the Institute for Sex Research, says, "It got them talking, and the greatest by-product is greater tolerance. This is quite marked among young college people today. How much of this tolerance is verbal, I'm not quite sure."

One reason that young people discuss sex more, according to Professor Kirkendall of Oregon State University, a leading authority on family life, is that they are trying to work out for themselves a new sexual code. "We are in a period when the whole approach to a consideration of sex standards has to undergo a change if we are to be realistic," he says. As Toynbee puts it, "People have rejected the conventional view of sexual morality and haven't found a new reality."

Aron adds, "Never was talking, writing, images, movies about sexuality as free as it is today. We have become, in terms of expressing ourselves, freer than any other time." This was also the comment of the British committee, headed by Sir John Wolfenden, that studied various sexual problems and reported, "Sexual matters in general are more openly talked about today than they were in the days of our parents and grandparents. . . ."

Most people studying behavior of youth believe that sexual activity is also increasing. "If it is not increasing," comments Professor Helen Perlman, "it would surprise me, considering the stimuli to sex and the rootlessness of the kids today."

Young people are breaking away from the counseling of parents and churches. They are experimenting to determine—almost by trial and error—the sexual morality they want to adopt. A London group of the Society of Friends in a pamphlet called "Towards a Quaker View of Sex" warns that "in subscribing to a moral code, some of which it no longer accepts, society merits the charge of hypocrisy and its authority is weakened. The insincerity of the sexual moral code may well be a cause of the widespread contempt of the younger generation for society's rules and prohibitions."

Dr. David R. Mace, executive director of the American Association of Marriage Counselors, blames the mass entertainment media for "regimenting" new moral attitudes about sex: "They are creating new mores of divorce and expectations of luxury." He criticizes the influence of the behavior of some movie and television entertainers: "Their patterns of living are so brittle as to be tragic. A whole generation are being deceived by the glamour. Never before have the entertainers been the pace setters."

Today's sexuality disturbs Dr. Mace: "It's hedonistic. Pleasure, having a good time, is the thing that matters. It's sexually amoral if not immoral. Exploitative! It's cynical in that it recognizes no higher values. It's irresponsible in that it takes no account of the consequences. Have a good time. Don't take anything seriously."

Even in sex, our society is pluralistic. Any number of subcultures within our nation have varying ideas about sex. And our laws form a confusing crazy quilt. In some places, for example, they permit common-law marriages, and in others, they do not; some states legally limit even what a wife and husband can do in privacy and with mutual consent. The variety of our divorce laws is absurd. One judge estimates that 80 percent of all men are, according to the laws, sex criminals. We are still heir to the puritanical concept that sex is fine, as long as one does not enjoy it; and this heritage is at war with an ever-present awareness of sex that is nearly grotesque. Says Professor Kirkendall, "Our young people are not sex-obsessed. The culture is. We use it to sell products, as a come-on."

One thoughtful college authority told me: "In any effort we make to bring discipline and prudence into sexual behavior, we will get little support from the general culture. We are bucking a tidal surge of sexuality and permissiveness that runs through all our society, in our literature, plays, movies, magazines, advertising and, indeed, in much family life. Still we must try."

Paul Gebhard concurs, "Our concepts of sexuality are terribly dependent on our mass media." Dr. Graham B. Blaine, Jr., chief of psychiatry to the Harvard University Health Services, believes, "Plays and movies where there is intercourse between unmarrieds do have an effect." He points out that in movies punishment no longer follows the crime. And Professor Perlman says, "Try to remember a novel in the last twenty years where the girl has illicit sex relations but there is real shame involved. The Scarlet Letter doesn't exist any more. When they see this, college kids feel they're square if they don't engage in this."

The city itself encourages anonymity and facilitates sexual activity which would have been at least more difficult in a smaller community. And we encourage youthful sexuality by enshrining beauty queens who are often legal minors; we make them alluring sex objects but do not want to permit sexual relations with girls their age. Dr. Gebhard judges that the age preference for females in our culture is from twelve to twenty-five—from Lolita to Miss America.

As David Riesman has written in a paper called "Permissiveness and Sex Roles": "Indeed, the availability of girls in America is an omnipresent and inescapable part of our visual esthetic—built into the widths of our cars, the reels of our movies, into the pages of our advertisements, and built into the girls themselves, I might add, in the way they carry themselves and dress."

Often a man from another culture can give us some insight into ourselves. Secretary-General U Thant says of the sexuality he found in America, "My concept of morality is different. I was brought up in a very different society. When I first came here in 1952, I was shocked to see public embracing in the park and people using a parked car as a bedroom. These values are so different." And he adds, "I still feel there is too much sex in the West."

There are many Americans who fear the visibility we give sex and demand watch-and-ward supervision of our mass media. It is true that a ten-year-old boy in our society is usually highly aware of bikinis, female nudity and the pictures of scantily dressed beauty-contest finalists in the evening paper. There are many groups that fight to remove "girlie" magazines from newsstands in their communities. But the problem with such measures is: Where do you draw the line on the censorship of sex? Do nudist magazines have a right to be sold? Will we forbid advertisements to suggest that smoking the right cigarette or drinking the right whiskey or driving the right sportscar will guarantee sexual "success"? Will we censor the entertainment advertisements in the "good gray" *New York Times*, where bosom-nudity and hard-sell innuendo is intended to stimulate sexual interest? Maybe the responsibility for drawing a line against smut or sadism lies with the individual parent rather than the community or the government.

Mrs. Oettinger at the Children's Bureau says, "We are too often lax about situations where experimentation goes on—the business of early dating, allowing youngsters so much freedom, sometimes promoting a boy friend at all cost. The youngsters who are unsophisticated have babies and are punished." The number of illegitimate births has tripled since 1940.

Many parents, who would be shocked if they realized it, are pushing their sons and daughters into earlier and earlier sexual activity. Says Mrs. Perlman, "In the class where the parents have 'made it,' they want their children to be happy. This is very widespread in our affluent society. Then there is a push to try to be happy. There is a pervasive fun morality: if it's fun, it's good."

These parents are appalled when a child "gets into trouble." Professor Hauser says, "It is a distorted society which gives sixteen-year-olds automobiles to drive, provides them with the opportunity to go out with the opposite sex, but does not teach them anything about sex or contraception. That's why they use Seven-Up and Saranwrap."

Parents often shove their children into social and sexual relationships before they are ready for them. "The desire is now very often to have children as status symbols," asserts Dr. Mace. "They are in a sense exploiting their children. This is why mothers push little girls into dances and such. This gives the mother a sense of satisfaction, since the goal of the woman in our society is to be sexually attractive and desirable."

Says Lester Kirkendall, "I'm concerned that it starts early and involves younger kids in more intensive relationships than they can handle. By the time they are in their teens, they are moving very close to a full physical relationship. The girl particularly is being pushed into marriage. A girl feels extremely pressured to demonstrate she has the kind of attractiveness that is going to satisfy a boy. For young women in their late teens and college students, it is becoming a more expected thing in dating relationships. The boy expects it, and they expect it to be asked of them."

This kind of pressure, often denied, creates a strong undertow of insecurity and competition among some young girls. Says Mrs. Oettinger, "In the early days this was covert behavior. Today it is overt—a matter of showing off." And Professor Perlman agrees: "You have to hold on to your boyfriend for status. Feelings of being uncertain about the self, this is the kernel of sexual experimentation—the attempt to become attached to another person, to have security in at least a body contact, and the attempt to test one's self for feeling."

This, in turn, leads to anxieties that not only stir youthful unhappiness but can eventually affect these girls' marriages and motherhood. Despite the dangers, young girls, to compete, are using every device from the padded bra to direct sexual enticement to land their young men. Dr. Kinsey used to say that the difference between a good time and a charge of rape was whether the parents were awake when the girl arrived home.

Dr. Milton Senn warns, "In the United States, we have more high school girls dropping out because of pregnancy, even girls who aren't yet in high school. They are twelve and thirteen years old and come from all kinds of families." Estimates of the number of abortions in the nation start with a low of 750,000 a year, and the number of illegitimate births far exceeds the abortion figures. (At least 90 percent of the abortions are reportedly performed on white girls, as many Negro girls cannot afford abortions and therefore have their illegitimate babies.) Approximately one in every twenty Americans is today born out of wedlock.

In 85 percent of all marriages in which both partners are high school students, the bride is pregnant. And in the entire fifteen- to twenty-years-of-age group, one bride out of every four is already pregnant. "This means," asserts Professor Kirkendall, "many more boys are being pulled into marriage through sex. Girls are becoming more aggressive in setting up dating relationships. They are devising more ways to take the initiative. Sometimes they press too hard and move too fast. The boy may back off or may exploit her in turn. Girl wants boy. Boy wants sex. So they get together on that basis."

To a significant extent, the practices of chastity and constancy have diminished. One psychiatrist who deals with college-age patients says that chastity "has been proven over the centuries to be impossible." And to a degree, Dr. Gebhard agrees, "Young males have a strong sex drive, and you are not going to stamp it out. It is a matter of alternatives. You are not going to compete with orgasm by offering hand-holding."

The greatest change in sexual morality is taking place among young women. The experts believe that teen-age girls especially seem to be less inhibited about sexual intercourse than in the past. Years ago, they say, only boys talked about sexual prowess. Now they report, college girls keep records, share experiences of a weekend, even borrow birth-control devices in sororities. Contraceptive pills are widely used, and some girls regard virginity as a "nuisance."

Says Raymond Aron, "There has been in the United States and other countries a change in attitudes toward the sexual life of young girls. Having sexual experience before marriage is more widely accepted today than it was a generation or two ago."

Professor Kirkendall agrees: "Although the number of men who have had premarital relations is high, it remains about the same. The proportion among women is rising. I think it is increasing very rapidly."

Concern over premarital sexual activity is, from one important point of view, a concern over the change in the partner-finding pattern of young people, from a pattern in which a young man found a sexual outlet with girls of a "lower class" or with prostitutes, to a pattern in which a young man can have intercourse with a girl he might marry. College-age males are finding sex partners on the campus, rather than in the dance halls and brothels. Says Professor Helen Perlman, "There are very few prostitutes now; you don't have to have prostitutes."

Some feel the change from prostitute to peer-partner is healthy, because it *can* replace exploitation with concern about the partner. But Dr. Blaine is worried about effects he sees. He says, "The double standard makes a lot of sense emotionally and physiologically." He finds distress and even rage among some young men who discover the woman they plan to marry has had previous sexual experience. And he reports many young women participate in sex relations but are seriously disturbed because they feel premarital sex is immoral. He says, "You have to deal with this thing called conscience. Girls do it to deepen the relationship—do it once—and find it complicates the relationship—and stop."

One result of the new attitudes has been a lowering of the marriage age; now in 50 percent of all first marriages, the bride is under twenty years of age. According to Mrs. Oettinger, "In some places it is almost a contagion. Young marriages can be immoral in the sense of not really under-standing what marriage means. Too often it is not to create a home for children but to have a status—to be able to say, 'I have a husband,' like a possession."

Mrs. Oettinger worries about the high divorce rate among such young couples and of the fate of the children they have. She says, "The children are tragic."

Father Imbiorski regards early marriages as a tremendous problem. He knows eighteen-year-old girls with two and three children. He says caustically, "Children have the right to have adults as parents."

Looking at another aspect of the sexual dilemma, Dr. Paul Tillich saw that the younger generation is often baffled by the pressures and uncertainty of today's world and seeks some kind of security. "Security seems especially true of the girls who force marriage on the young men by forcing children on them. And they begin a marriage that after a few years becomes a bore." He felt early marriages are one reason why the divorce rate is so high in the country today. Teen-age marriages are reported to have a divorce rate as high as 75 percent.

"The whole thing of sexual morality is part of the greater morality," explains Professor Perlman. "If you don't know what is really valued, the push is very strong for anything that seems real. A lot of these kids are trying hard to live hard and think sex is the way. If it's accompanied by love, it may be the way. If it hurts or scares, then you get promiscuity."

Frequently, sexual experimentation among young people arouses confusion and fear, according to Dr. Senn. "What we find among the adolescent is, some get involved in it and find it doesn't work too well, and they worry whether they are already frigid or impotent."

Comments Dr. Blaine: "One is going against one's up-bringing and conscience, and one has to suffer the conse-quences of that: guilt, anxiety and other kinds of neurotic symptoms. We see students pushed beyond what their con-science will let them do by a permissive system. They get sick."

Mrs. Perlman reports that analysts now encounter three kinds of problems among unmarried girls. One is the girl who has "given" of herself and is full of guilt. The second is the girl who has had intercourse but neither enjoyed it nor had an orgastic experience and is deeply confused. And the third is the girl who cannot bring herself to engage in what she regards as "illicit" sex and is scared that she is odd.

Most experts are convinced that, on balance, premarital sex relations among college-age youth are bad—but not for the reasons that have been given in the past. It has long been preached that premarital relations should be avoided because sex should not be pleasure, it endangers marriage, illegitimate children may result, it may cause venereal disease. Such teaching produced a morality based on fear. But for many youth these fears are no longer meaningful reasons for abstinence.

Professor Perlman offers a rationale: "The reason I think it is bad is because kids can get hurt psychologically. If I had a daughter, this is what I would tell her. A woman normally equates sex and love, whereas a man can have sexual experi-ence and feel he has had a good time. Women are hurt because they feel used or demeaned."

Harvard College's Dean Monro, who has two daughters himself, warns that a shock awaits young women: "They go along in twentieth-century attitudes until the girl gets preg-nant, and then nineteenth-century morality comes back into

play. Suddenly, everything reverts, and they are not prepared for this. There is poor communication between generations in the family on this. All parents are squares on this,
and all children are suspect."

One college official points to the consequences that face
college students who participate in sex relations without
restraint. He lists unwanted pregnancies, unexpected emotional entanglements, problems which young people are
unprepared to meet. One girl he knows tried to commit
suicide because the boy finally decided that their sexual
involvement was going to make it impossible for him to prepare for a professional career.

This incident dramatizes another significant element of
the change that has occurred: In the past it was the girl who
put a limit on her physical relationship with a boy; the girl
was expected ultimately to say "No!" Now the boy often
has to establish the limit; for one thing, he has to decide if
sex is going to cost him his career. Despite his biological
drives, he is often left with a dual responsibility—not only
to the girl, but to himself.

Says Dr. Blaine, "If you could have premarital sex without the danger of pregnancy, it might be a good thing. But
you can't. You are under the influence of forces beyond
your control." In his experience "pregnancy is the real
tragedy of all this." One part of the problem is that girls
sometimes do not use contraceptive pills and diaphragms
even when they have them. According to Dr. Blaine, some
who say, "If he really loved me, he'd take a chance," are
expressing their unconscious need to hold on to their man,
their fear of losing him. Dr. Blaine adds, "A lot of girls don't
want to admit to themselves that they are going to have
intercourse and won't buy a diaphragm or take pills."

At the same time, Dean Monro finds reason to applaud the new relationship between young men and women. "This is moving so fast it would surprise you. They are much closer together. Girls are much more independent. Birth-control information and devices help a girl be independent. This independence is great; comradeship is right. Women are people and should not think of themselves as dependents, second in line always. I see so many able women around here."

As Pope John XXIII said in *Pacem in Terris*: "Since women are being ever more conscious of their human dignity, they will not tolerate being treated as mere material instruments, but demand rights befitting a human person in domestic and in public life."

This new sense of independence and equality is important to Dr. Gebhard. He says, "Men still tend to look on women as objects—possessions. They think of them as some kind of sexual mannequins." He cites the "bunnies" in the Playboy Clubs. Dr. Blaine adds that the best argument in favor of removing the taboos from premarital sex is that it would "take the shame and guilt out of sex," and perhaps even "make sex in marriage better."

Increasing freedom for women, which now has spilled over into sex relations, is actually in the mainstream of what has been going on in America for the past half-century. As recently as 1914 only eleven states gave women the right to vote and it was 1920 before American women across the land gained the Constitutional right to vote. In early America, married women could neither hold property nor make a will; they had no right to sue or to sit on juries; they had access neither to formal education nor to most kinds of employment. Now they have won all these political and economic battles, have greater influence than in almost any other society and have been struggling, despite physiological and psychological differences, to achieve some form of sexual parity.

As Dean Monro suggests, there are many able women around, and they have achieved prominence in the professions, the arts and business. Able women have always been with us. The influence of Peggy O'Neale, Harriet Beecher Stowe, Mary Baker Eddy, Emma Willard, Elizabeth Caddy Stanton—and more recently Eleanor Roosevelt, Rachel Carson and Dr. Frances O. Kelsey—attests to that. Any student of the American frontier knows how women led the conversion of raw border villages and cow towns into communities where children could be brought up safely. They fought against child labor and adulterated foods; they waged running battles against the brothel and the saloon. In *The American Character* the British historian Dennis W. Brogan writes, "When the great department store, Macy's, moved uptown and built its vast new store on the site of some of the most famous brothels in New York, the early twentieth century opened with an omen of a new triumph for the American woman."

This triumph has had its price. A reporter recently asked two San Francisco priests for their impression of morality in the city from the confessions they heard. Most urgent, they replied, is the problem of the young woman in the city. The city is a magnet that draws young women to a transient, mobile social situation which is, to a substantial degree, manless—or at least most of the men are married. As a result, the priests felt, women are encouraged to become the aggressors in sex relations.

Despite this price, in view of American women's drive

for freedom and equality, it is hardly surprising to find educated women trying to unshackle themselves from the masculine-favoring double standard in sex. This effort is seriously disturbing college officials and parents back home.

Dean Monro says: "Needless to say, no sensible adult in our society, least of all a college dean, favors or encourages free love. But it is necessary to point out that the new facts of life for our time have brought about new and closer relationships between young men and women. Furthermore, for generations our sexual codes have been supported by the authority of parents and the church, and by age-old fears of consequences. In the thinking of many of our young people these old controls have diminished and are no longer effective. And, of course, in the area of sexual behavior, present adult behavior and example in our society are damaging and not helpful.

"If we are to develop a sensible and workable code of sexual behavior, we need to see these matters as they are. Our code of sexual behavior must be based less on authority and fear, and more on making clear to our students the social wisdom behind the old rules, the personal consequences of deep emotional involvement, and the enduring value of personal dignity and self-discipline. In all this, I deeply believe that the new-found independence and strengthening position of women will, in the long run, turn out to be a force, not for the further deterioration of our moral standards, but for their improvement."

Changing sexual mores have recently brought clashes between administrators and students at a number of colleges across the country. Students have sought to convince college administrations that sexual freedom is a fact of life today and that parietal rules permitting girls to visit boys' dormitories simply enable sexual relations to occur more pleasantly, comfortably and with some dignity. The students have repeatedly asserted that their sexual behavior is a private matter and none of the college's business.

At the University of Illinois, a biology professor who condoned premarital intercourse "among those sufficiently mature" was asked to resign. Cornell University was torn by an argument over a graduate student who shared an off-campus apartment with a coed from another school. Many undergraduate males there have their own apartments and well-developed patterns for using them; they recognize the value of convenience in campus sex life. When the president of Carleton College in Minnesota addressed the student body on manners and morals, he aroused a storm of protest from students who felt the administration should not supervise their personal actions. Student leaders charged that the college was trying to prevent more pregnancies on campus. A senior writing in the college paper declared: "Each person has the right to make his own decisions, right or wrong, about how he is going to run his life. Of course he should consult his elders—that is half of his education—but finally he must make his own decisions—this is the other half." The paper quoted a professor who said "inconvenience is not the greatest deterrence to premarital intercourse."

Sarah Gibson Blanding, while president of Vassar College, raised a national tempest by asserting that premarital sex relations, on campus or off, were taboo for students there. In the fall of 1965, officials of Brown University were shaken when it was reported that the university's health director had prescribed birth-control pills for two unmarried students at Pembroke College, Brown's undergraduate college for women.

Harvard College spent a good part of the 1963–64 academic year preoccupied with the sex problem, after the authorities learned that some students were using their college rooms for sexual relations. Dean Monro wrote to *The Harvard Crimson* saying that "the present set of parietal rules is now producing a succession of serious violations" that "move us closer and closer to outright scandal."

Explains Dr. Blaine, "Harvard seemed to the students to be promoting sexual intercourse." Student spokesmen took the position that sex is a matter of personal morality and decision. Economist and former ambassador John Kenneth Galbraith entered the lists, attacked college administrators' "frustrated maternalism" and said, essentially, that the college had no business policing undergraduate sexual activity. He declared, "No effort need be made or should be made to protect individuals from the consequences of their own errors, indiscretions, or passions. . . ." One student proposed that the university install wider beds in undergraduate rooms. But numerous older alumni failed to see any humor in the situation.

Dr. Blaine shares the administrators' concern about unwanted college pregnancies. He says, "Most of these babies were conceived in a Harvard dormitory," but he adds that their conception could not be blamed on the parietal rules, because they might just as well have been conceived in a field or a car.

One college official raises a serious point about a decision at Radcliffe, a woman's college now integrated with Harvard, to permit students to vote on whether or not to discard sign-out regulations that required the girls to report back to their dormitories by certain hours. The students voted to abolish the regulations, but more than two hundred girls voted to keep them. The official felt strongly that those two hundred girls needed such a rule as a safeguard against sexual involvements; they wanted to be able to tell a persistent young man that they had to get back to their dorms. He believed Radcliffe authorities should have kept the sign-out regulations for the sake of that sizable minority.

All this uproar on the campuses is faintly ironic, since the experts agree that college students are more restrictive and inhibited about sex than the rest of their age group in the nation. But it reflects the confusion, shared by college students and authorities, over the revolution in sexual mores now affecting, and often bewildering, American youth.

The growing demand from students for more sexual freedom has put many college officials in a moral quandary. Should they regulate—or attempt to regulate—students' sex lives? If so, should this regulation extend off-campus as well as on? If authorities ignore sexual activity off-campus and simply ban it on college property, are they not reacting as a landlord, rather than as educators who feel responsible for the students' total development? Dr. Blaine agrees that there has been a major change in behavior and feels that the colleges must guide it.

At the annual meeting of the American Orthopsychiatric Association in March, 1964, Dr. Paul A. Wallers, Jr., of the Harvard University Health Services, said: "There seems little doubt that among college women of today, chastity is not accepted as a necessary virtue. Young people have replaced it with a more ambiguous virtue—fidelity. . . . In this relationship each couple is expected to work out their own sexual code. . . . Chastity is not required, but looseness is not the result, for fidelity takes chastity's place. Thus, infidelity is frowned upon and promiscuity is completely unacceptable. Promiscuity is defined as either sleeping with more than one man in the present or as moving too quickly from one serious relationship to another."

Professor Kirkendall argues, "A college should not make a rule that chastity should be the rule. Because then you think if an act has or has not been performed indicates whether you have virtuous or non-virtuous students." He feels what is crucial is not the act but the nature of the relationship and the motivation for it. He adds, "This is not permissiveness, because relationships have rules. You can use sex in a hostile way just as you use a bludgeon.

"Rather than being concerned whether or not a sexual act has occurred, I would like to be concerned that we use all our powers and capacities with responsible concern for others. I'm more fearful about our inability to handle our aggressive and hostile impulses than our sexual impulses. It may violate the traditions of society, but at least they have warmth and a wish to make contact. That's why I can't get as upset about young people as many do, because I see them reaching out."

Kirkendall believes it is immoral when a boy exploits a girl—or vice versa. "There can be some very immoral things occurring without a sexual act taking place," he notes.

"What's changed isn't intercourse but the exploitiveness of intercourse," suggests David Riesman. He says, for example, that "going steady" is actually less competitive, less exploitive, than other dating patterns. "Going steady is a morality in which one doesn't steal others' boys or girls. The priests who see it as occasion for sin miss the point of it."

In his book *Honest To God*, the Bishop John Robinson has a passage on this point. He wrote: "To the young man asking in his relations with a girl 'Why shouldn't I?' it is relatively easy to say 'Because it's wrong' or 'Because it's a sin'—and then to condemn him when he, or his whole generation, takes no notice. It makes much greater demands to ask, and to answer, the question 'Do you love her?' or 'How much do you love her?' and then to help him to accept for himself the decision that, if he doesn't, or doesn't very deeply, then his action is immoral, or if he does, then he will respect her far too much to use her or take liberties with her."

Bishop Robinson went on: "Chastity is the expression of charity—of caring, enough. And this is the criterion for every form of behavior, inside marriage or out of it, in sexual ethics or in any other field. For nothing else makes a thing right or wrong."

Our confusion over sex morality is not limited to the problems of the young. Kirkendall says, "As long as adults focus on youth, they don't have to look at themselves. It is essentially an adult problem. When a person uses sex in marriage to punish, control, manipulate, this becomes immorality too." Gebhard voices the same concern: "If the wife is sore at the husband, this is what she withholds. Both genders have pretty good weapons."

Adult hypocrisy over sex is illustrated by the story of a large service club on the West Coast. The men in the local club became worried about the growth of juvenile delinquency in their area. They held meetings, discussed with seriousness and enthusiasm what they could do about it. They finally decided to sponsor and organize a baseball league for boys in the community. The next problem was to raise the funds for supplies and uniforms. So the service club decided to throw a big party to raise the money. For the party they brought in from the large city not far away stripteasers and pornographic stag movies. These attractions would bring out the men and the money. The sociologist who told me this story says, "Nobody saw anything incongruous in this. It was for a good cause. Nobody thought anything of their own immorality; it was going to keep the kids straight."

But the center of the present adult dilemma over sexual morality is in the home and in marriage. Most marriages stick pretty well, but the absence of communication that marriage experts find in many homes often results in the exploitive use of sex and in extramarital relations. The Reverend Gibson Winter calls this "the pathos of the search for communication." He cites one minister who told him that, with one or two exceptions, there was no real communication within any marriage in his congregation. "The sickness of this," says the Reverend Winter, "keeps us focused on the private sphere of morality."

According to Paul Gebhard, extramarital sexual activity has increased, and even more prevalent is the growth of extramarital petting. ("They won't have intercourse because their morality won't let them, but petting is different.") There are extreme situations like the Long Island housewives who organized as part-time prostitutes and the hundreds of suburban couples who, the *San Francisco Chronicle* revealed in 1963, were participating in "wife swapping," that is, adultery with mutual consent. The newspaper report quoted one wife as saying, in her husband's presence, "It will save your marriage from going on the rocks if it's sexually stale and you're bored with going to bed with each other. It saved ours."

Dr. David Mace believes many Americans pin false hopes

on marriage. He says, "Romantic love is based on unfilled sexual need—the yearning of sexual desire. After it has been discharged over a period of time, romance fades away. It is foolish to say it doesn't. We use up the romantic cycle and start over with a new partner. Marriage has become a series of ecstatic, romantic adventures."

The experts say we often practice "serial monogamy." Father Imbiorski of Chicago's Cana Conference says, "We have to a great extent divorced sexuality from procreation and from love. In certain segments, sex is used as entertainment, without personal commitment, without being related to family and marriage." On the other hand, Kirkendall asks, "Are we going to use sex only for propagation? Nobody confines their sex activity to that particular aspect." The fact is that neither propagation nor pleasure can be ignored.

It has been predicted that, as a result of our freedom and our confusion, one in every three couples married this year will be divorced within fifteen years. There are now about two million divorced women in the country and an estimated thirteen million children who belong to broken homes. Nationally, there is now one divorce for every four weddings. And in California, Dr. Mace reports, there is a divorce for every new marriage. He blames the national divorce rate on the mobility and rootlessness of our society, and says the Californians are virtually "semi-nomads."

One small silver lining to this high level of divorce is suggested by Mrs. Arnold Toynbee who says, "Where the family is broken up, there isn't the same hostility today. That's really a great improvement in charity. It is much easier on the children."

Says Dr. Mace, "What we have really done in our culture is turn marriage upside down. Goals and purposes used to be social and familial. Interpersonal relationship was a by-product. We've staked marriage on a fulfilling interpersonal relationship. We have created goals for marriage that are hard to achieve."

In a very deep sense, the central problem in our society is that we live so much without love. In the mass of human beings each of us is now in touch with—through the concentration of the city, the mobility of the automobile—we find few who are not competing for money, power or status. So our search for love centers in the marriage—and in the intimate premarital relationship. Husband and wife seek a surcease of loneliness in each other. And when they discover their humanness—their limitations, perhaps their pettiness or self-centeredness—more and more often these disillusionments flaw the hope of loving and put too great a stress on the marriage—and it cracks.

««17.

The Freedom To Be Concerned

—Conclusion

What the experts and thinkers are saying about almost every aspect of American morality is: In a rapidly changing world, we have lost our traditional moral guidelines. Our moral values are being reshaped under the pressures of our revolutionary times; for many of us, this is terribly difficult to admit.

We need not fear change. The great moral principles enunciated in our culture by the Golden Rule, the Ten Commandments, the teachings of Moses and Jesus Christ, the Bill of Rights are just as solid as ever. But man has never lived in a world of absolutes; he has always had to interpret the moral absolutes for his own time—or to have them interpreted for him by his chief or priest.

We are moving away from moral ritualism. We may begin to replace it with standards based on the realities of man's needs and responsibilities. But for the moment, we live our lives in a time of transition and confusion. We are groping, painfully and often blindly, in anger and often in fear, for a new moral code that will enable us to live morally and decently. Walter Reuther says we are searching for a moral "know-why" to go with our mechanical "know-how."

The forces of change are impersonal but, disconcertingly, they impose upon us a personal responsibility to choose. Some would meet this burden with wishful fantasies. They would tear down the threatening structure of technology and science and retreat to some New World Eden that never did exist. But most of us reject this response as irresponsible. We know that we must live with kaleidoscopic change.

On his Texas porch, I asked the late Frank Dobie who he thought was the greatest man of our time. He said, "Most of these 'doers' I don't think are very great. Maybe I won't even know his name. Some fella thinking. Only thinking can save us. We have all the six-shooters we can use."

The experts feel strongly that we cannot turn back to earlier, more rigid behavior and earlier, simpler obedience. "Moral codes are always the product of activities of men already dead in situations that no longer exist," says Philip Hauser. "When you begin to question morality, it is a sign that the individual is becoming free of the bondage of tradition. You may think that this is tragic or deplorable, but there's nothing you can do about it."

Dr. Hudson Hoagland said in a recent speech, "Empirically I cannot see how a modern society emancipated from magic, superstition and animism can function unless the individuals believe that they are free and responsible for their actions, and unless society can hold them responsible. Certainly our deepest convictions tell us we are free to make choices. The creation and advancement of civilizations appear to require this assumption."

If we refuse to accept this responsibility, we only echo

the former SS master sergeant at Auschwitz who admitted killing 250 inmates by injecting them with carbolic acid solution, but explained to a court, "I was just a little soldier carrying out my orders. I only did what was ordered, nothing more, and I didn't look to the right or left to see what else was going on." His rejection of moral responsibility helped make murder possible.

Our moral courage is being tried on many levels—from the threat of nuclear destruction to the mastery of our prejudices, our avarice, our appetites. Because much of our world is so new, the teachings of our established institutions are questioned and often rejected. We face the tests of moral courage as individuals. In the end, that is what freedom of the individual—freedom itself—is all about.

In a mass society such as ours has become, an individual can wait endlessly for his test. It never seems to come; no single moral point seems big enough to risk the loss of a job or the hostility of one's friends. As James Baldwin wrote in *The Fire Next Time*, "It is not necessary that people be wicked but only that they be spineless." This is the ultimate danger, for in a mass society there is some place to hide, not on a distant frontier but in apathetic anonymity.

Today each human being is challenged to think through what he really believes. Along the way, he listens to many voices, but he must eventually decide for himself which is the moral road. "You can believe in anything when it's easy," says Walter Reuther. "The real test of your inner convictions is where you stand in the hour of challenge."

Freedom always involves risks, and the freedom to let one's conscience decide on moral standards contains enormous risks. The individual conscience certainly is fallible. Some who have listened to the voice of their own consciences have obeyed with such fanaticism that they have, in fact, destroyed. A fanatic permits no room for doubt, for compromise, for adjustment—or, in the final analysis, for the other fellow's freedom to listen to his own conscience.

Actually, it is rare that the individual conscience directly and openly revolts against society. That agony is reserved for rebels, conscientious objectors and martyrs. Most men live with a more modest level of conflict. Their moral dilemmas exist within the matrix of society; they seek paths between such moral contradictions as their business loyalty and their personal ambition, their political principles and the interest of their party, their neighbors' standards of child-rearing and their own. The speed of change today has made even these conflicts agonizing. And yet how can we improve our society, if we cannot challenge ourselves?

"If history teaches us anything, it is that nations and societies decline as the moral fiber of their people decline," Mortimer Caplin warned in a speech. "We've had a series of rude awakenings over recent years; corruption in some local government; corruption in certain labor unions; illegal price-fixing and fixed bids; violations of fiduciary obligations by corporate officers; kickbacks and commercial bribery (cynically called 'payola') in the business world; expense-account abuses, some in fraud of our revenue laws; and seduction of college athletes by bribes or special favors. Many of us are genuinely concerned whether these signs are symptomatic of a general lowering of morality, ethics and decency, throughout large segments of our society." The range of our moral crisis is all-encompassing.

But we see that, in this age of extermination and experimentation and in this society that tries to turn people into numbers and to replace them with machines, there is deep concern over man's relationship to man. Each of us has to "reach out" to find the warmth that will give life meaning. As Bishop Robinson has written: "The only intrinsic evil is lack of love."

It is not strange that in such a dangerous time, when we walk on so many brinks, our concern is greater than ever. And because it exists, we can be hopeful about our moral crisis. Although the problems are complex, we can be optimistic because, unlike so many other societies, we have achieved some freedom of choice. We have choices to make about God, power, money, sex, prejudice and our responsibility in the world. We have, above all, the freedom to be concerned.

If we lack any freedom, it is that we cannot put down the burden of moral concern. We cannot be apathetic. We are no longer free to ignore each other, to hate each other, to destroy or exploit each other or to fail to hammer out a morality that will give mankind a chance to go on living. We must shape a moral code that will fit the needs of the society and age we live in. We have a large measure of freedom to carve out lives we regard as moral—if we will take the risks and pay the price. We need not wait for miracles. We now have the power. We need only find the courage.

Index

About the Author

J. Robert Moskin is a senior editor of *Look* magazine and has been on *Look*'s editorial staff for more than eleven years. Born in New York City, he was graduated from the Horace Mann School and from Harvard University, where he was managing editor of the *Crimson*. He also received a master's degree in American history from Columbia University.

In addition to serving on *Look*, Mr. Moskin has been a reporter on several daily newspapers, the editor of a weekly paper, a senior editor of *Collier's*, and the managing editor of the *Woman's Home Companion*. In 1965 he received two awards for the best magazine writing of the year: the Page One Award of the Newspaper Guild and the Sidney Hillman Foundation Prize Award. He is the co-author of the study *The Decline of the American Male*.

Mr. Moskin is a member of the National Freedom of Information Committee of Sigma Delta Chi, the national journalistic society. During World War II he served with the Army in the Southwest Pacific. Now, with their three children, he and his wife live in Scarsdale, New York.